CASES IN
BUSINESS ETHICS

2

CASES IN

BUSINESS ETHICS

THOMAS M. GARRETT
UNIVERSITY OF SCRANTON

RAYMOND C. BAUMHART
CAMBRIDGE CENTER FOR SOCIAL STUDIES

THEODORE V. PURCELL
CAMBRIDGE CENTER FOR SOCIAL STUDIES

PERRY ROETS
MARQUETTE UNIVERSITY

PRENTICE-HALL, INC.
Englewood Cliffs, N.J.

To American Jesuit Educators

Printed in the United States of America

ISBN: 0-13-118703-1

Library of Congress Catalog Card Number: 68-18034

10 9 8 7 6 5 4 3 2

PRENTICE-HALL INTERNATIONAL, INC., *London*
PRENTICE-HALL OF AUSTRALIA, PTY. LTD., *Sydney*
PRENTICE-HALL OF CANADA, LTD., *Toronto*
PRENTICE-HALL OF INDIA PRIVATE LIMITED, *New Delhi*
PRENTICE-HALL OF JAPAN, INC., *Tokyo*

Preface

It will not be enough merely to read this book; it is intended to be studied and pondered. Its purpose is twofold: (1) to familiarize the reader with the range and complexity of ethical problems faced by businessmen; (2) to provide the reader with an opportunity to consider and, preferably, to discuss the origin, context, and solution of these problems. It is hoped that this activity by the reader will result in an increased sensitivity to the ethical component in many business situations, and will provide the opportunity to develop a problem-solving approach which will prove useful in dealing with ethical problems in business.

The book is not intended as a dramatic catalogue of unethical practices in businesses, or as a study in business pathology. But discussions lead most surely to meaningful learning when the cases are drawn from real-life situations. In a casebook about business ethics, the situations typically involve at least a temptation or opportunity for someone to benefit personally from unethical behavior.

There is variety in the length and complexity of the cases offered. Each is intended to challenge the analytic powers of those interested in ethical decision-making. The longer cases require the reader to separate wheat from chaff, and to demonstrate his knowledge about business complexities as well as ethical theory.

Although all of the cases in this book represent situations which businessmen have actually faced, not all deal with identifiable persons and companies. Occasionally, when dealing with fictional companies, the editors have introduced statements of motivation and have tailored certain facts in order to prevent the reader from seizing upon simple open and shut solutions. The reader is warned against trying to identify the fictitious companies in this book with particular companies on the American business scene.

In some cases the editors have reluctantly used the names of real companies and individuals since the widespread publicity given to the cases made disguise impossible. Even in these cases, however, the editors do not pretend to give the whole story. The reasons are simple. In the first place, the private books and records of companies are not open to everyone. In the second place, motives and attitudes are generally not a matter of public record. For these reasons the editors believe that judgments about the case as presented should not be transferred automatically to the real persons and companies involved. The facts as presented provide material for discussion and analysis; they do not provide the basis for a final judgment about the real principals in the cases.

The cases do not represent the editors' views of either the right or the wrong way of handling the ethical and business problems involved. The cases are not meant as models of conduct but as challenges to the thoughtful reader. In all honesty, the editors admit that they have included cases designed to trap those who tend to make quick judgments.

The editors wish to express their gratitude to Mrs. Gladys Sperber, who spent long hours turning academic prose into readable English, and to Sheila Scanlon and Dolores Zappala who, with Mrs. Sperber, handled the correspondence and typing connected with the manuscript so capably. Various members of the Cambridge Center for Social Studies contributed valuable comments on individual cases.

The credit lines attached to contributed cases cannot really express our gratitude to those professors, businessmen, and publishers who granted permission to use their material. Moreover, nearly every case owes something to the excellent reporting of the American business press. In particular, *Advertising Age, The Wall Street Journal,* and *Fortune* provided us not only with starting points but with a great deal of background material.

Contents

I

Personnel Relations

Rungs on the Ladder

During Christmas vacation of his second year at the Kruger School of Business Administration, Jim Martin discussed his career plans at length with Harry Simpson, his prospective father-in-law. Mr. Simpson owned a small tool and die firm in Indiana. The company supplied several large manufacturing firms in the Midwest and had been quite successful. Mr. Simpson liked Jim and wanted him to join the firm. Because he had no desire to lose himself in a big organization, Jim felt this would be an outstanding opportunity. Mr. Simpson, however, had some misgivings about his joining the firm immediately.

Due to the small size of the Simpson firm, no training program was provided for new employees. In addition, the management echelon, consisting of six persons, had become somewhat stale and was in need of new ideas and systems. Mr. Simpson felt, therefore, that Jim should work with a large firm for a few years and then join the Simpson organization.

As Mr. Simpson put it, "Big companies have excellent training programs and you could learn an awful lot from them. Training sessions are taught by experts and they know all of the latest developments in their fields. I think the knowledge you would get from this would be invaluable to our firm. Let's face it, someday you'll

probably be running this company and you'll be a lot more successful if you have this background."

Since Jim agreed fully with this viewpoint, he interviewed several manufacturing companies offering broad management training
programs. By spring, he had decided on Chicago Steel Company.
Chicago Steel invited Jim to its headquarters for further interviews and a complete tour of the plant and general offices. The
manager explained that the company hired only four men a year
for its training program and invited Jim to be one of them. Jim accepted the invitation.

He started work immediately following graduation. The training period lasted about 22 months. During this time, Jim attended
many classes dealing with the functions and techniques of each operating department in the company; he also worked for a short
time in each of these departments. He took copious notes during
this period and tried to figure out how the techniques and principles he was learning could be applied to Mr. Simpson's firm.

At the end of the training program, Jim was called into the executive vice president's office where he was complimented on his
performance during the training program and offered the position
of an assistant plant manager.

Jim was surprised to receive such a responsible position. He
called Mr. Simpson and explained the situation. Mr. Simpson told
him to hand in his resignation immediately because he was needed
to replace the retiring vice-president in charge of production.

What Do You Suggest?

During the summer of 1966, the Portsmouth plant of Zimmerman Brothers was the subject of a research study by a university professor. When the report of the study reached the desk of Richard Erhardt, personnel manager of the plant, he eagerly read the results.

Zimmerman Brothers was a large foodpacker, employing about 62,000 people. Most of these employees worked in 46 foodpacking plants, of which Portsmouth was one. Built in 1902, this plant had 1,600 employees on its payroll when the professor made his attitude study. One hundred fifty-two Portsmouth workers had been chosen by random sample, and in private interviews they stated their opinions concerning their company and their union. One of the areas investigated was the workers' attitude toward Zimmerman's suggestion plan. Because Erhardt was ultimately responsible for the success of the suggestion plan at Portsmouth, he read this chapter with particular interest.

The Zimmerman suggestion plan enabled employees to submit ideas for improving equipment, working conditions, or methods. Suggestion blanks were readily available throughout the plant. If the company adopted a worker's idea, he received a cash award or, if he preferred, merchandise. The amount of the award varied with the savings realized from the suggestion. In addition, shares of Zimmerman stock were occasionally awarded for the best suggestions received during a given period of time. The company newspaper publicized some of the award-winning ideas.

Erhardt was interested to see that 75 percent of the workers were favorably disposed toward the suggestion plan, with an average score of 2.4 for the 152 workers interviewed.[1] But he also noted that the score was less favorable than the same workers' attitude scores toward the company, the union, their foreman, and their job. One topic which the report brought forcibly to Erhardt's attention was the workers' fear of suggesting themselves or other workers out of a job. According to the report, mention of this fear had been spontaneous and recurrent in many of the interviews. Erhardt had been aware of this attitude, but had not realized its intensity. The report stated that workers who had been with the company for a long time felt this way more strongly than those who had been with Zimmerman for a shorter time.

One old-timer, Thomas Leyden, said, "I won't turn suggestions in where they'll knock three or four men out of work. I never could see that. I know when I first started to work here, we used to carry the fresh fruit all the way down to the coolers. They got a chain in there now. There used to be twice as many men working there as there are now."

Another veteran employee, Charles Harwood, stated: "If I cut ten men off for $25 or $30, I can't see it. If I can improve something to help the men along, I do it. But whenever you cut a man off, you feel bad. It may not only hurt him, but it may hurt ten or twelve other people besides."

Foreman Keith Kinnamon commented: "The suggestion system is good; but one of your problems with the hourly paid is that they're so afraid of putting themselves or another man out of work that some of them have resolved never even to submit a suggestion."

A union steward, Andrew Dietz, had devised a way to prevent one worker's suggestion from putting another worker out of a job.

[1] Each attitude was graded by the interviewer on the basis of the worker's comments. A score of 1 indicated a very favorable opinion; a score of 5 indicated a very unfavorable opinion. Between these extremes were 7 other grades at successive ½-point intervals. Thus a score of 3 indicated a neutral opinion.

Dietz: I try to tell all of my people that if ever they have any suggestions, I'd like to see them before they're turned in. They want to know why. I tell 'em: "I'd like to see whether you're decreasing employment." It's good to make suggestions, but it isn't good to suggest so that somebody isn't able to feed their children at home. I want to increase employment, not decrease it. When you suggest something, actually what you're doing is suggesting machinery or a gadget that would take some of the labor out of the job. Mostly the suggestions are all right, provided they're looked over by somebody that has a little authority on whether the job itself is going to be eliminated by it. I think the union should have somebody there, or suggest to the people to bring it to their stewards or somebody that knows the job before they're turned in.

Interviewer: Otherwise somebody might lose a job, is that it?

Dietz: I would never, if I could suggest something in science, I would never say "no" to that, because they're out for something to help everybody, but management is out for something to help themselves.

Interviewer: So there's a big difference between science and management?

Dietz: There sure is a big difference. If I could tell one of those big professors how to make a heart tick constantly, I'd tell him. But I wouldn't tell management how to make their machines operate more efficiently.

Willy Brown, an employee who was very favorable to the suggestion plan, made a distinction between two kinds of suggestions. "If I thought of a suggestion—which I have thought of several— usually after someone else—but if I'd see where it would cut somebody off, I'd never turn it in. But if I see where it would make working conditions better, well, I'd turn it in."

Erhardt was interested to note the comments of 53-year-old Neil Mitchell, a skilled worker:

Mitchell: I've put in two or three suggestions. I don't think I ever got any money out of 'em. (laughs) But I think it's a good thing. Lots of people will tell you that every new invention kept somebody out of a job, but it isn't true. 'Way back over the time, the more inventions we got, the more people that have work, and it's cheaper— the products have come down. But a lot of people just can't see.

Interviewer: I was just up in the coffee department. They have a new packing machine which seals and closes those one-pound packages. That displaces three or four girls.

Mitchell: Yeah, but they got more girls in there than they ever did have.

Interviewer: Have they? It's hard to get people to see that, isn't it?

Mitchell: So many people, they don't stop to analyze the thing. They just look at it quick and jump to conclusions.

Joseph Rudolph, a union steward who was favorable toward the suggestion plan, saw both the workers' and the company's point of view. "In its way, the plan is all right. But there is a feeling against it. Like some of the men have turned in suggestions to cut out two or three men—well, that don't go over so big amongst the people. They get $50 out of it, and it maybe knocks some whole family in the head. It knocks that man out of a job—he's got a family—it looks bad. But on the company side of it, I can see their side because they are looking for improvements. And they are going to have improvements whether *you* suggest it or not—somebody is going to get it up. Like the guy that says, 'It's going to happen anyway, so why shouldn't I get something out of it?' It's a ticklish question."

Shrinkage and the Seeing Eye

The management of Jay Dee Department Stores was proud of the stores' low shrinkage figures. Where the national average was one percent of sales, Jay Dee lost less than .8 percent of sales through theft, damage, or the improper handling of markdowns. This was due to careful control of inventory and to the fact that shrinkage could seriously lower a manager's or buyer's bonus. Monthly and quarterly reports helped to keep managers on their toes.

Inventory and shrinkage reports over a period of three months indicated that the glove department in one of the smaller stores was experiencing a gradual rise in shrinkage. In one month the shrinkage was three percent, equal in dollar value to the net profit on sales for that particular department. A careful checking of the records by the store manager, Christopher Unger, failed to reveal any serious mistakes in markdowns. Little damaged material had appeared, and the security officers had failed to detect any wholesale shoplifting. It seemed safe to conclude then, that the shrinkage was due to theft by employees. Since store policy required that employees have purchases and packages checked and initialled by the proper buyer, a careful watch was kept on the store guards who had the job of controlling packages carried out by employees. Nothing

9

came of all these efforts, and shrinkage in the glove department continued at about three percent.

The chief security officer, Ralph Talkin, suggested to Unger that a hidden television camera to watch the check-out stations and the glove department might help to catch the thieves. The cost would be high for a small department, but Talkin felt that unless something were done, other departments might start to suffer in the same way. In addition, Talkin wanted to install hidden microphones and recorders in the stockrooms and the restrooms. In this way he hoped to pick up careless remarks that might pass between confederates, since he felt sure that several people must be involved.

Unger admitted that the problem was serious, but was uneasy about the solution proposed. If the employees learned of the camera, thefts might diminish but morale would suffer. On the other hand, if no one but Unger and Talkin knew of the cameras, the thieves might be caught but Unger would feel like a Gestapo agent. Moreover, if the use of the cameras were ever revealed, public outcry might damage the reputation of the store. As for the microphones and recorders in restrooms and stockrooms, this was out of the question. People had some right to privacy, even in a business.

Nothing was done at the time, but when the shrinkage continued for another month, Unger gave in and allowed the secret installation of the cameras and the mikes. Within a week, the cameras had caught the assistant buyer of the glove department in the act of stealing. He was fired and the shrinkage immediately dropped to a reasonable level.

The mikes provided no useful information about the shrinkage, but Talkin and Unger learned that there was a small numbers ring operating among the employees; that one girl was having an affair; and that one buyer was determined to discredit Unger. Unger, who felt guilty about the entire operation, decided that he could not use any of this additional information; but he admitted to himself that his attitude toward the people involved was no longer the same.

The Double Expense Account

PART A

Heinrich Picaro is a senior in the School of Business at Kruger College. Although he has had many job offers, he continues to go through interviews arranged by the college placement service. He reasons that the interview experience will be valuable and may even turn up a better offer. In fact, Heinrich has discovered a way to make money from job interviews.

On one occasion, two firms invited him to New York for a tour of the home office. He managed to schedule both firms on the same day, and then billed each of them for his full travel expenses. In this way he was able to pocket about $100. When a friend objected that this was dishonest, Heinrich replied that each firm had told him to submit an expense account so that he was not taking something he had no right to. One firm had not even asked for bills, which he interpreted as meaning that they really intended to make him a gift of the money.

PART B

Thirty-nine Chicago businessmen read of the action of Heinrich Picaro. Then they were asked to answer the following question: If you were personnel manager of one of these two firms and discovered what Heinrich had done, would you hire him or would you hire another student who had the same talents, grades, and personality as Heinrich, but who had split the total expenses for his trip between your company and the other company? (Please check only one.)

       (a) I would hire Heinrich.
       (b) I would hire the other student.
       (c) I see no reason for preferring one student over the other.

Four businessmen chose (a), 28 chose (b), and 7 chose (c).

The Traveling Wife

John Voyage is the national sales manager for Runabout Motorcycles, an English firm attempting to establish operations in the United States. Since John is the only fully-trained salesman, he needs to give continual assistance to his men in the field. In the past year he has been on the road two or three days every week.

His wife has started to complain and does not seem to understand his position. In order to restore some peace to the family, John has started taking his wife with him whenever he travels to any point of interest. Since he approves his own expenses for accounting, he bills the company for some of his wife's expenses, though this is against company policy. He tries to keep the over-all bill to the company within reasonable limits by taking a double room at a slightly less expensive hotel, and by flying tourist instead of first class. Frequently the bill he puts in is no higher than it would have been if he were traveling alone.

John argues that the company policy does not really apply to a case like his. Moreover, he feels the company ought to be willing to help him in keeping his family intact.

Policy, Principle, or Ethics?*

Continental Foods is a large, well-established food processor with plants in North and South America and Europe. The company produces cereals such as "Dynamo Flakes," livestock and poultry feeds, pet feeds such as the well-known "Sport" dog food, flour, and various cooking and baking mixes, such as "Pioneer Waffle Mix." In 1959 gross revenue exceeded $340 million with an operating profit margin of 8.2 percent. Dividend payments have been made regularly since 1905.

In February of 1960 Richard Carlson, Vice President in charge of Personnel Relations, called a meeting at the Continental Foods general offices in Chicago. The conferees were Robert Peters, Industrial Relations Vice President; Raymond Malley, Public Relations Vice President; and Donald Wood, the company's legal counsel.

Mr. Carlson began. "The reason for this meeting is a letter from John Tydings, our Lemoyne, Pennsylvania plant manager, requesting that extra payments be made to one John Lewis, because of a serious compound fracture of the right leg. Mr. Lewis is a plant employee with two years' service. He fell off a step ladder in the plant.

* With the permission of the author, Raymond C. Jancauskas, S.J., Loyola University of Chicago; Loyola-Danforth Case Material.

"Under the Pennsylvania Workmen's Compensation Law, the Industrial Commission of Pennsylvania has awarded Lewis payments of $42 a week until he is fully recovered, which may be at least sixteen weeks. Forty-two dollars is the Pennsylvania maximum. (The Illinois maximum is $45.) That's about half of Lewis' gross pay. But Lewis has six children and is in serious financial straits. The children are too young to work regularly. The two oldest sons have part-time jobs after school. The wife has been moderately active in her church group until the time of the accident, and the ladies have already had a small card party for the family. Jack suggests that we add $20 to the $42 payments so that there would be no danger of Lewis being forced to turn to some public agency for help. The request is supported by Bill Stern, Jack's personnel manager."

Robert Peters, Industrial Relations Vice President, was the first to comment. "This is a tough case. Number one: we should not make unilateral changes in what might amount to being contract terms with the union. The union might think we were trying to undercut their demands in the negotiations coming up this summer. (In view of the Pennsylvania Workmen's Compensation Law, Continental Foods does not have any clause in its union contracts covering in-plant sickness and accidents; it has a benefit plan for off-plant sickness and accidents. Beneficiaries receive half-pay, beginning after the first week away from work and running for a maximum of sixteen weeks.)

"Then there is the problem of retroactive payments. The last case we had here was pretty rough too—that packer in Tennessee who was up to his ears in installment payments when the accident occurred. He may ask why we didn't do something extra for him.

"And then, of course, there is the problem of precedent. What about the next accident?"

The legal counsel, Mr. Wood, agreed. "I think the last reason is very strong. We should not start taking over the work of the Industrial Commission of Pennsylvania.

"We have to think of the other companies too. If the N.A.M. code thinks 'equal pay should be given for equal work performance within the wage structure of the local business establishment,' I think we can argue *a pari* that 'equal awards should be given for equal injury within the compensation structure of the local legal regulations and determinations.' I would suggest we stay in line."

Mr. Malley, Public Relations Vice President, objected. "You are quite correct about the legalities of the situation. But I suspect the reason Dick called us together on this is that we should get at the public relations and the morality.

"What's the use of letting Jack Tydings have a $1000 fund for 'small local contributions in view of public relations' if the whole work force and most of Lemoyne find out one of our workers had to turn to public relief? Why should the community help carry one of our workers? Are we the Continental family, or aren't we? I just can't help thinking that the ladies might run a bingo, and then all Lemoyne will know about it too."

"You almost hit it on the head," said Carlson. "The problem, as I see it, starts with that figure of $42. I can't get it out of my mind. How would you or I start managing on $42 a week?

"Another facet is our policy for salaried people. Remember the Foote case? He was an office manager in our Ohio plant. We carried him at full pay for almost two years until he got rid of his ulcer. He had hospital insurance, as I recall, and a good backlog of savings. If we did right by Foote, are we doing right by Lewis?

"Still another thing is our loan policy for transferred employees. If we help them round out a down payment on a new house, or carry them till they get rid of the old one, it seems we should at least be able to lend in this hardship case. What would you say to making a representation to Ron Graham (the Treasurer) for a loan, if Lewis would want it?"

Mr. Wood said, "Ron will not have to give it, Dick, as you implied. And you know how he feels about his job. He doesn't mind being Treasurer of Continental, but he doesn't like this branching out into the small loan business one bit. He would have to set up special books, set up new rules, etc. It's the problem of precedent again."

At this point Miss Rentrow, Mr. Carlson's secretary, walked in and handed a memorandum to her boss. "We now have a little more information," he said, reading the message. "It seems that Lewis has two major installment debts: one involving monthly payments on his home, the other involving monthly payments on his car. Now I wonder if Lewis should not be expected simply to give up his car and use the money for his real necessities?"

"This case is getting harder all the time," Robert Peters remarked. "I know that the union has not approached the company in this case. Has Lewis asked for help?"

"He hasn't," replied Carlson. "But this does not make our problem easier. As you know, Tydings is one of our best-liked plant managers. He has real empathy for the workers. On top of that he is pretty shrewd. I remember his telling me once that it's easy to do something special for the men once in a while. It doesn't have to be much, as far as money goes, but it must fit some extraordinary situation that everyone is talking about. He might be applying that formula here—though it is hard to see how Lewis is not in a real jam.

"And then there is the point we have not faced fully so far. You brought it up, Bob. Do we have any moral obligation, either in justice or charity, to do something for Lewis, law or no law?"

Old Secrets in a New Job*

William Stapleton, a chemical engineer with considerable experience in offset printing processes, had been hired recently as an engineering supervisor in Western Chemical's Printing Products Division. Until then he had been employed as a research chemist by a competing firm and during the past two years had personally developed a new formula and manufacturing process for press blankets. The new blanket was now on the market and was gaining an increasing share of the market for Stapleton's former employer.

In the offset process, the rubber blanket cylinder on the press receives the image from the inked printing plate and transfers this image to the paper. The blanket is thus an important determinant of printing quality. Stapleton's formula and manufacturing process resulted in a blanket which not only produced superior quality but also gave longer wear, reducing the cost of materials and the cost of press down-time for blanket changes.

Western executives who had interviewed Stapleton had made no mention to him of the new offset blanket. They had indicated it was his managerial potential which interested them since the com-

* With permission of the author, William McInnes, S.J., Fairfield University; Business Ethics Case Material.

pany was expanding and would soon need many more managers with scientific experience than were presently available. Stapleton had been anxious to move out of the laboratory and into management work for some time, but his former employer had not afforded him the opportunity.

The responsibilities of supervision and administration had brought Stapleton to grips with new kinds of problems, as he had hoped would be the case. One problem, however, currently sitting on his desk in the form of a memo from George Curtis, the Division's director of Engineering, was giving him particular concern. It read as follows:

> Please see me this afternoon for the purpose of discussing formulas and manufacturing processes for offset press blankets.

This was the first reference anyone had made to the use of specific past technical information in his new job. Stapleton realized he would have to decide immediately to what extent he would reveal data concerning the secret processes being used by his former employer.

Thefts and Threats

The Minneapolis Office Supplies Company employs 58 men and women to attend to the business of selling, servicing and supplying office equipment to business firms in and near Minneapolis. Among the items stocked by the company are typewriters, adding machines, and cash registers. The volume of business has been, and promises to be, extremely rewarding. Wages are relatively high, working conditions are most satisfactory, and the employees appear to be working in harmony. In short, the company seems to be the model of success.

Henry Adams is one of the company's employees. His duties consist of routine stockroom work. John Nett, Arthur Couch and three other men work with him at unloading, checking and repacking office equipment. Included in their operations is a tally of all materials received and shipped. In this way a continuous inventory is made available to the company officials. There is a certain amount of responsibility and trust placed in these men, because it is here that theft is most likely to occur.

One afternoon Henry returned to the stockroom for his car keys. He surprised John Nett in the act of carrying a typewriter out of the side door and into his waiting car. Henry reacted quite normally by asking John what he was up to. John replied unexpectedly

by threatening Henry with physical injury if he reported the incident to the foreman. Being a practical man, Henry decided to tell
John not to worry about such a report. John left with the typewriter and Henry went home for a sleepless night.

Henry was worried about what would happen if he reported the
theft; he worried about not reporting the theft and being impli-
cated in it if John were caught; and he worried about John's ac-
cusing him if John happened to be apprehended through other
means. John was a quick-tempered man. After working with him
for two years, Henry knew that John wouldn't hesitate to use brute
force if the theft were reported.

In search of advice, Henry confided in Arthur Couch, who was
a good friend. Much to Henry's surprise, Arthur said that he knew
about John's activities. It seemed that Arthur too had been a victim
of intimidation only two weeks earlier. When asked if he intended
to report the incident to the foreman, Arthur explained that he
wanted no part of anything that John might do if he were caught.

A week passed without Henry's reaching a decision. However,
by checking the tallies for the week and comparing them to what he
had counted, Henry discovered that two other typewriters could not
be accounted for. He naturally assumed that John had taken them
too.

Henry Adams was in a dilemma.

The Company Man

       Walt Jones is a student at a large Midwestern university. In order to contribute toward his expenses, he has held a summer job with an Illinois utility company at which his father is a vice president. During four of his five summers at the utility company, Walt was a meter reader. His job was to go from house to house taking readings off the gas and electric meters for monthly billing purposes. Each day he would report to the company office and pick up his route for the day. The number of meters assigned varied with the distance to be covered.

       Walt was proud of his job with the company. He considered himself a "company man." He had been highly praised by his supervisor, who regarded him as a conscientious and efficient worker. The company had a family employment policy which would prevent Walt from taking a job with them after graduation. But several officials had expressed the desire to stretch the rules in his case. One executive pointed out that it would be foolish to lose his services and potential contributions because of a general policy ruling.

       There was one problem that persistently plagued Walt's conscience throughout the years he worked as a meter reader. For the first month in which he read meters, it took him the full eight hours to complete a route; but as he became experienced it took less and less time to do the work. This was the case with all new men hired to read meters. There were many days it would take him only four hours to complete a route. After finishing, having no further duties, he would go home. The next morning he would turn in the previous day's route and pick up the new one. Walt was not the only person in this situation, for none of his co-workers put in an eight-hour day. He usually worked six hours per day, but the full-time readers averaged around five hours of work per day.

The supervisor knew of this situation—it had existed long before Walt started with the company—but he merely warned the men not to get caught. It was common knowledge and a source of humor to the employees. They kept it an inside joke, however, for the men did not want the information to reach the higher-ups for fear of having a new system installed.

Walt found many reasons to justify his behavior. Everyone knew that the newer men took the full time to read a route, and he attributed the shorter work day to the hustle of the more experienced man. Furthermore, he rarely took more than 20 minutes for lunch and felt that the remaining 40 minutes should be considered as an addition to his working time. Also, Walt was a fast worker to whom speed came naturally. Another justification Walt used was the condition of the houses he was required to go into. At times he was almost overcome by the stench and dirt in the basements. He had also been in basements where rats would run across his feet and stairs break away under him. Then there was the constant threat of harassment from dogs. On the whole, many meter readers felt they were not paid a high enough wage for their required duties.

Walt's attitude was that because of his part-time status he was not required to report the lack of work assigned to him. He could easily have discussed the situation with his father, but he did not feel that he was in a position to do so. He knew that he would not return to this particular job after graduation from college. All of his co-workers were family men, and he did not think it was fair to those who depended on this job for a living, for him to instigate an investigation. He also felt he would endanger his supervisor's position—an employee with a record of 30 years with the company. Walt would not like to have seen any of the meter readers laid off for lack of work. He felt that enough permanent employees in fairly responsible positions knew of the situation. They should be the first to report it.

Middle Class Gypsies

Utility Stores is a chain of department stores with gross sales of $400 million. The central office in Boston handles financing, planning and some buying for subgroups, each of which has its own officers, who exercise considerable authority. The subgroups are comprised of one central store and from one to six satellite stores. Each satellite store has its own manager, merchandise managers and buyers, subject to supervision by the central store's general buyers, who oversee and coordinate the work of particular departments in the subgroups.

The central office keeps an eye on promising young men and moves them through the system as part of an apprenticeship program. In this way management found it possible to train the buyers and managers they need at all levels. Experience has taught them that this is the best method, since the nature of their stores and local markets varies so much that a man needs wide experience before he becomes a likely candidate for an executive position in a central store or in the Boston office. A single subgroup, for example, may have one store which caters to the low income group and two which try to maintain a quality image. Some stores are in the inner city and some in shopping centers.

In the past ten years Utility Stores has grown rapidly. Twenty

24

new stores have been added and another ten are planned for the three-year period ahead. As a result of this rapid expansion, men have been moved around frequently in order to increase their exposure to various aspects of the business. While there is no written policy on the question, it is understood that if a man is not willing to move, he will soon be out of the company or at least permanently frozen in a job. The company has been fairly generous in granting moving allowances but has no machinery to help the employee in relocating.

Until recently there had been few complaints about the moving. During the last year, however, Charles Jelser, the Corporate Vice President in charge of executive personnel, has been worried. The need to move frequently has discouraged several good prospects for employment as trainees. Moreover, some of the younger men have opted to stay where they were despite the implied threat. Many others have complained, and moved only with great reluctance. Some, indeed, have raised the ethical issue.

Jelser had been at a convention recently in which a professor had reported on the problems created by relocation of employees. The report included typical comments from the people interviewed in the study. Several of the comments are as follows:

"One loss incurred by the frequent moves that is not reimbursed is the high interest. You never work mortgage payments down to high payment on principal and low interest."

"It sometimes appears that transfers are made for transfers' sake, not for the needs of the business or the growth of the individual. In my opinion, relocations should be held to a minimum and should be accompanied by a promotion and/or raise to minimize the financial effects of the move."

"If the individual wants to go, fine. If not, he should not be asked to, and the 'no' answer should not have the effect, as it does now, of putting the man on the shelf."

"It has been hard on my family. The girl attended four different high schools. The boy attended five different high schools. Tough on youngsters. They've never belonged anywhere."

"During the period between job transfer and the movement of the household, a liberal policy in regard to trips home on weekends should be employed."

"If at all possible, moves should be made during the summer

months rather than during the year for those employees with school-age children."

As Jelser sees it, the problem can be summed up in the career of John Fahren. Fahren joined the firm as a trainee ten years ago, just as the company was starting to move. Because of the need for talent at that time, he became an assistant buyer for men's wear within six months. At the end of a year, he was transferred from one of the central stores to a satellite about 60 miles away and was made a buyer. Fahren did well financially in the new job. Though his salary was only $6,000 a year, he earned a bonus of $6,000 in his first year. The bonus may have been partly luck since the store was so new that the quotas on which bonuses were based had been set too low. At the same time Fahren had introduced some vigorous retailing methods into the store. At the end of two years Fahren was transferred to a store 300 miles away. He was still only a buyer, but he had been given hints that he was in line for the job of merchandise manager if things turned out well. During his five years in the new store, Fahren did fairly well. His combined salary and bonuses came to about $15,000 in the fifth year. Then, he was asked to move again.

Fahren moved, but he was not happy about it. In the process of selling his house, he had to take a loss of $1,000. In addition, the timing of the move forced his wife, Maria, to remain behind with the children for six months, while Fahren rented an apartment in the new location. It was a case of running two households or disrupting the children's education, and Fahren had decided for the education of his four youngsters. In one way or another, the move cost the Fahrens some $2,000. This was in addition to the company's paying $1,200 in moving expenses.

Upon arrival in the new location Fahren decided to buy another house because rents were extremely high. He also had to pick up a second car. The new home was so far from doctors and shopping areas that Maria would have been unable to run the household without one.

The Fahrens had only been in the new location for eighteen months when the company asked him to move again. This was to be a short move of only 50 miles, and management strongly implied that this was Fahren's big chance. They intimated there was an opening for a merchandise manager that he was almost certain to fill, once he had the feel of the new store. In any event, his salary was to be raised $1,000.

Fahren was disturbed this time and spoke to Jelser on one of his infrequent visits to the central office in Boston. Jelser calmed Fahren with a standard speech about the price of advancement and the cost of not moving when asked. Jelser, however, was not happy since no one had the authority to even hint that the move meant a promotion. Indeed, Fahren's efficiency reports indicated that he was at about the end of his potential even though he was only 34 years old. Jelser's uneasiness was magnified by the fact that the local store manager had told him that the moving seemed to be upsetting Fahren's home life. The wife, Maria, was a timid type who found it difficult to make friends. She was unhappy with the continual change of location and had been pressuring her husband to quit and take a more stable job.

Jelser sees Fahren's case as typical of what has been happening in the last ten years and of what will happen more frequently in the next three. Does the company really have a right to transfer men around this way without very good reasons? Must more consideration be given to the impact of moves on both finances and family life? Even from a purely business point of view there is trouble brewing. One Fahren would be no great loss, but what about the dozens like him? Furthermore, frequent transfers seem to be inefficient. The confusion of moving and the pressures of adjustment do not make for peak performance.

A Letter of Recommendation*

John Crowley, general manager of Halberg's Shoe Company manufacturing plant, received a phone call from a business acquaintance, Charles Erl, stating that one of Crowley's supervisory employees, Clayton Munson, was seeking employment with him. Erl, who was manager at another local shoe factory, added that he thought it proper that he should inform John of the situaation. He stated that he was mailing a confidential "personal recommendation" form and would appreciate having John fill in the indicated comments regarding Munson and then return the form. John replied that he would give prompt consideration to the matter, assuring Erl that it was his policy never to hold back his people from such a move if it meant advancement for them.

Munson was not a good administrator. In fact, Crowley considered him to be his poorest performer. Therefore, when John began to fill out the recommendation form, he went at it with the idea that the best way out of the situation for both the Halberg Company and Munson would be to have Erl hire the supervisor.

* With the permission of the author, William C. McInnes, S.J., Fairfield University; Business Ethics Case Material.

One question on the form made him hesitate. It read: In comparison with all other supervisory personnel you have observed, how would you rate the applicant as a leader and an administrator?

Above   Below

Average _____   Average _____   Average _____

Crowley felt that if he rated the man "Below Average" his chances of being hired would be greatly reduced, but he wondered whether worse consequences might result if he were to give Munson a higher rating. Crowley knew that he had his own reputation to consider as well as that of the Halberg Company. He also felt that it was his duty to treat his employee with fairness.

Another question that made him pause was: "Do you believe that this man is a dependable worker?" Crowley knew that Munson had occasionally missed work because of heavy drinking, but he also knew that the man had been burdened financially and emotionally by personal troubles at home.

The last item asked: "Give your general appraisal of this man as an employee while working with your firm."

Mr. Crowley, in preparing his recommendation, is wondering how he should answer these questions.

This I Believe . . .

In a college course in personnel management, the students were asked to write ten statements which described what they believed about people.

Here are some of their statements which have ethical implications.

ABOUT CUSTOMERS

A. Each customer feels that rules, regulations, and procedures are intended for the other customers and do not apply to himself since he is the exception.

B. Customers have lost the joy of giving, but continue to buy gifts to fulfill their obligations.

ABOUT WORK

C. There is an absence of pride in one's work these days.

D. People tend to overestimate the importance of their job in relation to other jobs.

E. Those who help in making a decision will work harder to see that their idea is successful.

F. On-the-job problems should not be discussed at home or at social functions.

G. Anxiety is productive.

H. Employees who have violated a company rule and are faced with disciplinary action almost always tend to view their violation as an exception and feel they deserve lighter disciplinary action.

ABOUT MANAGING

I. Close personal relationships between an employee and his supervisor create an unhealthy business climate; neither will work as efficiently as he would if this relationship did not exist.

J. Most people would rather be told what to do on the job, than assume the responsibility themselves.

K. If a superior is too lenient with a person or gives him too many chances, he will soon be taken advantage of.

L. Criticism should be used as little as possible, because it kills ambition, puts the other person on the defensive, and makes him strive to justify his actions.

M. Since many people are unsure of themselves, they want some authority to guide or direct them to their goal.

N. Tell the employee why he is doing a good job. It is of utmost importance that the employee know not only that he is doing a good job but also how and why he is doing it.

O. It is imperative to have all the facts in formulating good decisions.

P. Bosses are pals nowadays, mainly because they haven't got strength enough to be bosses.

Q. Persons must be handled, and handled purposefully—but they must never know that they are being handled.

R. If people have guidance in doing their work they will generally be able to accomplish a higher quality and a greater amount of work than if they are left to their own initiative.

S. Remember to praise people for their successes, and to say as little as possible about their failures.

ABOUT PEOPLE

T. There are both good and bad in every race and nationality; only by judging each person as an individual can we escape the tragic pitfall of classification into stereotyped social groups.

U. People that say the least to your face are the ones that say the most behind your back, and vice versa.

V. People always stick with you when you are a winner but desert you when you are down.

II

Hiring, Firing, and Promotion

Early Retirement at Milmark

In 1964 Milmark and Company was one of the largest manufacturer of road construction equipment in the United States. In the preceding fifteen years the company's aggressive management had established a reputation for building efficient, high quality, durable products consistent with the needs of the road construction industry.

Between 1954 and 1964, thanks to superhighways and other demands, Milmark's sales increased by 50 percent and profits by 6 percent. Milmark secured a larger share of an expanding market. The Marketing Department at Milmark is broken into five separate sections, each responsible for a complete line of equipment. The fifth section was formed in 1958 because of expanded sales volume and the introduction of a new product line.

The objective of the five marketing sections is to find new applications for existing equipment and also to develop new products. All sections are responsible for writing specifications for new products and for working with Milmark's engineering department to insure customer acceptability. Each section consists of a manager, two or three supervisors, and from ten to fifteen product engineers. Each manager reports to William E. Boyd, the Marketing Vice President.

Frank Treadway, manager of the standard equipment marketing section, had two supervisors and twelve product engineers working for him. Upon graduating with a degree in mechanical engineering in 1934, Mr. Treadway joined the company as a product engineer in the standard equipment section. In 1940 he was promoted to supervisor. As product engineer and supervisor, Frank Treadway did a commendable job. Several new products were developed and successfully marketed under his supervision. He had the reputation of being very thorough. In 1948 he was made section manager. At that time Milmark had not yet begun to experience its real growth. The manager's job was comparatively simple.

Sales for the standard equipment section in 1948 were $2.4 million; in 1954, $4.5 million. Sales increased to $9.0 million by 1963. Milmark's share of the market for this type of equipment increased from 21 percent in 1948 to 27 percent in 1954, and remained at this level for the next ten years. Profits remained stable at approximately 5 percent of sales.

The rate of growth at Milmark provided a good opportunity for personal advancement among the management. In 1963 Milmark employed a total of 3,500 people, an increase of 1,100 since 1954. Very seldom was Milmark forced to go to other companies to recruit management personnel. Approximately 95 percent of the supervisor and manager vacancies were filled from within the company.

Boyd's Department at Milmark had doubled in personnel since 1954. Treadway's section had grown from one supervisor and five product engineers to its present position of two supervisors and twelve product engineers. A product engineer within the section was promoted to supervisor in 1959.

The recruiting of new product engineers was done by the combined efforts of the personnel department and the marketing managers. The marketing managers were responsible for the final approval of a prospective employee's qualifications. Treadway had personally hired ten of the fourteen employees who were under his supervision. The other four had been transferred into the section with Treadway's full approval. All fourteen employees had excellent educational records and their previous employers or managers had rated their capacity for growth as good to excellent.

Vice-President Boyd was aware that the turnover of product engineers in Frank Treadway's section was much higher than in the other four marketing sections. The engineers leaving Treadway's section had been with Milmark about five years. The typical reason they gave for leaving was that they wanted a job offering more responsibility and greater opportunity for advancement. They felt that Treadway had denied them authority to make decisions, and that their every action was subject to his final approval. Also some feared they were becoming too specialized, since they were coming in contact only with the products sold by their section.

Since 1954 many managerial and supervisory positions had opened up at Milmark. Some of these positions were filled by supervisors or product engineers from the Marketing Department. But out of the sixteen promotions coming from the Marketing Department, only one came from Treadway's section. In the past, when Treadway was asked to recommend a candidate for a manager's position, or a supervisor's position even in his own section, his usual comment was that he simply did not have anyone who could assume the responsibility of such positions. Boyd tried to get Treadway to spend more effort on developing management personnel.

The situation did not improve, and early in 1964 Vice-President Boyd began an investigation into the backgrounds of the standard equipment section engineers and supervisors. After taking a long look at the college work of these men, at their scores on Milmark's employment tests and at their company records, Boyd concluded that many of these men really did have managerial talents that were not being developed.

In September, 1964 Vice-President Boyd brought the problem of the standard equipment section to the attention of Milmark's president, Dwight Loomis. Loomis and Boyd then invited in a management consulting firm. This consulting firm made a thorough study of the standard equipment section, its history, its men, and especially of Frank Treadway. The consultants reported that, unfortunately, Treadway would probably not improve in his ability to develop men. Treadway had formed his idea of his job at a time when Milmark did not stress the development of subordinates. Secondly, Treadway was technically oriented rather than people-centered. At his age a change was possible, but not probable. The consultants noted, however, that Treadway was adequate for other phases of his job.

Boyd was undecided whether to ask for Treadway's retirement, even though he was ten years from the mandatory retirement age of 65. He knew that Treadway would be given 35 percent of the pension he would have received at age 65, and that full retirement benefits were equal to 76 percent of Treadway's present salary. In addition, Treadway and his wife would be covered by Milmark's medical insurance plan. Boyd realized that early retirement would be very distasteful to Treadway, who was in good health. And Boyd also felt that the company had some kind of obligation to Treadway, who had been a loyal employee for 30 years.

Mores, Morals, and Company Rules

Located in a Western city of 65,000 people, the Hart-Tasch Company manufactures, assembles and distributes small parts for a variety of machines. The company employs 275 persons, of whom about one-third are women.

The president of the company, Harry Hart, believes in letting employees know the objectives of the company and what he expects of them; he gives every employee a copy of the "22 Company Rules." The introduction to these rules states: "Violation of any of these rules will make an employee subject to discharge or lesser disciplinary action, depending on the gravity of the offense as determined by supervision." Among the 22 rules are:

1. Careless or inefficient performance of duty . . .
3. Willful restriction of production . . .
15. Conduct on or off the job that is contrary to the common decency or morality of the community or that reflects unfavorably upon the corporation . . .
22. Horseplay.

In a letter to a friend, Albert Maher, in February, 1966 Hart wrote: "Moral and business ethics have always been of great concern

39

to me in that I live up to the highest possible standards I can. Yet at the same time we are constantly confronted with the necessity to live within the circumstances in which we find ourselves in our community and business life . . . I feel we will continue trying to upgrade our moral ethics, our corporate ethics and our personal ethics in all areas, even though we are not successful all of the time."

In March, 1966 Hart learned that a man and a woman who worked for his company had been guilty of immoral behavior. The man and woman were married, but not to each other. One afternoon when the woman was not scheduled to be working, the man obtained an excuse for time off due to a headache, and the two had gone together to a motel. After an inquiry, Hart felt certain that they had committed adultery. Several people at the plant said that it was not the first time, though nobody knew if the spouses of the two were aware of the affair.

While Hart was debating what to do about the affair, he accidentally bumped into Maher, and the topic came up for discussion. Hart felt that the reputation of his company was at stake, as well as the future enforcement of the "22 Company Rules."

Maher asked Hart whether he thought there was any limit to his authority over employees' off-the-job behavior. Hart replied that the man, at least, was not really off the job; he should have been on the job, though admittedly it would be hard to prove that he did not have a headache. Maher also asked whether dismissal might not be too severe a penalty. If the employees were fired, word would get around town; their families would be hurt; and it might be difficult for them to get the kind of work and pay to which their skills entitled them, and which they might need to support their families.

Because the man provided the only income for his wife and two children, Hart was inclined to be less severe with him than with the woman, whose husband was also working. But Hart wondered whether firing only the woman would give her grounds for a complaint under Title VII of the Civil Rights Act of July, 1964, which requires that all employees be treated without regard to sex in every phase of employment.

In April Maher received the following letter from Hart: "I thought you would be interested in hearing the outcome of the conduct problem which I discussed with you recently.

"The woman quit and I decided to fire the man. Upon going

to the Personnel Department to carry out this decision, I was informed that I had been cheated. He had already quit. I think this is a cowardly way to act. I sometimes am disappointed in the shifty character of human nature and in people who will not stand up and have someone poke them in the eye when they have it coming.

"However, I did initiate an action through the Personnel Department and the union, whereby all the people were aware of what our action was going to be had they not left the company. We also made it clear we had planned on taking positive and drastic action in this instance. So maybe we have accomplished the same end result, in an easier manner than might have been anticipated. Perhaps the lesson will serve as an example for some time in the future. I do not have too much confidence that I have solved the problem permanently unless sex goes out of style."

City Auto, Incorporated*

City Auto, Incorporated, is a large retail automobile agency located in the auto row area of an Eastern city of 350,000 people. City Auto has a franchise with a major automobile manufacturer retailing new cars and trucks. Used cars are also handled. A large service shop is maintained and new replacement parts are distributed to smaller garages and service stations.

Dick Fleps has been employed by City Auto for six years and has been sales manager for the past two years. Fleps has been in the auto business for fifteen years, working for a number of auto outlets. At one time he owned a used car lot.

When he started as sales manager he had five salesmen. Fleps trained these men to use a low pressure approach in their selling work. He was a stickler for details. The salesmen were required to attend weekly sales meetings at 8:00 A.M. sharp on Monday, to be on the sales floor at all times unless with a customer, and to submit weekly reports on the present status of prospective customers. He also required the salesmen to attend to a number of clerical details. The men resented a few of his rules, but in general morale was high and Fleps had the respect of his entire sales force. Sales had in-

* With the permission of the author, William C. McInnes, S.J., Fairfield University; Business Ethics Case Material.

creased and four new salesmen were added to the staff by the end of Flep's first year as manager.

Before the spring of 1961, no salesman had been assigned to the used car lot. Each salesman on the floor would take a day or two on the lot. This lack of attention to the used car business developed because the owners of the agency took the attitude that the profit on used cars was not great enough to warrant a large used car lot. As a consequence most trade-ins were sold at wholesale. For six months Fleps had urged his boss to reconsider this policy on the ground that profit margins on used cars were higher than on some new car sales. He finally received approval to expand the lot in size and to hire a man to run it.

After a number of interviews, Fleps engaged Frank Clow, who was unmarried, 31 years old, with five years of auto sales experience. He was hired on the basis of a personal interview and two letters of recommendation.

Clow had served in the U.S. Army for three years. After his discharge from the service, he had enrolled in a small college in California, which he quit a year and a half later. He then started selling used cars, remaining only a few months at each of several lots, mainly—he said—because of a lack of job security. Fleps realized that Clow was a restless, hard sell type and might be hard to handle. However, he felt that possibly just such a personality would be required on the used car lot.

After six weeks on the City Auto used car lot, Clow was averaging three car sales a week, which was on a par with the other nine new car salesmen. Two and a half months later, he had increased his sales volume from three cars a week to an average of 2.5 cars per day. Fleps was congratulated by the owners for both his idea and his skill in selection and training. It even looked as if the increased retail volume in used cars was going to have a significant impact on profits.

Though Clow was an excellent salesman, he resented authority. He missed more sales meetings than he attended. He also maintained his own hours, sometimes arriving at noon on Mondays. His reply to Fleps' questioning on this matter was: "As long as I am outselling every man, there is no reason for me to abide by all the rules." Clow pointed out that he was working more than 70 hours a week making calls and demonstrating cars at night.

The other salesmen were apparently affected by Frank's behavior. They began to question some of the rules, and attendance at the Monday morning sales meeting began to fall off. Several of the men had expressed the opinion that time was a salesman's greatest asset and all the laborious details that they were required to attend to took too much time. Fleps explained that they could maintain a quality image only if the new car department kept everything under control.

Privately Fleps felt that Clow's attitude and work were all right on the used car lot. However, since it was affecting the discipline of the entire sales force, something ought to be done. He finally laid down the law to Clow. "You will abide by the rules or else. Perhaps *you* will sell fewer cars, but I consider the general discipline of the work force more important than a few extra sales. I'm sorry but that is the way it is."

Fleps mentioned his actions to Mr. Brianti, the principal owner of City Auto, about a week after the showdown. Brianti said that Fleps was in charge of everything, but suggested that perhaps discipline could be relaxed in the interests of higher sales. Indeed, Brianti hinted that Fleps might be unnecessarily imposing his own need for order on the sales force.

Fleps was upset by this and started to question the fairness of his own work rules. Clow's free and easy ways, however, continued to annoy him, especially since other salesmen now refused to play the game by Flep's rules. At the same time, he had to admit that sales were improving despite the breakdown in discipline.

Having confronted Clow, Fleps felt he must fire him. He wondered, however, whether it would be fair. He even doubted whether it would do any good. Worst of all, he was certain that with Frank Clow gone, profits would go down, at least temporarily.

Coach of the Year

On December 23, 1965 Lou Saban of the Buffalo Bills was named coach of the year in the American Football League. This marked the second straight year that Saban had been chosen for that honor by the players. The Bills had won the AFL championship in both seasons.

On January 2, 1966 Saban resigned as coach of the Bills, saying that "there can be little left to conquer in professional football." His resignation surprised the team owner, Ralph Wilson, Jr., who said that Saban "expressed a desire to retire because of the pressures involved in coaching professional football today. He wanted to spend more time with his family." Saban and Wilson had come to terms each year on a handshake, without a written contract. In 1965 Saban was reported to have received $30,000. There was no report of friction between the two men.

On January 3 the 44-year old Saban was named head football coach at the University of Maryland. He succeeded Tom Nugent, who had been dismissed a month earlier. Saban agreed to a four-year contract, starting at $22,500, with gradual increases to $25,000 after three years. This contract made him the highest paid football coach in the history of Maryland. Additional benefits, including radio and television contracts, were expected to put his annual income near $30,000.

During the 1966 collegiate season, the Maryland Terrapins won four games and lost six.

On December 9 Saban visited Denver, Colorado, where he spent most of the day with the management of the Broncos, a professional football team in the AFL. When a report of this meeting was circulated on December 14, Saban denied it. Later he explained: "The only reason I denied it was that Denver still had a ball game left and I didn't want to disrupt Denver's play against Buffalo."

On December 16 the newspapers reported that Saban had agreed to a ten-year contract as coach and general manager of the Denver Broncos. Gerald H. Phipps, owner of the Broncos, said that the salary was about $50,000 a year. Saban said, "It's kind of hard to walk away from the proposition Mr. Phipps made."

The University of Maryland announced Saban's resignation. A statement by the university's president, Wilson H. Elkins, and two members of the Athletic Committee said that Saban was being unfair. "We believe that serious consideration of the job with Denver at this time is contrary to what he told the University he was going to do, is indicative of his consideration of breaking his contract, that it is unfair to the University, and that it will hurt the University's football program," the statement said.

"The first time the University had heard of any consideration of such a position by Coach Saban was yesterday morning when it appeared in the newspapers. At that time Coach Saban indicated, according to the news report, that he didn't know anything about it."

To Test or Not To Test

On March 14, 1966 the Supreme Court of Illinois settled the Motorola case by finding the company innocent of discrimination in its hiring practices. The Court, however, did not decide whether or not Motorola's first screening test is discriminatory. This issue, which had been raised by the original Hearing Examiner of the Illinois Fair Employment Practices Commission—but did not enter into the Court's decision—is still being debated.

Companies use tests in order to cut down the cost of secreening and training applicants. In the case of a company like Motorola, which screens some 20,000 applicants a year, the cost can be considerable. Motorola, moreover, found that in the three years from 1963 to 1966, the use of tests enabled it to halve the maximum number of days required to train applicants for wiring and soldering. As early as 1960 the company had used tests on applicants and then hired them without consideration of the test scores. A follow-up study made some time later revealed ". . . that a significant proportion of those accepted who had since terminated would not have been accepted originally if their test scores had been considered at the time of employment."

The problem is not unlike that of colleges which use tests to select students who stand a good chance of finishing college, even

47

though admissions officials know that the tests will eliminate some applicants who could make it successfully through the particular school. Whether or not such tests are fair depends on the reliability and validity of the tests. However, since tests take time and money to administer and score, the cost of testing relative to the job to be done is also relevant.

In 1960 the Motorola Company started using Test No. 10 as an initial, low-level screening device. Developed by Shurrager, Shurrager and Ross in 1949, the test consisted of 28 items that were to be done in five minutes. Those who received a raw score of at least six on this test were given additional tests for the particular job they desired. Test No. 10, which is used also by Montgomery Ward, Brunswick, and the Jewel Tea Company, involves verbal comprehension and simple reasoning. Its authors keyed it to the original standardization group, which was predominantly white.

According to a Motorola report,

. . . the ability of the test to yield acceptable consistent measurements is indicated by a test-retest reliability coefficient of .8. This value was reported in the original standardization of the test and subsequent studies have demonstrated reliabilities ranging from .7 to .9. Test No. 10 correlates .8 with the Otis 30 minute paper and pencil test and has been correlated with other standard measures of intelligence. Its relationship with the Wechsler-Bellevue, an individually administered test of intelligence, was also found to be .7.

The company's studies indicated the following results, which have a bearing on the validity of the tests:

Significant variations in mean scores obtained by various groups have been found. In Chicago area plants, wirers and solderers obtained a mean score of approximately 8 correct items. In Motorola's Phoenix, Arizona plants, the mean score of a comparable group of production people was approximately 11. More highly skilled groups tend to score higher. For example, each group of television phasers and analyzers in Chicago obtained mean scores above 14. The mean score of this job is 6 points higher than the mean of wirers and solderers and 8 points above the cut-off score used on applicants.

In another study, 215 electronic students in a technical school were given Test No. 10 plus a short technical achievement test used by Motorola foremen in selecting phasers and analyzers. The correlation between these two tests was statistically significant. There is a demonstrable relationship between performance on Test No. 10 and the ability to acquire technical information.

Psychologists who testified before the Fair Employment Practices Commission were divided as to whether or not the tests were unfairly discriminatory. The authors of the test and four other psychologists said that the test would only discriminate in terms of trainability. Four other experts said the test was inadequately reliable, *probably* not too relevant to the job and *probably* unfair.

The issue, according to Dr. French, Vice President for Research and Testing with Scientific Research Associates, was whether or not the tests discriminated on the basis of education and skills which were not actually needed on the job or could be easily learned or compensated for by other skills. Leroy N. Vernon, in an article in the *Illinois Psychologist,* noted that to prove the tests discriminatory in this sense, "they will also have to demonstrate that the job performance of Negroes as compared with whites is erroneously predicted by test scores. Proof or disproof of this point is likely to be extremely difficult with the numbers of people involved, and in situations where criteria of job effectiveness are difficult to establish, will probably be difficult or impossible."

Recommendation C 15 of the 1954 Technical Recommendations of the American Psychological Association is pertinent to this problem:

If the validity of the test can reasonably be expected to be different in subgroups which can be identified when the test is given, the manual should report the validity for each group separately or should report that no difference has been found.

The case thus involves questions of both ethical and professional responsibility for the validation and administration of tests.

The person involved in the Motorola Case decided by the Illinois Supreme Court was Leon Myart. Myart, a Negro, had attended Forrestville School and Dunbar Vocational High School. In 1955, at age eighteen, he left school without graduating. Until 1959 he served as a communications lineman in the army. During this period he continued his education and received a high school equivalency diploma as well as earning an FCC third class radio-telephone operator's license. Upon being honorably discharged from the army, he took a 432 hour evening course in electronics. In May of 1961 he completed an additional course as an electrical technician at the Coyne Electrical School. In December of 1962 he completed a television-radio technician course. From time to time he also worked as a television repair man.

In July of 1963 Leon Myart applied for a job as an analyzer and phaser at Motorola's Franklin Park plant. After filling out an application form, he was given the General Ability Test No. 10, which was described earlier. He scored four, or two points below the minimum requirements. As a result no further tests were given. He was then interviewed very briefly by a Motorola personnel man. It would appear that the entire process took only fifteen minutes.

Although Myart testified that he had never taken this test before, the Personnel Services Manager of Montgomery Ward testified that he had taken it in October of 1962 and obtained a score of six. Mr. Walter Ducey of the Illinois Fair Employment Practices Commission administered the test orally to Myart, and he scored seven. Ducey, however, had not followed the standard procedure for administering the test, nor did he have the official scoring key.

Because scores on a given test can vary, Myart's passing grades at Montgomery Ward do not prove whether or not he would have passed at Motorola. Experts point out that variations of two or three points are not unlikely, even on a short test.

CORE Protests to Benson Foundry

Benson Foundry employs about three hundred persons. Of these, about one hundred are either supervisors or have technical or clerical positions. The business is family owned and the president and chairman of the board is Charles E. Benson, grandson of the company's founder. The company operates a single facility located in Milwaukee, manufacturing small and medium-sized gray-iron castings for many different customers.

The labor force is composed principally of unskilled and semi-skilled workers. Approximately 25 percent of the labor force is Negro, 72 percent is white and 3 percent is of Spanish descent. The first line supervision consists of 15 foremen, all selected from the work force. All of them are white. The average laborer has a ninth-grade education, while the average foreman has completed two years of high school.

The upper supervision, about 25 in number, is made up primarily of men educated in engineering, metallurgy, or business. The remaining office staff is composed of technicians, secretaries, and general clerical help. Most of this group are high school graduates.

Benson is a nonunion shop, but management has made it a policy to keep wage rates on a par with union shops in the area, whose rates are classified as "average" for the foundry industry. It has been company practice to hire Negroes for the labor force for over 30 years.

In recent months the local chapter of CORE (Congress on Racial Equality) has been contacting local companies concerning their hiring and promotional policies in an effort to convince them to take positive action to end any form of *de facto* discrimination. Many firms have agreed to discuss the matter, and some have instituted programs and policies aimed at gradually correcting the injustice resulting from discriminatory practices.

On Friday, November 6th, Charles Benson refused to meet with local CORE officials, saying, "We don't need CORE to tell us how to run our business. We've been hiring Negroes for 30 years. Let them worry about those who haven't." On Monday, November 9th, CORE began picketing Benson Foundry.

When questioned about CORE'S action, Martin Jones, president of the local chapter, said,

We have made repeated attempts to discuss this matter with representatives of Benson Foundry, but they have refused to do so. As we see it, Benson Foundry is practicing discrimination in both their hiring and promotion polices. They have never hired a Negro for any but the lowest class of jobs. Although one-fourth of the labor force is Negro, they have no Negro foreman and there are no Negroes among the office force. We feel that if one-fourth of the laborers are Negroes, it is reasonable to expect that one-fourth of the foremen and office force should also be Negroes. We are picketing Benson Foundry to draw attention to this discrimination, and we urge all fair-minded businessmen to refuse to support this discrimination.

In a press release on November 10th, Mr. Benson made the following statement:

You might say that I am surprised and somewhat angry at this action by CORE. I am sure that this will have no effect on our business. Our employees are loyal, and our customers are not apt to be influenced by these high-handed methods. I am surprised at this action, because we have a record of 30 years testifying to the fact that we do not discriminate in hiring. The only criterion we have used is whether or not an applicant is willing and able to do the job. I am shocked and angry at this public act of intimidation. Neither CORE nor any other pressure group has the right to tell a man how to run his business. We just don't do things that way in this country.

In private conversation, Mr. Benson was vehement in speaking about the incident.

If CORE really wants to help the Negro, let them encourage him to become better educated so that he can qualify for supervisory and technical positions. If we don't have Negroes working in our office, it is simply because Negro applicants aren't as qualified as the personnel we do have. What am I supposed to do—fire some of my present people to make room for unqualified Negroes? Somehow that doesn't seem fair to me. And as far as Negro foremen are concerned, it just wouldn't work. Any business-man knows that one of the principal functions of a foreman is to get along with his people—to get them to work for him. Now, many of our people come from various ethnic groups and, like it or not, they're prejudiced. They wouldn't work for a Negro. So even if we could find a qualified Negro, he wouldn't work out. It would severely hurt our morale and we can't afford that. Five or six years ago I had a Negro foreman. He was a good man but he quit because the workers made life too tough for him. I'm no crusader. I'm just a common businessman trying to make a buck. I think that these things take time, and irresponsible actions by Negro groups such as CORE aren't going to help things. They just get people riled up.

CIVIL RIGHTS ACT OF 1964
Excerpts from Title VII—Equal Employment Opportunity

DISCRIMINATION BECAUSE OF RACE, COLOR, RELIGION, SEX, OR NATIONAL ORIGIN

UNLAWFUL PRACTICES.

SEC. 703. (a) It shall be an unlawful employment practice for an employer—

EMPLOYERS.

(1) to fail or refuse to hire or to discharge any individual, or otherwise to discriminate against any individual with respect to his compensation, terms, conditions, or privileges of employment, because of such individual's race, color, religion, sex, or national origin; or

(2) to limit, segregate, or classify his employees in any way which would deprive or tend to deprive any individual of employment opportunities or otherwise adversely affect his status as an employee, because of such individual's race, color, religion, sex, or national origin.

EMPLOYMENT AGENCY.

(b) It shall be an unlawful employment practice for an employment agency to fail or refuse to refer for employment, or otherwise to discriminate against, any individual because of his race, color, religion, sex, or national origin, or to classify or refer for employment any individual on the basis of his race, color, religion, sex, or national origin.

LABOR ORGANIZATION.

(c) It shall be an unlawful employment practice for a labor organization—

(1) to exclude or to expel from its membership, or otherwise to discriminate against, any individual because of his race, color, religion, sex, or national origin.

(2) to limit, segregate, or classify its membership, or to classify or fail or refuse to refer for employment any individual, in any way which would deprive or tend to deprive any individual of employment opportunities, or would limit such employment opportunities or otherwise adversely affect his status as an employee or as an applicant for employment, because of such individual's race, color, religion, sex, or national origin; or

(3) to cause or attempt to cause an employer to discriminate against an individual in violation of this section.

TRAINING PROGRAMS.

(d) It shall be an unlawful employment practice for any employer, labor organization, or joint labor-management committee controlling apprenticeship or other training or retraining, including on-the-job training programs to discriminate against any individual because of his race, color, religion, sex, or national origin in admission to, or employment in, any program established to provide apprenticeship or other training.

EXCEPTIONS.

(e) Notwithstanding any other provision of this title, (1) it shall not be an unlawful employment practice for an employer to hire and employ employees, for an employment agency to classify, or refer for employment any individual, for a labor organization to classify its membership or to classify or refer for employment any individual, or for an employer, labor organization, or joint labor-management committee controlling apprenticeship or other training or retraining programs to admit or employ any individual in such program, on the basis of his religion, sex, or national origin in those certain instances where religion, sex, or national origin is a bona fide occupational qualification reasonably necessary to the normal operation of that particular business or enterprise, and (2) it shall not be an unlawful employment practice for a school, college, university, or other educational institution or institution of learning to hire and employ employees of a particular religion if such school, college, university, or other educational institution or institution of learning is, in whole or in substantial part, owned, supported, controlled, or managed by a particular religion or by a particular religious corporation, association, or society, or if the curriculum of such school, college, university, or other educational institution or institution of learning is directed toward the propogation of a particular religion.

(f) As used in this title, the phrase "unlawful employment practice" shall not be deemed to include any action or measure taken by an employer, labor organization, joint labor-management committee, or employment agency with respect to an individual who is a member of the Communist Party of the United States or of any other organization required to register as a Communist-action or Communist-front organization by final order of the Subversive Activities Control Board pursuant to the Subversive Activities Control Act of 1950.

(g) Notwithstanding any other provision of this title, it shall not be an unlawful employment practice for an employer to fail or refuse to hire and employ any individual for any position, for an employer to discharge any individual from any position, or for an employment agency to fail or refuse to refer any individual for employment in any position, or for a labor organization to fail or refuse to refer any individual for employment in any position, if—

(1) the occupancy of such position, or access to the premises in or upon which any part of the duties of such position is performed or is to be performed, is subject to any requirement imposed in the interest of national security of the United States under any security program in effect pursuant to or administered under any statute or the United States or any Executive order of the President; and

(2) such individual has not fulfilled or has ceased to fulfill that requirement.

(h) Notwithstanding any other provision of this title, it shall not be an unlawful employment practice for an employer to apply different standards of compensation, or different terms, conditions, or privileges of employment pursuant to a bona fide seniority or merit system, or a system which measures earnings by quantity or quality of production or to employees who work in different locations, provided that such differences are not the result of an intention to discriminate because of race, color, religion, sex, or national origin, nor shall it be an unlawful employment practice for an employer to give and to act upon the results of any professionally developed ability test provided that such test, its administration or action upon the results is not designed, intended or used to discriminate because of race, color, religion, sex or national origin. It shall not be an unlawful employment practice under this title for any employer to differentiate upon the basis of sex in determining the amount of the wages or compensation paid or to be paid to employees of such employer if such differentiation is authorized by the provisions of section 6(d) of the Fair Labor Standards Act of 1938, as amended (29 U.S.C. 206 (d)).

INDIANS.

(i) Nothing contained in this title shall apply to any business or enterprise on or near an Indian reservation with respect to any publicly announced employment practice of such business or enterprise under which a preferential treatment is given to any individual because he is an Indian living on or near a reservation.

PREFERENTIAL TREATMENT.

(j) Nothing contained in this title shall be interpreted to require any employer, employment agency, labor organization, or joint labor-management committee subject to this title to grant preferential treatment to any individual or to any group because of the race, color, religion, sex, or national origin of such individual or group on account of an imbalance which may exist with respect to the total number or percentage of persons of any race, color, religion, sex, or national origin employed by any employer, referred or classified for employment by any employment agency or labor organization, admitted to membership or classified by any labor organization, or admitted to, or employed in, any apprenticeship or other training program, in comparison with the total number or percentage of persons of such race, color, religion, sex, or national origin in any community, State, section, or other area, or in the available work force in any community, State, section, or other area.

OTHER UNLAWFUL EMPLOYMENT PRACTICES

SEC. 704. (a) It shall be an unlawful employment practice for an employer to discriminate against any of his employees or applicants for employment, for an employment agency to discriminate against any individual, or for a labor organization to discriminate against any member thereof or applicant for membership, because he has opposed any practice made an unlawful employment practice by this title, or because he has

made a charge, testified, assisted, or participated in any manner in an investigation, proceeding, or hearing under this title.

(b) It shall be an unlawful employment practice for an employer, labor organization, or employment agency to print or publish or cause to be printed or published any notice or advertisement relating to employment by such an employer or membership in or any classification or referral for employment by such a labor organization, or relating to any classification or referral for employment by such an employment agency, indicating any preference, limitation, specification, or discrimination, based on race, color, religion, sex, or national origin, except that such a notice or advertisement may indicate a preference, limitation, specification, or discrimination based on religion, sex, or national origin when religion, sex or national origin is a bona fide occupational qualification for employment.

John Mills, Engineer*

Marcel Kowalski is a product design engineer for Superior Motor Car Corporation. He works in a large engineering facility, responsible for advanced brake design. He has five graduate engineers assigned to work with him in this area. His men work under considerable pressure with deadlines that require the group to work at full speed and with very little margin for error or delay.

Recently one engineer was transferred, and Kowalski has been assigned a new engineer, John Mills, to work in his group. Mills is a Negro. In the process of familiarizing the new engineer with the operations of the group, Kowalski plans to send him to one of the assembly plants to become acquainted with the way in which the brake is finally put together. But he discovers from conversation with friends in the assembly plant that there is considerable resentment there on the part of middle and lower management. "They'd better not send that fellow down here!" Chances are he will be given a hard time when he appears in that location.

In addition Kowalski discovers that Mills is having difficulty with some of the support groups in the engineering area when it comes to getting cooperation on small jobs that he needs to have done. These groups do not openly refuse to do the work, but they

* With the permission of the author, Detroit Industrial Mission; *Life and Work*, Vol. 8, Number 4; April, 1966.

drag their feet as much as possible and cause delays in getting Mills' work out for him.

Given the time pressure under which Kowalski's group works, he is concerned about what John Mills' presence will mean for meeting the deadlines he has been given by his superior. Kowalski feels he has three lines of action he can follow:

(1) He can continue to use Mills as he would any other member of the group and take a chance on the slow-down that this will create. Kowalski is convinced that if he does this he will be unable to meet the deadlines he has been given, and consequently his own performance will be marked down by his superior.

(2) He can remove the Negro engineer from responsibilities that put him in direct contact with the plants or the supporting services in the engineering area, and restrict his work to things he can do at his desk. This would avoid the tensions and problem—but would put more work on other members of his group and raise some resentments among them. This would still reduce Kowalski's ability to meet his deadlines.

(3) He could go to his boss, explain the situation, and ask to have Mills taken out of the area and given a job where there would be less time pressure.

A Man's World

In the summer of 1964 Richard Ritt took part in an "on-the-job" educational program for high school teachers conducted by the local plant of Brader Products Company. The plant was the largest employer in a city that regularly had more workers than jobs. During the school year Mr. Ritt taught economics and bookkeeping to seniors in one of the city's three high schools. While at the plant, Ritt divided his time among the four departments of the comptroller's division. He was assigned a desk in the cost accounting department and came to know the seven members of this department well.

One Friday morning, Earl Puls, the cost accounting supervisor, took a few minutes to explain how white-collar employees were paid. He showed Ritt a sheet listing the workers and the hours worked; the supervisor had to sign this sheet. Ritt inquired why there was one sheet for the six men in the department and one for the lone woman, Josephine Beelus. He pointed out that there was obviously room enough to put all seven names on one sheet. Earl said that it was a policy of Brader Products to keep the payroll for women separate from the payroll for men, but that he did not know the reason for this separation. This answer prompted the teacher to inquire into the implications of a few facts he had learned along similar lines.

He had noticed that the six men in the department regularly worked overtime, once putting in 60 hours of work in a week; but Josephine never worked a minute overtime. Earl replied that July and August often saw the cost department working overtime as it prepared the budget for the next fiscal year, but that the plant comptroller had insisted that no women in his division work overtime.

Earlier, Ritt had learned from Al Kunkel, one of the older members of the cost group, that it was rare for a woman in the comptroller's division to get a classification like "Junior Accountant" no matter how proficient she was. For example, Al singled out two competent, middle-aged women who had been with the company for more than ten years but had not been promoted to "Junior Accountant." It was common knowledge that women did not advance in job classifications or in pay rating as rapidly as men at the plant. When Ritt asked Earl whether Brader Products had any policy concerning the employment of women as supervisors, Earl replied that he knew of one female supervisor in another city, but that she was certainly an exception. Earl felt that the paucity of female supervisors was due to "the fact that no man likes to work for a woman."

Ritt also learned that Josephine was being paid about 20 percent less than a couple of men in the department who had been with the company a shorter time than she, had the same education as she, and were doing basically the same kind of clerical work. In his economics class Ritt had taught that industry generally practices the maxim "equal pay for equal work" and was surprised that a big, well-known corporation seemed to be ignoring it. He also recalled a speech in which an executive of Brader Products had stressed the idea that productivity must always be the ultimate criterion in any wage contract.

When Ritt asked Earl whether Josephine or the other women in the comptroller's division ever complained about men receiving more money than women, Earl answered that there were very few complaints on that basis, but that there were complaints about pay differences between women who were doing the same kind of work in different departments. The plant did not have a standardized wage scale for white-collar jobs.

After Ritt returned to his desk, he thought over what he had learned about the treatment of women at the plant. He wondered whether he should mention the matter to the comptroller when the two men met at the end of August. The comptroller had told him at the beginning of the summer that any ideas for improvement or any criticism of current practice would be welcome. Ritt knew that several of these practices probably violated Title VII of the Civil Rights Act passed early that summer, which would not go into effect until July, 1965. But he felt that the question of overtime was purely an ethical issue.

Ritt was ambivalent about the inclusion of women as a special group in the Civil Rights Act. He knew that the sex amendment, which was introduced in an effort to delay a vote, had gotten into the bill on a fluke. He wondered whether the amendment would not work hardship in time of recession on men who were the heads of households, but who had less seniority than women who did not have similar family responsibilities.

The Boss's Son*

William Bateman, the plant manager of a manufacturing firm, is faced with the problem of appointing an assistant. The two best qualified candidates are Dean Thomas, Jr. and Henry Roberts.

Thomas, the son of the company's president, is 25 years old. A graduate of a liberal arts college, he is bright and willing to learn. He has been with the company for two years and has held jobs as machine operator's helper, production control clerk for the plant production manager, production manager for the assembly department, and customer service manager (inside salesman) in the sales department, spending about equal time in each job. Thomas has been working on his M.B.A. degree at night, and his professors rate him as definitely superior. Although the speed of Thomas' promotions and the breadth and variety of his assignments have exceeded that of other recent employees, he has also shown unusual competence.

Roberts, 38 years old, is a graduate of a leading technical and professional school, where he received simultaneous degrees in industrial engineering and business administration. In his seven years

* With the permission of the author, William C. McInnes, S.J., Fairfield University; Business Ethics Case Material.

with the company he has held several jobs in the sub-assembly department, including eighteen months as general foreman of the department. He has been in his present position, plant manager of production control, for one year. In each assignment he has, according to his boss, "shown sound judgment and knowledge of all plant operations." Bateman has considered him to be the company's leading candidate for promotion to assistant plant manager.

Roberts has been dropping hints about tempting job offers from a competitor. This disturbed Bateman, who is not sure that he can easily replace him. Certainly there is no one within the plant with Roberts' combination of education, experience, and drive. At present the market is tight since most firms in the industry are operating at capacity.

An additional factor affecting the decision is the expected retirement of the company's general manager in four to six months. Bateman, who is 50 years old, thinks it likely that he himself will be named to succeed the general manager, thus making the newly appointed assistant the logical choice for plant manager at that time. As a matter of fact, Bateman feels that his success in developing and promoting the right man will greatly influence his own advancement.

The feelings of Dean Thomas, Sr., president of the company, are a mystery to Bateman. He believes that his recommendation must include a defense of his decision both in terms of the qualifications of the man appointed and the continued developmental progress of both young Thomas and Roberts. The president has always emphasized the concept of promoting from within the company and on the basis of proven merit. It is commonly felt, however, that Thomas, Sr., now 62, has his heart set on his son taking over the business. Indeed he made an exception to the company's policy prohibiting the employment of managers' sons when he permitted his son to start with the company.

Bateman feels that the promotion of Thomas would be acceptable to most subordinates since people have accepted the fact that he will move rapidly up the ladder. Roberts and his close friends will be upset if Thomas gets the job, but—aside from quitting—they would probably not deliberately hurt morale. Bateman is torn between fairness and fear for his own career.

Statistics for Meditation*

I. A study of the 50 largest commercial banks in the United States revealed the following interesting information:

Senior officers in the 50 banks studied totalled 632. The survey found that 8 of these senior officers (1.3 percent) were Jews.

Of 3,438 middle management executives, only 32 (0.9 percent) were Jewish. These 32 were employed in 12 of the 50 banks studied.

Of the 50 banks under study, 9 are located in New York City. They had 173 senior officers among them; only one of these was identified as Jewish in the survey. The middle management of these 9 banks included 927 executives in all, of whom 9 (1.0 percent) were Jews.

It should be noted that 25 percent of the population of New York City are Jews, as are 50 percent of its college graduates.[1]

II. Another study gave this result:

Eighty-two percent of New York City's 50 mutual savings banks have no key Jewish officers, and 60 percent have no Jewish

* The studies from which these data were gathered were sponsored by the American Jewish Committee, Institute of Human Relations, 165 E. 56 St., New York.

[1] "Patterns of Exclusion from the Executive Suite: Commercial Banking," August, 1966, pp. 3-5.

trustees. Less than 2.5 percent of the more than 400 officers and under 3.5 percent of the approximately 750 trustees are Jews.[2]

III. Yet a third study of the utility industry in the United States indicated that:

1. Officers in the 50 companies studied number 755. Of these, only 8 (1 percent) were identified as Jews.

2. Of the 50 corporations surveyed, 43 apparently have no officers who were identified as Jews.[3]

---

[2] "The Mutual Savings Banks of New York City: A Survey of the Exclusion of Jews at Top Management and Policy Making Levels," October, 1965, p. 1.

[3] "Patterns of Exclusion from the Executive Suite: The Public Utilities Industry," December, 1963, p. 15.

III

Industrial Relations

Union Rules

My name is Lewis Johnson. For the past two years I have been both a member of the International Union of Operating Engineers and an engineering student at the University of Minnesota.

Last week, when school ended, I began looking for a summer job to earn the money for next year's expenses. I called my Local's business agent and was told that, although there was nothing near my home town, there was plenty of work in Minneapolis. When I agreed to go there, he said, "Report to work at midnight tomorrow operating an HD-6 with an end-loader, at ABC Steel under the Wabasha Street Bridge. You'll be working for the XYZ Construction Company; the rate of pay is $3.49 an hour; and your master mechanic is Bill Ownes."

When I arrived at the job, Mr. Ownes put me to work operating the HD-6 and loading dump trucks with dirt. About two hours later my HD-6 began to boil because of a leaky radiator. I stopped working the crawler and went to look for water to put in the radiator to keep the HD-6 going until it could be properly repaired.

About 100 feet ahead I spotted a five gallon pail. On the way to get it I happened to pass an operating engineer, an old union man, who was tending an air compressor. He shouted, "Where are

69

you going?" When I told him, he replied, "I've got news for you. You're not going to get that pail. Understand? If you want to work on this job you'd better start acting like a union man—or I'll report you to the master mechanic. You'd better get back on the HD-6 and wait for the foreman to get a couple of laborers to help you. Remember, if you stop your crawler because of a boiling radiator and there's no pail within 40 feet of where you happen to stop, it's not your job to get a container."

I was pretty much confused, but I didn't want any trouble, so I went back to the HD-6 and waited for the foreman. It was two hours before the foreman came up, and in the meantime seven dump trucks and their drivers were idle. When the foreman finally did come, and I explained the situation to him, he said, "I'll get you a couple of laborers to draw some water." I explained to him that I could easily have gotten the water myself earlier but that the operator at the air compressor had told me to lay off. The foreman answered, "That's the way things are on this job. I don't want any trouble, so I do what the union boys want."

There were more such incidents during the summer, and the basic idea was always the same. Various craft unions decided on a lot of crazy restrictions that made a full day's work unusual. My employer, the XYZ Construction Company, had a contract with ABC Steel on a cost-plus basis.[1] So, the more the employees loafed on the job and raised the costs, the more the construction company made. But the steel company was the one bearing the costs, or rather, in the long run, the consuming public, because this labor waste would contribute to the increasing cost of steel.

---

[1] In a cost-plus contract, the buyer agrees to pay all costs plus a certain percentage. By contrast, in a fixed-fee contract the actual costs may be higher or lower than the contract figure.

Freedom of Speech for Businessmen

John Hooker, Director of Employee Communications for Intaglio Tool and Die Company, was in a quandary. A National Labor Relations Board news release of December 16, 1966 has made him wonder whether his plans for employee communications during contract negotiations are unethical.

The release read in part as follows:

The National Labor Relations Board ruled today that the General Electric Company had failed to bargain in good faith with the International Union of Electrical, Radio and Machine Workers, AFL–CIO, in their 1960 contract negotiations.

By a 4-1 vote, the Board held that the nation's largest electrical manufacturer utilized an essentially take-it-or-leave-it negotiating technique that was not true collective bargaining. The Board majority based its decision on GE's 'entire course of conduct.' It determined that the totality of GE's actions before and during the 1960 negotiations fell short of the requirements of the National Labor Relations Act, and ordered the company to cease to refuse to bargain in good faith in national negotiations with IUE.

In finding that GE had violated the labor relations statute, the Board cited both major facets of the company's 1960 bargaining technique—an intensive communications campaign among the employees before and during negotiations to disparage and discredit the IUE as bargaining representative, and adamant insistence at the bargaining table on GE's 'fair and firm' contract proposal.

*   *   *   *

Good-faith bargaining, the majority noted, also requires both parties to recognize that collective bargaining is 'a shared process in which each party, labor union and employer, has the right to play an active role.' The employer must recognize its obligation to deal with the employees' statutory representative in conducting bargaining negotiations and must acknowledge 'that it can no longer bargain directly or indirectly with the employees.'

'It is inconsistent with this obligation for an employer to mount a campaign, as Respondent did, both before and during negotiations, for the purpose of disparaging and discrediting the statutory representative in the eyes of its employee constituents, to seek to persuade the employees to exert pressure on the representative to submit to the will of the employer, and to create the impression that the employer rather than the union is the true protector of the employees' interests. As the Trial Examiner phrased it, "the employer's statutory obligation is to deal with the employees through the union, and not with the union through the employees." '

*   *   *   *

Member Jenkins, in his concurring opinion, said:

'There is adequate evidence in this record to support a finding that the Respondent by its course of conduct sought to bypass the Union and deal directly with the employees, to discredit the collective bargaining representative with which it was obligated to deal and carry on negotiations with others.'

*   *   *   *

Member Leedom disagreed with his colleagues' views of GE's over-all bargaining conduct. He wrote:

'I am particularly disturbed by the (majority) treatment accorded Respondent's communications. Surely the Respondent can lawfully communicate with its employees. Yet here, although the communications are held to be some evidence of bad faith, the majority neither in its decision nor in adopting the Trial Examiner's recommended order provides the Respondent with any guides by which it can with reasonable certainty determine what it can lawfully say to its employees.'

As Hooker read this material, he felt that the *legal* question of employer communication to employee was still an open issue. After all, the NLRB insisted that it was judging the totality of G.E.'s bargaining procedures. The Taft-Hartley Act, Section 8(c) provides only that:

The expression of any views, argument, or opinion, or the dissemination thereof, whether in written, printed, graphic, or visual form shall not constitute or be evidence of an unfair labor practice under any of the provisions of this Act, if such expression contains no threat of reprisal or force or promise of benefit.

Hooker, however, was concerned about the *ethical* quality of the communications which he planned to use during the coming negotiations. His plan had four parts.

(1) The Department of Employee Communications would put out a daily bulletin describing the negotiations. This would go by teletype to all company plants so that it might be communicated to local workers and media. Although the bulletin would give the offers and arguments of both sides, the emphasis would be put on the company's position since the Union would certainly emphasize its point of view in its own news releases. Since Hooker felt that the members of locals knew all too little about the negotiator who would be representing them, he intended to give reports on the conduct of this individual, who often acted like a wild man at bargaining sessions.

(2) Hooker had also prepared material to be shown in each local plant, which would make the company's position clear. In addition to film strips, the kit included a question and answer manual to be used by the local management in answering workers' questions. In addition to presenting the company's offer in detail, the materials also stressed the fact that the company wanted to avoid a long strike which would benefit no one. It also pointed up the fact that several older plants might have to be closed if wage demands made those particular operations unprofitable. Here and there in the material there were hints that if the package were too big, the company's competitive position would suffer and endanger the jobs of *all* employees.

(3) Each plant was to conduct meetings on company time for the presentation of the material; workers were free to attend or not. Local media were also to be urged to use the material so that the entire community would know the state of affairs. Where possible,

local managers were to have meetings with employees' and citizens' groups in order to explain both the offer and the justifications for it. The Union was not to be allowed to address the employees on company time or under the same circumstances. If the Union wanted to educate its members, it had its own newspapers and meeting places.

(4) If the negotiations became particularly difficult, Hooker had plans for an added community campaign which would cause a ground swell of public opinion to influence the local union's attitude toward the national negotiator's positions. Among other things, this provided for letters and pamphlets to be mailed to neighbors of workers. The letter would include a list of Intaglio employees living in the neighborhood, and urge the recipient to impress the workers with the seriousness of the situation. The letter would stress the fact that many local jobs and businesses were involved in the settlement of the contract talks. Where appropriate, the latter would also warn of the possibility of plants being removed to more favorable locations.

While going through the files in his department, Hooker found samples of his predecessor's work. The following paragraphs from news releases and other company publications were the type that worried him.

From a newspaper advertisement just before a union strike vote:

Make your vote count! If you vote for a strike . . . you will jeopardize your pay, your family's welfare, and your job.

From a press release:

Intaglio's Cutward Division will automatically be excluded from bidding on 30 to 40 contracts a month if a strike occurs at the local plant.

From a letter to employees:

. . . a strike could wipe out indefinitely all the 100 new jobs created since 1958. It would also bring about a direct reversal of promotions, and result in a great many downgradings in reassignment.

From a management newsletter to guide supervisors in speaking with workers:

As you know, the Company has more and more in recent years looked to the south and the west for its growth and expansion. . . . The company has not forsaken its old-line plants. Despite the greater costs, it has maintained reasonable employment levels and has continued to invest money in them. But it does not make sense to continue to invest money in the older plants when they may, upon the whims of union officials, be shut down at any moment. There is no reason why the Company should continue to keep all of its eggs in several large baskets, unless employees demonstrate that they are willing to compete with newer locations. . . . So as the Cutward workers come to the strike vote, they are voting about their future. A pro-strike vote will have disastrous consequences that reach far beyond a strike itself.

From a company newspaper:

A strike may not put the old plants out of business, but it can make the job of keeping them competitive a lot more difficult.

Fraternity Versus Seniority

The A. O. Smith Corporation supplies frames and other parts for General Motors cars and trucks. Federal Labor Union 19806 represents about 4,000 workers in A. O. Smith's Milwaukee automotive products division. When sales of cars and trucks declined in the fall of 1966, the A. O. Smith Corporation management decided that a manpower cut back was necessary, and informed the union officers of their decision. The labor contract stipulated that when a 40-hour work week could not be provided for all union employees, the change had to be approved by the union.

A. O. Smith's management offered the union two alternatives: (1) that 200 employees be laid off for about six to eight weeks; or (2) that all production facilities be shut down, and none of the 4,000 employees work on Friday, December 23, and Friday, December 30. Since Christmas Eve is a paid holiday but New Year's Eve is not, the workers would receive five-days' pay in the week before Christmas and four-days' pay the following week.

At the request of the union officials, management agreed to give the employees a choice between the two-day closing for 4,000 and a six-to-eight week layoff for 200. If the latter were chosen, the layoff would start on December 19. Union leaders recommended the two-day closing to their members.

The balloting was held at the headquarters of the union on Monday, December 12. The vote was 1,220 to 954 in favor of laying off the 200.

Standard Dynamics, Incorporated*

Standard Dynamics, founded five years ago by a young engineer, John Lacy, to develop and market the ideas which his previous work gave rise to, today is listed on the New York Stock Exchange. It has ten million dollar annual sales, and has 250 employees with an average tenure of three and one-half years.

The company has been free of labor strife. It offers the usual fringe benefits to employees such as sick leave, Blue Shield, vacations, and life insurance. It uses the standard pay scale and incentives for the industry, pays a bonus at year-end, and offers opportunities for advancement. Management is well-regarded generally.

Seven weeks ago, a representative of a large international union met with James Cox, the general manager of Standard Dynamics, to ask for recognition. Standard Dynamics had never been unionized, and Cox assumed that it was a matter of a handful of employees desiring to organize. Playing for time, he told the representative he would take the matter under advisement.

Within ten minutes, eight pickets appeared in front of the plant. Lacy and Cox adopted a "wait and see" attitude. In the following weeks, the situation deteriorated as truck drivers refused to cross the picket line and the entire work operation slowed down. In the fourth

* With the permission of the author, Roger Sonnabend; Seminar material for Young Presidents' Organization.

week, 120 employees walked out while 130 employees remained, but since these were primarily supervisory, clerical, research, and engineering people, the plant for all practical purposes was shut down.

Lacy and Cox reviewed the situation. The union seemed to have half the employees in hand. The remaining 130 people, however, refused to be unionized. The union had indicated, for reasons that were not revealed, that they would not sign a contract except for the entire plant. Customers primarily involved with the space program were pressing for delivery because they were in danger of shutting down themselves. Suppliers were insisting on the company taking shipments in warehouses if necessary. Whereas Standard Dynamics had previously been successful because of its outstanding and consistent performance, the company was now faced with a loss of customers, suppliers, and good will, and possible bankruptcy.

Lacy and Cox had tried in numerous meetings to come to agreement with the union. The union demands, however, included an increase in base pay and a substantial increase in incentive and wage rates that would give the company a labor expense 10 percent above industry scale. In addition, demands for four extra holidays and three more sick days would, if met, move Standard Dynamics further out of a competitive position. Unfortunately for the company, the union representative had assured the employees he would obtain these wage rates and benefits when he urged them to strike.

When the situation was at its worst, management was approached by Oscar Hale, who represented himself to be a friend of both labor and management and had been an arbitrator in many labor disputes similar to this one. "For a fee payable in cash," Hale said, "I could settle the strike and guarantee that Standard will obtain a reasonable contract, enabling it to maintain its competitive position and to go back to work in a strife-free atmosphere." On checking with other executives in the industry, Lacy determined that Hale could in fact accomplish this, apparently because of an understanding he had with the union leaders.

Lacy debated whether to accept Hale's offer.

How Long Must a Good Man Fight?

Inigo Olla went to work for the Harcore Ironworks in October of 1956. Although he was hired as a layout man, it soon became obvious that he was expected to act as an informal supervisor whenever Joseph Pignatelli, the partner in charge of shop operations, was absent. Inigo did not mind this since it was only a small shop employing 35 people. Within a short time, however, Inigo realized that something strange was going on.

The Harcore Ironworks was located in an area of chronic unemployment, and unless a man had special skills, he generally needed the help of a politician or a prominent businessman to get a job. Jobs, indeed, were very precious, so that people were not liable to complain or make trouble for their employer. There were, however, real grievances. More often than not, grievances were not processed, for the simple reason that both the employer and the worker's political or business sponsor pressured men into keeping quiet. Even when grievances were recognized by the union, it was difficult to get action. The procedures used and the individuals involved help to explain this.

The shop steward was supposed to present grievances at union meetings. If the union voted in favor of processing, it was put into the hands of the business agent. Once the business agent was in charge, no other union officer was allowed to do anything about that particular grievance. Unfortunately for union members, the business agent had an agreement with the partners who owned Harcore. As far as Inigo could find out, the business agent received money for letting grievances pile up or delaying arbitration. In many cases, workers just gave up when nothing was done about their case.

Inigo Olla decided to run for the presidency of the local union, in the hope that he could do something about this situation. As soon as he announced his intention, he was approached by the two owners of Harcore—Frank Xavier, in charge of the office; and Joseph Pigna-telli, in charge of the shop. They informed Inigo that they had great things in mind for him if he withdrew his candidacy. Inigo rejected this vague offer and was ultimately elected president of the local.

After the election, the partners who owned Harcore tried to make Inigo superintendent of the shop. When he refused, they started to make threats. "Something could happen to you." "Don't forget we have already had one dynamiting in town." "The District Attorney may want to look into your case." Inigo did not know why they were so anxious to get him out of his position as president. He suspected that he was rocking the boat in some way, but he had no facts which would indicate that anything more than fear of griev-ances was behind the threats. Yet he felt that there must be some-thing more.

When Inigo's term as president of the local expired, he did not stand for reelection, but was elected shop steward. Inigo promptly started presenting written grievances to the two partners so that there could be no dodging the issues. This not only short-circuited the business agent's control of grievances but caused the partners to re-new their threats. On one occasion Xavier went so far as to say, "We have ways of getting rid of anyone we want to, and we don't care how much it costs." When Inigo persisted, Xavier informed him that he had seen a representative of the International Union and that all grievances were to be considered as settled. Inigo did not accept this. He said that grievances were going to be settled properly, and that the International had no right to wipe the slate clean on its own authority.

Shortly after this last interchange, Inigo was fired. No reason was given. Since he was in no position to present the grievance directly, he had to process it through the union meeting and the business agent. The agent stalled for two months and finally acted when Inigo threatened to take the case to court.

Ultimately the business agent and the employers agreed to arbitration. The hearing became so noisy that the arbitrator called off the proceedings before Inigo had a chance to put all of his evidence in the record. The arbitrator had heard enough, however, and made his ruling within two days. He ordered the reinstatement of Inigo without back pay. He had evidently sensed something unusual, for his award included the sentence: "As for Inigo Olla, a word to the wise is sufficient." The union itself voted to pay Inigo for the time he had lost and the expenses he had incurred. He refused to accept this offer because he felt entitled to unemployment compensation.

When he had been fired, Inigo had applied for unemployment compensation. He had, however, received no checks. The interviewer at the Bureau of Employment Security kept telling him that he would not act since he understood that the union was going to take care of everything. Inigo did not know what the interviewer meant.

Inigo sensed that he was being blackballed. He had answered an ad for a job as a layout man, but was informed that there was no one available to interview him. When he applied for a second job opening, he was told that the personnel office was out of application forms. He knew that that particular job had not been filled. Inigo insisted that he be given a hearing. He had tried to get work, and the arbitrator's ruling established that he had been out of work through no fault of his own. In the end, the Bureau of Employment Security authorized the payment of seven weeks' unemployment compensation.

A few weeks after Inigo had returned to Harcore, he was ordered to report for work on a Saturday morning. He showed up half an hour early on that day and let himself in by reaching through a hole and lifting the latch. This was a regular procedure since no one had a key. By 8:00 A.M., Inigo had laid out his tools and blueprints in the work yard, and started to do layout work on the beams. No one else had showed up for work. At 8:10 A.M., two policemen rushed into the yard with their hands on their guns. They questioned Inigo about his presence. It appears that Xavier had called the police and informed them that the shop was going to be robbed at 8:00 A.M. The policemen were supposed to have staked out the shop but had arrived late. Now Inigo knew the meaning of the vague threats about having the District Attorney "get" him.

At this point, Inigo became really afraid. Before he had only been angry and determined to fight for his own rights and the rights of his fellow employees. He still did not know why Harcore wanted to get rid of him. He certainly had no future with the company. Should he keep up the fight or move out of the area and get a new job?

IV

Production

Is a Clear Conscience Enough?

The Midwestern Fuel Company is a highly success-
ful, middlesized firm engaged in drilling for oil, and also in the production and distribution of gasoline. In 1958 Midwestern invested in
a $100,000 pump installation for its Whiting, Indiana refinery. Shortly
after the installation was completed, the supplier, Industrial Pumps,
Inc., presented Robert McPhelin, Midwestern's general manager,
with a Studebaker Lark. McPhelin was seriously concerned as to
whether or not he should keep the Lark.

The pump installation had been made to replace equipment
installed in 1957 when Midwestern constructed a modern cracking
plant at a cost of approximately $4,500,000 as an addition to its
Whiting refinery. The original pump equipment had consisted of
two large piston pumps, which cost about $190,000. These two
pumps had proved to be unsatisfactory in operation and had caused
plant shutdowns, and excessively high maintenance costs. Finally
McPhelin discovered that these original pumps were quite specialized and had never been designed for the kind of use the Midwestern
refinery required. In 1958 McPhelin concluded that the pumps
would never give satisfactory service, and decided that an entirely
new pump installation, with a different design, would be necessary.

Midwestern did not follow its usual purchasing procedure in

negotiating for the installation of the new pumps. For standard equipment and for ordinary purchases, the purchasing agent was responsible for the selection of sources of supply, the securing of bids, and for conducting all negotiations involved in purchase transactions. Midwestern did not hesitate, however, to deviate from this procedure when special engineering or design problems were involved. The pump specifications in this case were unusual with respect to operating temperatures, pressures, and the quantity of oil to be handled. As a result, after the decision to secure new equipment had been made, McPhelin instructed his engineering department to make a preliminary survey of possible suppliers and to get their recommendations and rough approximations for the cost of equipment to handle the job satisfactorily.

Midwestern Fuel Company usually bought about $50,000 worth of standard types of pumps from various suppliers every year. McPhelin and his refinery engineer discussed Midwestern's special problems with five regular suppliers who were known to be reliable. Estimates of costs were submitted. McPhelin and his associates finally accepted the bid of Industrial Pumps, Inc., the lowest bidder at $100,000. Midwestern's engineering department assisted in the planning and installation of the pumps according to the rough plans developed by McPhelin's refinery engineer.

The Prometheus Mine*

The Prometheus Mine was located in a very remote part of one of the mountain states. Because of its remoteness it had been necessary to build a "company town." In this "company town" homes were provided for all employees of the company. In the residential district the homes of the mine executives and the supervisors were clustered in one corner; the homes for the miners occupied another sightly spot on company land. Each of the homes was distinctive and employees were free to select the color of their houses and otherwise to modify the homes to suit their own individual tastes and preferences. The company had built a school building, but the school itself was under the supervision of state education authorities. The company had also built various stores and a post office. Moreover, the company had built three churches, but it exercised no control over the selection of the ministers of the three denominations represented. They were chosen in the manner usual to the respective denominations. The nearest small town, with a population of about 5,000, was about 20 miles away; the nearest town of considerable size, a city of 50,000 people, was about 100 miles away.

* This case was prepared by John A. Glover of the Harvard Graduate School of Business Administration as a basis for class discussion rather than to illustrate either effective or ineffective handling of an administrative situation. Copyright © 1952, by The President and Fellows of Harvard College.

More than 30 years ago, the Prometheus Mine had been the site of bitter labor-management disputes. These disputes had led to considerable violence and several people had been killed. Ultimately, these disputes had been resolved, and the company had entered into a "closed shop" agreement with a national union. At about this same time, the safety record of the Prometheus Mine had been one of the worst in the country. There had never been any major single disaster, but many individuals had been injured seriously and a number of men had been killed in and about the mine. However, in more than a decade prior to 1950, not a single man-day of work had been lost due to work stoppage of any kind; and in the eighteen months prior to August, 1951, not a single man-day had been lost due to an accident in the mine. There had been no fatal casualties in over five years.

The nature of operations at the Prometheus Mine, as in all mines, offered many opportunities for accidents. A good part of the mine was dug into solid granite, and mining operations involved considerable blasting, drilling, and cutting of the solid rock. Inside the mine there were about twenty miles of narrow-gauge railroad track, over which trainloads of ore were brought out of the mine to the processing mill. These trains were made up of from 16 to 20 cars, each of which contained about six to eight tons of ore. The clearances in the mine's tunnels on either side of the cars were only a couple of feet, and the over-head clearance was in many cases less than a foot. In the processing mill itself, the rock—sometimes coming from the mine in chunks as large as pianos—was reduced to a dust and various ores were extracted by various methods. About a mile from the center of the company town, there was a large dump of high explosives. At any one time the company had in storage in this dump upwards of 20,000 tons of high explosives. The annual consumption of explosives was several times that figure.

Just before World War II, the company had sent to the Prometheus Mine a new superintendent, Albert Wriston. Mr. Wriston had been in the company's employ for many years and had had considerable experience in mining operations in various parts of the world. After coming to the Prometheus Mine, Wriston had acquired the firm reputation in the mine of being vitally interested in the matter of safety. Over the years he had often delivered many impromptu "lectures" on safety to men at all supervisory levels. He had, also, often spoken to the miners about the importance of safety practices. He had tried to bring home to them the inherent dangers in the nature of the mine and the work in which they were engaged.

Wriston had set forth a number of rules concerning safety. These rules concerned many operations such as blasting, drilling, loading, running of the ore trains, and the use of safety equipment and clothing. Infraction of some of these rules, especially those concerning the use of explosives, carried the penalty of immediate dismissal.

The mine provided the men with safety shoes, safety helmets, goggles, and other safety equipment as needed. All through the mine, the mill, the offices, and scattered through the town there were posters, placards, signs, and exhibits relating to safety. Some of them carried slogans. Some presented statistics comparing the safety record of the mine to that of other mines, and to various safety statistics published by government agencies. Some of the exhibits contained goggles which had been shattered along with a "testimonial" signed by the man who had been wearing them at the time—"I'm sure glad I had my goggles on!" Other exhibits contained safety shoes which had been smashed, helmets which had been dented, and the like with similar "testimonials." The company had never employed a safety director nor had it ever employed a personnel officer.

Inside the mine, the actual mining operations were something as follows: At each of several levels, a system of several "tunnels" had been excavated. These are as shown in Table 1 and are indicated by the numbers 1 through 6. Most of the actual mining operations proper were done in transverse "galleries" which intersected these tunnels at angles of about 90°. The galleries leading off tunnel No. 1 are lettered A through F. The transverse galleries were located about 100 feet or more apart. At the ends, on the sides and above these galleries, the blasting and drilling operations necessary to drill out the rock were carried on. Thus, blasting and drilling took place at points such as at the ends of D-1, D-2, E-1, and E-2. From the galleries, the rock was then transported by portable powered conveyors to the tunnels, such as No. 1, where it was loaded onto dump cars. When a trainload of cars was filled, it was then hauled by electric engine to the mouth of the mine tunnel and conveyed to the mill.

Blasting was always done by teams of two men. When a team of blasters had prepared a charge, for instance, at the end of gallery

E-1, they then withdrew to the tunnel and stationed themselves on either side of the opening of the transverse gallery they were blasting in, at points X and Y, for example. It was a firm rule that the blasters were not to permit anyone to go between the points at which they had stationed themselves and the mouth of the transverse gallery where they were blasting. That is, no one was to be permitted to be in the area in the tunnel between X and the mouth of gallery E-1, or between Y and the mouth of gallery E-1 at the time of the blasting. Blasters were also responsible for seeing that no one was in the other side of the gallery across the tunnel, such as at E-2. It had been long established that the violation of the two rules would result in immediate dismissal.

Table 1

PROMETHEUS MINE

		Tunnels #1	#2	#3	#4	#5	#6
	F-1 (X)	F-2					
	E-1	E-2					
Transverse Galleries	D-1 (Y)	D-2					
	C-1	C-2					
	B-1	B-2					
	A-1	A-2					

From the mouth of tunnel

Blasters at the Prometheus Mine were among the most highly skilled workers and were among the highest paid. The annual income of an experienced blaster at the Prometheus Mine was about $8,000 a year. Experienced and skilled blasters were not very numerous. The Prometheus Mine had, itself, trained several of its most experienced blasters; others had come from other mines.

While working inside the mine, blasters were under the line

direction of the foreman of the level in which they were working. The level foreman was fully responsible for all operations on his level. His responsibilities included such matters as production, cost, and safety. Engineering for the whole mine was the responsibility of the chief engineer. To some extent blasters also took orders from the subforeman of the particular tunnel in which they were working. While working inside the mine, blasters received only technical assistance and guidance from the head blaster.

One of these teams of blasters was made up of Nils Jensen and Peter Kovici. Nils Jensen was about 50 years old. He had worked in mines from the time he was a young man. In the summer of 1951 he had two sons working in the mine. The younger was a student in the high school in the company town; the older was studying mining engineering in a state university in another mountain state.

Peter Kovici had been a blaster at the Prometheus Mine for over ten years. He had had much experience as a blaster, not only in the United States but also in mines in South America and in Africa. Kovici was about 45 years old, married, and had four children. His oldest boy, who had finished his freshman year in mining engineering, was also working in the mine that summer.

One afternoon in July, 1951, Nils Jensen and Peter Kovici had just placed a charge at the end of gallery E—that is, at E-1. They had taken up their positions at points X and Y, respectively, in tunnel No. 1. Jensen, as the senior member of the team, was in charge of the electric battery detonator. Just after Jensen had shouted that he was ready to push the plunger on the detonator, Sam Bennett, the level foreman, heading toward gallery E, walked past Kovici who was sitting on an up-ended empty box. Bennett had not gone more than about 20 feet beyond Kovici when Kovici suddenly shouted, "Hey Sam!" Sam turned quickly around. At that very instant the charge went off. Pieces of rock were blown with great force out of gallery E-1 into the tunnel by the blast, but Sam, being about 100 feet away from the mouth of gallery E-1 was uninjured.

Specifications and Information

Paul Peel, president of the Peel Company, recently purchased a rock-crushing unit from the Magnus Corporation. Unfortunately the machines have not been performing up to expectations. The unit was expected to produce 750 tons of crushed rock per hour, but has in practice been producing only 500 tons per hour.

Peel has been complaining vociferously and angrily to Gordon Goodbody, sales manager of Magnus. He revealed that, relying upon the expected capacity of the machine, he had made a number of contracts for furnishing crushed rock to various customers. Now he was finding it difficult to fill those contracts. In fact, in some instances he has been required to go to other gravel companies in order to purchase—at retail prices—the crushed rock which he contracted to furnish to his customers. Furthermore, when Peel borrowed the money to purchase the new rock crusher and its attendant equipment, he had planned to repay the loan with the income which he expected to receive from increased production.

The loss of expected income, together with the payment of the loan installments has driven Peel to exasperation. After shouting at Goodbody and excoriating his equipment at length, Peel threatened to sue unless Magnus agreed to return half the purchase price of the equipment.

Frank Napp, the foreman of Peel's new rock-crushing installation, and Elmer Urmston, the company's chief engineer, are not happy with the new equipment, but they are not sure that the Magnus Corporation and Gordon Goodbody are at fault. The contract for the new equipment specified that the unit should be able to crush 750 tons of "properly graded limestone" per hour. Magnus had tested samples supplied by Peel and based its promise of performance on these tests. Peel, however, had been using stone taken from several different company quarries. Both Napp and Urmston had objected to this since much of this stone was harder than that in the sample given to Magnus. The equipment had not broken down, but there had been several jams, and the machines had been consistently unable to turn out as much crushed rock as they were supposed to.

Napp and Urmston talked over this matter and decided to present the problem to Mr. Peel. If Magnus fought Peel's suit, Napp and Urmston would certainly be called on to testify. Moreover, they both felt that the Magnus Company had a right to know that Peel has been using a harder rock than that used in the tests.

Peel listened to Napp and Urmston but was not convinced that he ought to inform Magnus of the difference in hardness. Peel thought that the performance guarantee covered the crushing of rock for any and all of the company's quarries.

The Air We Breathe

John Brownling is a member of the board of directors of the Deecy Power Company. He has a successful law practice and sees himself as a representative of the public as well as of Deecy's stockholders. Recently he has been disturbed by reports on the problem of air pollution in the United States. The problem became very personal at a recent directors' meeting called to discuss the construction of a new power plant.

Electrical power plants are one of the largest sources of sulphur dioxide in our atmosphere. While sulphur dioxide is not poisonous to man in the ordinary concentrations found in the air, it can cause crop damage. In some areas it causes nickel and copper to erode rather rapidly. Under certain conditions it can kill people suffering from respiratory ailments. Sulphur dioxide, for example, was blamed for 400 "excess deaths" during a two-week period of heavy smog in New York City in 1963.

Brownling feels strongly that the company should build the plant so as to reduce the discharge of sulphur dioxide. His fellow directors, however, point out that the only means available for doing this would raise costs considerably. If the company substitutes No. 2 oil (which is low in sulphur) for residual fuel oil, fuel costs will go up 80 percent. Even if the company buys residual oil with part of the sulphur taken out, fuel costs would be 20 percent higher. Brownling points out that fuel represents only one-seventh of the total cost of generating and distributing electricity, so that the over-all increase in cost would not be prohibitive.

The other directors feel that any increased costs would have to be reflected in higher prices, and any increase in the price of electricity would involve them in endless trouble. In the first place, the Public Utilities Commission might delay rate increases to cover the higher cost. In the second place, consumer annoyance over increased prices would hurt the company's public image. The majority of the board feels that they should not use methods which would increase expenses. The cost of collecting fly ash already has added a little under one percent to their total costs. Besides, other industries and motor vehicles were far more guilty of causing air pollution. As one director put it, "Why should we be leaders in this area when it is going to cost either stockholders or consumers a good deal of money?"

Brownling sees the force of their arguments but is not really convinced. He feels that the company has an obligation to protect public health as long as it can stay reasonably profitable. Indeed, he wonders if he can continue to serve on the board of a company which allows purely business considerations to dominate its decisions in an area which he feels is critical.

Automobile Safety

PART A: FAULTY EQUIPMENT

The American auto industry claims that it produces the safest cars in the world. The public, however, seems to be more interested in automobile styling than in safety.

In 1965 Ralph Nader, a lawyer, published a book on auto safety entitled *Unsafe At Any Speed*. Along with other criticisms, he exposed the dangers of the Chevrolet Corvair. Most particularly, the car was prone to tuck its wheels under and roll over. Though the 1960 Corvair had been built to understeer, it began to oversteer as the car picked up speed. As a result, even a good driver had to be very careful to turn the car properly at 40 miles per hour. According to Nader, General Motors had already settled 100 suits arising out of the Corvair's peculiarities. In 1966, the March issue of *Consumer Reports* noted that the 1966 Corvair still oversteered on a fast curve. Although this car was safer when the front tires had eleven pounds less pressure than the rear, the driver was at the mercy of a service station attendant who might inadvertently inflate all tires to the same pressure.

In 1965 more than 49,000 Americans were killed on our highways. Another 1,800,000 were disabled and an equal number injured less seriously. Auto accidents are the leading cause of death for Americans between the ages of 5 and 30. Although it has long been recognized that driver education and better highway design can reduce the number of accidents, 1966 saw an increase in agitation for improved vehicle safety. The General Service Organization, which purchases automobiles for the Federal Government, set down a series of safety standards for the cars they would purchase. A first set of standards were to go into effect in 1967 and a second in 1968. In addition, Congress is studying a proposed National Safety Act, which grants discretionary authority to the Department of Commerce. Local groups such as the Illinois Citizens for Automobile Safety, Physicians for Automotive Safety, and the American Trial Lawyers Association are deeply involved.

There are rumors that certain insurance companies are going to base their premiums on the safety record of car models as well as on the records of various classes of drivers. In addition, the courts are extending the doctrine of strict liability, which makes an automobile manufacturer responsible for accidents resulting from defects in his car whether or not he knew of them. In short, automobile safety has become a major issue.

The auto makers countered the rising agitation and publicity. General Motors published a pamphlet, *Designed For Safety,* which implied that driver behavior was the only major unsolved problem (Cf. Part C of this case). In December of 1965 and in January of 1966, Ford spent more than $1 million in promulgating basically the same idea. The auto makers also announced that the safety features demanded by the General Service Organization would go on their new cars. However, they did not want government-promulgated standards, and suggested instead the establishment of a committee made up of the presidents of the manufacturing companies and an outsider chosen by the presidents and approved by the Secretary of Commerce. They argued that their long-range planning would be disrupted if Washington had the power to set standards.

The issues became clouded and emotions heightened when it was disclosed that General Motors had hired private detectives to watch Ralph Nader, whose book brought him before a Congressional committee as an expert witness (Cf. Part B of this case).

The automotive makers were further embarrassed by the New York State Safety Car, which was developed as a result of a $100,000 grant given to the Department of Motor Vehicles. The prototype car, developed by the Republic Aviation Division of Fairfield Hiller

Corporation, is designed to be mass produced. According to *Consumer Reports* for April 1966, preliminary findings indicate:

Its outstanding finding was that for a forward crash impact speed of 50 mph, a car built from the project's design would reduce by more than 50 percent all types of injuries—including fatalities—compared with cars now on the road.

This car includes, among other things, a swing-gate bumper which deflects impact; an engine designed to move under passengers rather than into them; full door pillars and roll bars; a built-in rear collapse structure; and lights that can be seen from the side.

Some critics of the automobile industry are asking if manufacturers should not be required to reveal the safety results of their own tests. There are even those who claim that cars, like drugs, should not be approved for sale until they have been proved safe. In short, the question of full disclosure has been raised. The automobile manufacturers admit that in some cases they have concentrated primarily on styling but feel that basic standards would hamper their work without necessarily contributing to the safety of the public. Some critics feel that the proposed bill, which gives discretionary authority to the Secretary of Commerce, protects the industry from regulation rather than the public from accident.

Henry Ford II struck out at critics in April of 1966 and warned Congress against upsetting the economy by passing irrational legislation. James Roche, president of General Motors, said, "Government regulation would discourage competition as we have known it." He also pointed out that minimum safety standards would tend to become maximum standards with the result that real progress in safety would be held up. Others in the industry felt that the outcry for safety was motivated by a small group of lawyers, and they feared that government investigation and regulation would give rise to a large number of poorly grounded liability suits. General Motors denied that the Corvair has any real safety problem, but later admitted that some changes had been made in the car "to improve driveability." The public outcry, however, had hurt the sales of the Corvair, which fell from 200,000 in 1965 to 86,000 in 1966.

As noted above, the automotive industry promised to take care of the auto safety problem itself and proposed to establish a committee composed of the presidents of the auto companies and one outsider. So that this group might set standards freely, the industry asked Congress to waive the anti-trust laws. It was claimed that fear of prosecution had prevented them from exchanging safety information up to the present time. Shortly after this, however, the industry capitulated and agreed to federal legislation. The auto makers then asked that the law contain guidelines which would require a balancing of costs versus benefits, and provisions for judicial review. Furthermore, they wanted penalties kept to $1,000 per violation, with a ceiling of $100,000 for any related series of violations.

Shortly after the shift in tactics, Walter Reuther, president of the United Auto Workers, testified before the House Commerce Committee. He insisted that safety design need not add to the present cost of cars. The auto makers need only take off the frills which are standard equipment and substitute safety features. Moreover, Reuther claimed that auto profits were so high that the increased costs of safety features should be absorbed by the manufacturers themselves.

Although there is evidence of some safety problems in particular cars, the picture is not entirely clear. On the basis of statistics supplied by the auto companies, Senator Ribicoff, chairman of the Senate subcommittee investigating auto safety, estimated that between 1960 and 1966, 18.5 percent of the autos produced were defective in some respect. The auto makers hold, however, that these statistics are exaggerated since they are based on the number of cars called in for inspection and not on the number of cars actually found to be defective. On the other hand, the statistics say nothing of defective cars which were not formally called in.

A study made at the Harvard Medical School indicates that mechanical defects may cause half of the 50,000 traffic deaths which occur each year.

Traffic Deaths per 100,000 Population

	Whites	*Non-Whites*
States with inspection	25.1	37.9
States without inspection	38.2	64.2

The higher rates for non-white citizens are probably due to the fact that their lower income leads them to drive older cars. Deaths in cars over eight years old are twice as frequent as deaths in new ones.

On a miles-traveled basis, the statistics are even more startling. Inspection reduced traffic death rates from 57.8 to 17.1 for non-whites between the ages of 45 and 55. Such statistics show that car safety involves maintenance as well as manufacturing problems.

There are no accurate figures on research expenditures on auto safety. In 1958 Andrew Kucher, vice-president for Engineering and Research at Ford, said:

Because we are thoroughly sold on this philosophy, the motor vehicle manufacturers spend between $5 and $6 million each year in safety-oriented research programs. This expenditure is aimed at solving basic problems and also is a searching for new and better solutions to old problems.

In 1965 Ford listed expenditures of $700,000 for its automotive Safety Center and $300,000 for research and development of safety cars. Scientists in the Bureau of Public Roads estimated that, in 1964, industry spent approximately $2 million on highway traffic research. General Motors claims that the cost of safety research cannot be separated from engineering and development costs.

Although civil aviation fatalities are only in the neighborhood of 1200 a year, the Federal Government spent a minimum of $35 million a year on air safety research and development between 1960 and 1965.

PART B: HARASSING A CRITIC

Aloysius Power, general counsel for General Motors, ordered a background investigation of Ralph Nader in November, 1965. Power said he wondered whether Nader was in some way connected with 106 lawsuits involving $40 million in claims against GM. In January, 1966, intermediaries for GM arranged to hire a former FBI agent, Vincent Gillen, to handle the investigation. Assisted by other ex-FBI men, Gillen directed an investigation under the pretext of a pre-employment inquiry. Gillen instructed his co-workers: "Our job is to check his life and current activities, to determine 'what makes him tick,' such as his real interest in safety, his supporters, if any, his politics, his marital status, his friends, his women, boys, etc., drinking, dope, jobs—in fact, all facets of his life."[1]

1 *The New Republic* (April 2, 1966), p. 9.

The detectives questioned 50 to 60 of Nader's acquaintances and members of his family. From February 4 to 9, detectives had Nader under constant surveillance. Gillen filed reports with GM from February 7 to March 4.

On March 21, James Roche, president of General Motors, who had earlier denied that the company had authorized the investigation, apologized to Nader and to a Congressional committee. "I think there has been some harassment," Roche said. Senator Abraham Ribicoff, who had read all the detective reports, said to Nader: "You and your family can be proud. They [the detectives] have put you through the mill and they haven't found a damn thing wrong with you." Senator Ribicoff added that he hoped the hearing "will have a salutary effect on business ethics and the protection of the individual. There's too much snooping going on in this country," he said.

PART C: FAULTY DRIVERS

Not without reason, auto makers have answered criticism about the safety of their products with references to "the nut behind the wheel." The driver is undoubtedly the cause of many auto accidents, but little research has been done to clarify the driver's role and responsibility in highway safety. Driver indifference, human error, and drinking are several aspects certainly relating to the driver's role in highway accidents. One problem linked quite directly to driver responsibility is that of the drinking driver. Alcohol has been shown to be a factor in 50 percent or more of fatal traffic accidents. Problem drinkers cannot control their drinking, and only removal from the highways can keep them from causing accidents. The social drinker can be made aware of the grave responsibility he assumes when he drinks and drives.

Driver irresponsibility and indifference probably account for those accidents caused by driving too fast for conditions, ignoring right of way regulations, and other traffic violations. In the current controversy about mechanical defects in automobiles it is interesting that although safety devices such as seat belts can reduce injuries by 35 percent, at least half of the people whose cars are equipped with seat belts do not use them. When mechanically safe cars become common on our highways, unless they are manned by responsible drivers, the present highway carnage will continue.

Moralists have long insisted that it is unethical for a person to endanger his own life or that of others, without a serious reason. For example, Pope Pius XII, speaking to the leaders of the International Highway Federation on October 4, 1955, stated:

(The International Highway Federation) carries on an important work of social education to which we are glad to pay tribute. We mean the formation of a highly developed sense of responsibility toward all users of the highway. . . . It is also necessary to inculcate in everyone his grave duty to respect the lives of others. A salutary fear of immediate and adequate repressive measures undoubtedly will contribute toward this end. But the police alone cannot avert all the dangers created by drivers scarcely masters of themselves, carried away by the craze for speed or, at times, intoxicated. It is important to impose on one's self a strict discipline, conforming to established and generally accepted rules. The often dramatic effects of violating the traffic code give it an extrinsic obligation much more serious than people generally imagine. Drivers cannot rely solely on their own skill and watchfulness to avoid accidents; they must maintain a proper margin of safety in order to cope with the careless driver and unforeseen difficulties.

V

Pricing

A Perfect Bust

In a routine transaction, a New York art gallery acquired a 26-inch stucco sculpture. In October, 1965 the gallery offered it for sale at one of its regular auctions. The gallery's auctioneer started the bidding at $150, which indicated that the gallery's appraisers, who regarded the sculpture as a reproduction, did not think it valuable.

Experts from the Metropolitan Museum of New York had seen the bust on display and, after a quiet investigation, had decided that it was an original work of either Andrea de Verrocchio or Leonardo da Vinci. The Metropolitan sent one of its men to bid on the bust. He was able to purchase it for $225. Some art appraisers estimate that the Metropolitan would have gone as high as $225,000 to obtain the bust. One prominent art dealer put its value at $500,000. The sculpture is now mounted in the Metropolitan for the public to enjoy free of charge.

Holman Screw Machine
Products Company*

In the fall of 1955 the Holman Screw Machine Products Company received an inquiry from the Geraldine Company, an old customer, for a price on 10,000 spacers. Mr. Rudolph Holman, the proprietor and General Manager of the 35-employee concern, handled customer contacts and determined and quoted prices on products himself.

In discussing the spacer order with Mr. Holman, the customer displayed a tentative assembly sketch of a new gear assembly in a design stage, showing a spacer in relation with other component parts. It was apparent that each spacer[1] was to be a cylinder of $\frac{5}{8}''$ diameter, $\frac{1}{4}''$ long, and that the spacers could be made out of brass or steel, solid or with a $\frac{3}{8}''$ clearance hole,[2] whichever was cheaper.

Mr. Holman's plant was equipped with automatic screw machines, and it appeared to him that a Brown and Sharpe Automatic

---

* This case was prepared by P. Jacobson, under the supervision of Franklin E. Folts of Harvard University Graduate School of Business Administration, as the basis for class discussion rather than to illustrate effective or ineffective handling of an administrative situation. Copyright ©, 1949 by The President and Fellows of Harvard College. Used by permission.

1 See Table 2 for sketches of spacer.

2 Hole could be $\frac{3}{8}''$ diameter or slightly larger.

Table 1

HOLMAN SCREW MACHINE PRODUCTS COMPANY

Costs and Prices for ⅝" Diameter Spacers

Using Steel or Brass Rod or Tubing

(Figures are dollars per 1,000 spacers if 10,000 spacers are made)

	Steel Rod No Hole	Steel Rod Drilled Hole	Steel Tubing	Brass Rod No Hole	Brass Rod Drilled Hole	Brass Tubing
Material cost	$1.76	$1.76	$4.77	$6.15	$6.15	$6.75
Less scrap value	0.00	0.00	0.00	0.35	1.19	0.10
Net material cost	$1.76	$1.76	$4.77	$5.80	$4.96	$6.65
Hours required to set up	0.2	0.25	0.2	0.2	0.25	0.2
Setup charge at $3	0.60	0.75	0.60	0.60	0.75	0.60
Hours required to machine	5.4	3.2	3.6	1.3	1.3	0.9
Machining charge at $2.50	13.50	8.00	9.00	3.25	3.35	2.25
Pricing Figures	$15.86	$10.51	$14.37	$9.65	$9.06	$9.50

Screw Machine No. 0 would be suitable for the job. He determined, upon analysis, that he had six alternative methods of producing the spacers from which to choose. He could use:

(1) ⅝" diameter B-1113 cold-drawn steel rod and drill no hole;
(2) ⅝" diameter brass rod and drill no hole;
(3) ⅝" diameter B-1113 cold-drawn steel rod and drill a ⅜" diameter hole;
(4) ⅝" diameter brass rod and drill a ⅜" diameter hole;
(5) ⅝" outside diameter SAE 1020 steel tubing (with a .385" diameter hole); or
(6) ⅝" outside diameter brass tubing (with a ⅜" diameter hole).

Table 1 is a summary of alternative costs and prices as figured by Mr. Holman on steel and brass rod and steel and brass tubing, including an estimated material cost, estimated setup charges, and estimated machine charges. In estimating costs, Mr. Holman figured setup at the rate of $3 per hour. This figure, according to Mr. Holman, was a "pricing figure," not a cost figure. It was made up of a labor charge plus an average overhead charge and a profit margin. He charged machine time at $2.50 per hour. This figure also was a composite of labor cost, an average overhead charge including depreciation and a margin for profit. All workers were paid hourly wages.

In December, 1955, the Holman plant was running at capacity.[3] There was one setup man who set up the six automatic screw machines with which the department was equipped, checked their output for quality, and kept them adjusted. Practically all of his time was devoted to setup work. During the night shift no setup man was on duty. Mr. Holman had been advertising in local papers for a second setup man but had been unable to find one. The day shift setup man made sure that the machines to be run on the night shift were in good adjustment when he left at the end of the day shift. The night foremen checked the work coming off the machines occasionally but did not adjust them. If the work coming off a machine failed to meet specifications he shut the machine down and the setup man adjusted and started the machine again when he came on duty the next morning. The machines were kept supplied with bar stock

[3] At that time screw machine work was in great demand. Every shop in the area was running at full capacity and six-months deliveries were common.

HOLMAN SCREW MACHINE PRODUCTS COMPANY
SKETCHES OF SPACER

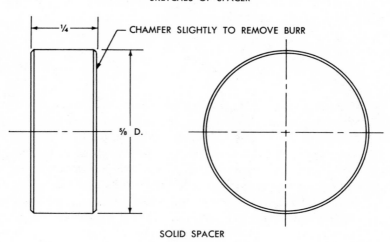

SOLID SPACER

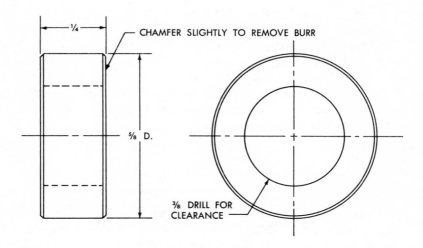

by one or more of several unskilled workers who did common labor
work in the several departments in the shop. Only a fraction of their
time was spent in supplying the screw machines with bar stock, re-
moving trays of finished parts, sweeping, and cleaning. The machines were completely automatic and no attendant was needed
while they were in operation.

QUESTIONS

(1) What price should Mr. Holman quote on the Geraldine inquiry?
(2) Which of the six alternative methods should be used for the production of 10,000 spacers if the order is obtained?
(3) In February of 1957 the Holman Screw Machine Products Company plant was operating only 36 hours per week.[4] Screw machine business throughout the community was slack and Mr.
Holman, like other screw machine company operators was
actively soliciting business. On Thursday morning, February
21, Mr. Holman received a telephone call from the purchasing
agent of the Geraldine Company. Geraldine was in the market
for a second lot, this time of 20,000 spacers, similar to the 1955
order. Mr. Holman told the Geraldine purchasing agent he
would like to discuss the order with him and arranged to be at
the Geraldine Company office an hour later. Before he left to
keep the appointment Mr. Holman checked the price he had
quoted on the 1955 order. What price should Mr. Holman quote
on the present inquiry? If he obtains the order how should Mr.
Holman have the spacers made?

NOTE

In principle the automatic screw machine is much
like a turret lathe. The difference is the automatic cycling action of
the automatic screw machine. Once it is set up the entire action of the
machine is automatic. The rotation of the turret is automatic. The
machine automatically feeds bar stock into position for cutting. All

4 The setup man was paid on a 40-hours per week basis.

tools advance to cutting position and retract automatically at the end of the cut. The entire cycle of sequential action is automatic and the only attention required of an attendant is to keep a supply of bar stock in the machine. The setup man periodically checks parts as they come out of the machine and makes any infrequent adjustments that are necessary as the result of tool wear or other minor failure of the automatic functioning of the machine.

Full Line Prices

The Hubbard Company manufactured and merchandised a line of shampoos, hair sprays, and hair lotions—fifteen different items in 40 different containers. The company's latest addition to the product line was Softy, advertised as the first men's shampoo able to clean the scalp, remove dandruff, and leave the hair with enough oil so that it combed easily. Actually, Softy was not much different from Smooth, another Hubbard Company shampoo, which sold for $1.00 per bottle. With the usual markup, including a reasonable profit for both the manufacturer and the retailer, Softy would sell over the counter for $.75 per bottle.

However, the Hubbard Company was in financial difficulty. Sales had fallen off badly during the last six months, and Bernard Flannery, the President, foresaw the need to skip dividend payments for at least two quarters. Furthermore, the company might operate at a loss for the year unless Softy was a success.

Since Softy was a brand new product and a big advertising campaign was planned ("great new breakthrough in hair care"), Flannery decided to price it at $1.50 per bottle. His conscience bothered him a bit because the price was so far out of line with the costs. However, he felt that the price was justified by the low profit margins and slow sales of other items in the Hubbard Company line.

112

For items like women's hair spray, the price competition from other companies was currently so stiff that Hubbard's profits were slight. An ethical price should not be determined by the individual item, he felt, but by an entire line; that is, by the structure of prices of all of a company's products. In this business, it was practically impossible to compete unless a company offered a large number of related items. Department stores and drug stores would not handle one or two items; they wanted a full line, a multiplicity of products able to satisfy a wide variety of customers' preferences. A full line also made some kinds of advertising more economical.

Reading Peter Drucker's *Managing for Results,* Flannery saw that his problem was not unique. "Most large companies end up with thousands of items in their product line—and all too frequently fewer than twenty really sell. However, these twenty or fewer items have to contribute revenues to carry the costs of the 9,999 non-sellers."

Flannery also noted that product-line pricing was in use by non-profit organizations. As a member of the board of trustees of Claver University, he knew the University's tuition policy. The tuition in the various Schools in the University was based more on what the market would bear than on the cost of running the School. This was obvious since the Evening School and the Business School annually showed substantial surpluses of tuition income over expenses, while the Graduate School and the Medical School regularly showed substantial deficits. The former Schools had lower costs because they did not use science laboratories, their faculty-student ratio was higher, and their faculty members received smaller salaries. The pricing practice at Claver, thought Flannery, was not much different from that at the Hubbard Company.

The Salesman and
Psychic Needs*

Marlin Day is a sales representative for Acme Corporation, a distributor of shipping supplies. His customers include a wide variety of companies, and Marlin is, therefore, given much latitude in setting prices with individual customers. For example:

No. 2 Box—Cost $2.00

Possible selling price	$4.00	$3.00	$2.50
Mark-up (percent)	50	$33\frac{1}{3}$	20
Commission (percent)	20	12	5

Marlin Day imagines himself a practical psychologist. He knew he was selling a staple product and realized that his ability to get a good price was based on the personal relations he established with each customer. He had a number of buyers whom he could convince to pay the top price for No. 2 boxes.

One of these was Jerry O'Dowd, purchasing agent of the Concord Company. Day filled a great need for O'Dowd by building up his importance on every call. He recognized that O'Dowd felt that he lacked status in his own company.

* With the permission of the author, Edward Jamieson, and the NATIONAL CONFERENCE OF CHRISTIAN EMPLOYERS AND MANAGERS.

Day found that many of his customers had psychic needs that he could help fulfill. If handled properly, this would result in getting a better price for his products. Some of the men were lonely and needed a friend; some wanted to feel important; and some needed a father and wanted reassurance.

Of course, Day also had many accounts who bought shrewdly and paid the lowest price. These were the difficult ones to deal with from his standpoint.

Mark Moody, Salesman*

In 1963 Mark Moody was hired as West Coast sales representative for Cottons, Inc., a medium-sized wholesale firm selling a wide line of textile products to small retail, department, and general stores.

Moody's remuneration was based entirely on his commission earnings. Each week the company advanced him $150, to be charged against his commission earnings once a month. Moody paid all of his travel expenses. His gross commission earnings in 1963 were $8,500, in 1964 were $9,000, and in 1965 they were $10,000. His travel expenses in each of these years was $3,000, $3,500, and $3,700.

Moody was advised when he was hired that his commissions were 40 percent of the gross profit on each item he sold. For example, a certain towel costing Cottons, Inc. $8.00 per dozen was sold to the retail stores for $10.00 per dozen, giving a 20 percent gross profit on sales or $2.00 per dozen. Moody received 40 percent of the $2.00 or 80 cents.

Moody was authorized to change prices so as to increase the gross margin, and hence his commissions; or, where necessary, to reduce the gross margin. For example, on the towel selling for

* With the permission of the author, Edward Jamieson, and the NATIONAL CONFERENCE OF CHRISTIAN EMPLOYERS AND MANAGERS.

$10.00 per dozen, Moody had sold five different retail stores at the following prices in a three-week period:

Price	Gross Profit	
$ 9.00 doz.	$1.00	11 percent
10.00 doz.	2.00	20 ”
11.00 doz.	3.00	27 ”
13.50 doz.	5.50	41 ”
14.00 doz.	6.00	43 ”

When the subject of the various prices he charged came up during a conversation with another salesman, Moody said, "Where I can get a big price, I do it; if the buyer is tough, I shave the price closely."

When Moody attempted to break in with a large account, he would cut his selling price to cost, if necessary, in order to undercut the competing product then being purchased. If he was successful in dislodging the competitor, he would then attempt to raise his price later.

Cottons Inc., had many highly competitive items in the line which were sold at mark-ups so low they were unprofitable. In 1958 the firm assigned the brand name "Superba" for the major items in this group, such as sheets, towels, and spreads. Superba brand was promoted as a better quality product through media and word-of-mouth advertising by all the company salesmen, including Moody. However, he also continued to carry the identical items without the Superba brand name.

The figures below give a comparison of the prices he received.

	Unbranded	Superba Brand
Towel A	$12.00 doz.	$14.00 doz.
Spread B	3.00 each	5.00 each
Sheet C	22.00 doz.	24.00 doz.

Wherever Moody had the opportunity, he switched customers to the branded, higher mark-up line even though quality was identical with the lower-priced unbranded line. He did this by stressing the superiority of the Superba branded item over the unbranded item. By 1959 Cottons, Inc. and Mark Moody were making substantially more money on items that had formerly been unprofitable.

Looking a Gift Horse
in the Mouth

Father Barr, who taught courses in business ethics, had an ethical problem. A stomach ulcer had led to the problem. The ulcer, which was at least as active as Father Barr, required that he take three pills a day. When purchased at a drug store with prescription, these pills cost twelve cents each, including a ten percent clergy discount.

Father Barr's uncle was a "detail" man, a drug company salesman who introduces new drugs to physicians for a large drug manufacturer. Wondering whether his uncle could get the pills at a better price, Father Barr wrote to the uncle. Several days later he received this letter:

Shortly you will receive a package containing 30 physician sample folders. Each folder contains six pills of the kind you described. There is, of course, no charge for these samples. I was able to arrange this deal because a detail man for the drug company which makes these pills has a sinus condition. One of my company's products is the best treatment for his sinus condition. So I provide him with samples of what he needs, and he provides me with the pills you need. This is the way I like to do business. Let me know when you need more pills.

Father Barr debated whether or not to accept the gift. He wondered whether he would be setting a bad example by keeping the

118

pills, and whether his being a priest and an ethics teacher made any difference. He thought that the best course might be to use what had been sent, but to write to his uncle not to send any more. He was bothered by the problem . . . which wasn't helping his ulcer.

Hide and Seek*

A spokesman for the Cooperative League of the U.S.A. has criticized the new packages of Ralston Purina Company's Wheat Chex, Rice Chex, and Chex Mates cereals. David A. Angevine, public relations director of the League, claimed that "the new Wheat Chex package contains 14.5 ounces compared with 18 ounces in the old package—almost 20 percent less. The new package has the same dimensions as the old, and all four supermarkets where I've checked are selling it at the same price."

"Net contents of the new Corn Chex package dropped from 9 ounces to 8 ounces. Despite this 11 percent reduction, the new box has the same dimensions as the old, and it's selling at 25 cents, just as the old package was. The new Chex Mates package also has the same dimensions as the old, sells at the same price, and net contents have dropped from 9 ounces to $7\frac{7}{8}$ ounces."

Ralston Purina's position is that there are perfectly sound and reasonable explanations for the smaller packages. It seems that a few years ago the company came up with the research finding that its wheat cereal was "too tough," too hard to chew." J. V. Getlin, director of marketing of the company's grocery products division, discussed the problem with the researchers, who indicated that the

* Adapted with the permission of the copyright holder, *Advertising Age*.

Wheat Chex could become more chewable, while still maintaining its shape and flavor, by making the product of lighter consistency.

While the company was working toward this end, however, the government raised the parity price on wheat; and most of the major cereal makers raised their prices. Ralston Purina decided to hold the line, mainly because it didn't want to raise prices and then have to lower them again when the lighter Wheat Chex was introduced. As for Corn Chex, Mr. Getlin said there had been several increases in corn prices in recent years which warranted the price rise.

Mr. Getlin further said that Ralston Purina had two packaging possibilities for its lighter cereals. It could have invested more than $100,000 in new packaging machinery to increase the size of the package to accommodate the greater volume of the lighter cereal—and at the same time raise the price of Wheat Chex. Or, it could keep the size of the package the same, change the weight on the label to 14.5 ounces and keep the price the same. It chose the latter course. This was tantamount to taking a price increase—as other manufacturers had done the previous year—by reducing the net weight of the packages.

The same explanation applied to the corn product, which was "buffered" and also made lighter to give a "cornier" taste. The Rice Chex cereal remained the same. Ralston Purina, in order to "dramatize" the new chewability of its Wheat Chex and Corn Chex, dressed the packages in new "appetite appeal" colors.

Advocates of the Truth-in-Packaging Bill object that such methods *hide* price increases and so deceive buyers even when the increase may be justified. As they see it, the way prices are raised can sometimes be as important as the raise itself.

The Price of Milk

Joel Laitier was an independent dairyman who owned a herd and distributed his milk to small groceries. In early May of 1966, Laitier's herd was producing a temporary but large surplus, so he decided to move into the volume market provided by supermarkets and the larger grocery stores. The "normal" price to the retailer was 50 cents for a half gallon carton of milk. Laitier decided to sell gallon glass jugs for 90 cents. Since the jugs were good, on an average, for 35 refills and deliveries, he would be able to keep costs down at the same time that he increased volume temporarily.

Retailers found Laitier's price attractive. Milk is a high volume item for the food retailer so that it can return a nice profit even at a mark-up of ten percent. Some of the retailers decided to lower prices in order to bring more business into the store. Since milk is a large item in many family food budgets, this measure proved quite effective. In order to retain business, nearly all retailers in the area were forced to cut milk prices.

By May 15th, the volume distributors who had lost business to Laitier cut their prices to the retailer from 50 cents to 44 cents a half gallon. They were actually selling half gallons at approximately cost.

Average Costs For Half Gallon Carton

To the farmer	25.1 cents
Handling and transport	2.2 cents
Processing	5.0 cents
Container	3.2 cents
Delivery to store	8.0 cents
	43.5 cents

Laitier could not match these prices, and by May 30th his new customers in the volume market had switched back to their regular milk distributors. At the end of June, the volume distributors raised their prices to 55 cents a half gallon in order to make up for the decreased profits during the price war.

A Good Deal for the Doctor

Healthway, Inc., is a drug repackaging company located in a southern state. The company specializes in mixing, tableting and bottling, under private label, well-known drugs that are no longer protected by patent. Healthway differs from other repackaging firms in that 1,500 of its 3,000 stockholders are doctors practicing in Healthway's primary marketing area. The doctor stockholders are encouraged to write prescriptions using the Healthway private label, even though these same drugs could be obtained more cheaply under their generic name.

One letter to stockholders read in part as follows: "Doctor stockholders have generated sales averaging only $1.00 per day per doctor. This represents only one Healthway prescription every third day. What would happen if each doctor stockholder had written one Healthway prescription per day? The answer is astounding. Sales would have increased by $135,000 in November alone and profits would have been up $45,000!"

The effects of stock ownership were studied by monitoring the prescriptions of two groups of fifteen physicians matched for age, location, and type of practice. One group owned Healthway stock, the other group did not. More than 7,000 prescriptions written over a period of two years were studied.

The studies showed that the stockholder doctors prescribed Healthway products in 16 percent of their prescriptions, much more frequently than did nonstockholder physicians. The patients of the stockholder doctors also paid an average of 25 percent more for drugs than did the patients of the nonstockholders.

Healthway did not engage in research, which would have increased costs, and it did little promotion except to its doctor stockholders. On the whole, Healthway's promotional costs were negligible. Within three years of its inception, Healthway was returning a net profit of 14 percent of sales after taxes. This high return was attributed by competitors in part to Healthway's captive customers, whose existence enabled the company to mark up its drugs. For example, Healthway was able to buy one drug from generic-name suppliers for $2.75 per 1,000 tablets, and to resell it to druggists under the Healthway brand for $30 per 1,000. The same tablet was being sold under its major brand name for $39 per 1,000 by the company which had developed the drug in its laboratories. Another drug was sold by a major drug company for 7.2 cents per capsule, by Healthway for 5.4 cents, and by generic companies for 2 cents.

Zappala Department Store

Located in a suburban shopping center, the Zappala Department Store sold $2,100,000 worth of merchandise in 1965. The stationery department, managed by Edward Hertel, accounted for $50,000; the records department, managed by Walter O'Berg, for $30,000. These two departments are situated on different floors and at opposite ends of the building.

In January, 1966 Joseph Wirth, a distributor from an adjoining state whose selling efforts rarely brought him to the city in which the Zappala Department Store was located, made an unusual offer to O'Berg. He offered record albums of big-name singers at the price of $1.00 apiece, with the provision that unsold records could be returned. Wirth wanted to sell the albums in lots of 3,500, which would include some very slow-moving items. And he could not supply at this price records of some of the most popular singers.

O'Berg pays his regular distributor $1.95 for albums like this, but can order the kind and number that he wants. Not wishing to alienate his regular distributor, and dubious about the quality of Wirth's records because of the low price, O'Berg turned down the offer.

Wirth then went to Hertel and made the same offer. Reasoning that he was risking only shelf space and insignificant shipping costs, Hertel accepted.

Pricing the records at $1.95, Hertel sold 14,000 by the end of the year. One consequence was that O'Berg's sales declined markedly because his prices for these records were higher. Hertel got rid of some of the lemons by selling them to a local record store for $1.50; the rest he returned to Wirth.

O'Berg discussed the situation with the store manager, Carl Gole, but received no sympathy. Gole felt that O'Berg should have been more imaginative. Besides, Gole receives five percent of profits above a quota figure, and Hertel's sale of records added $500 to Gole's income for the year.

Brand Names, Prices, and Consumers

The Borden Company sells its evaporated milk under its own brand name and with private labels. In 1957, the average price per case for the nationally advertised brand was $6.2655. The private label evaporated milk sold at an average price per case of $5.1716. In some individual instances, however, a private brand buyer had to pay only $4.95 per case f.o.b. as against $6.60 for the nationally advertised brand. Small evaporated milk producers claimed that Borden was injuring them by selling to private brand merchandisers at a discount price.

Borden answered these complaints by pleading that the difference in cost justified the difference in price. They said that the average cost per case over and above direct labor and material was $1.5045 for the national brand and only $0.2326 for the private label evaporated milk. The difference in average cost was thus greater than the difference in average price.

Borden's cost figures depended on certain accounting decisions which did not go without challenge. Critics claimed that if costs were allocated as a percentage of sales, the advertising charges for the nationally advertised brand would be reduced from $0.1249 per case to $0.1188. Similarly, costs for the advertised brand would be lower if sales expenses other than advertising were allocated on a basis of gross profit from each brand rather than on a basis of the sales of each. In addition, Borden had allocated a premium redemption cost of $0.2316 per case to the nationally advertised brand. However, Borden owned 25 percent of the premium company. Borden noted the premium company had not paid a dividend and operated on a break-even basis.

If one allows all the objections to Borden's allocation of costs, the difference in price is greater than the difference in cost between the private label milk and the nationally advertised milk. The significance of this difference depends on the answers to two questions. Are the two products identical in grade and quality? Does advertising make a difference for physically identical products?

Borden contended that advertising made a difference since the advertised brand commanded a higher price in the marketplace. The FTC did not agree with this contention. "The Commission view is that labels do not differentiate products for the purpose of determining grade or quality, even though one label may have more customer appeal and command a higher price from a substantial segment of the public." This interpretation was based on precedent and on the fact that Congress had rejected an amendment to the Robinson-Patman Act which would have allowed price discrimination on the basis of branding.

Preferential Pricing

Harry Downing, president of H. R. Downing Company, is sales agent (at 5 percent commission) for the Huntington Steel Company, a producer of specialty steel. Huntington publishes a price list on all grades of steel it produces, and the prices listed are identical to those published by its ten competitors. Over the past four years, one or the other of their competitors has reduced prices a total of five times, and each time all producers lowered their prices to the same level to remain competitive.

Downing has tried repeatedly to sell Solo Manufacturing Company, a large potential user, but without success. He was told by Richard Blake, president of Solo, that in order to receive some of his business, he must give Solo an additional 2 percent discount. Blake states that he is already receiving this discount from the sales agents of the Lowell Steel Company and the Pacific Steel Company, two of Huntington's most formidable rivals. Solo Company has tried samples of Alloy 108 (the only grade of steel it uses) from all three competitors, and in Blake's opinion all three are identical for his purposes.

Downing at first resists giving the discount but, realizing that his stand is cutting him out of some business which his competitors are enjoying, finally decides to go along. Since Huntington Steel ships and bills directly to the customer, Downing gives Solo the discount in the form of a rebate after he receives his commission from the order. He continues to sell to his other customers at the published price. These customers are unaware that Downing is selling Solo the same grade they are using at a lower price. Huntington, which itself adheres to a firm price policy, is not aware that Downing is making this concession.

The Code of Ethics for the Society of Manufacturer's Agents, Inc., of which Downing is a member, makes the following statements about agent-manufacturer relationships.

I-5. The Agent will conform to the Manufacturer's policies in regard to prices, terms and conditions, guarantees, etc.

III-3. Being trained for his profession, backed by many years of successful selling and managerial experience, the professional Manufacturer's Agent with these assets, combined with reserves, is kept free from the coercions of necessity. He often represents 'the rock of integrity in selling.'

Downing's comment on the Code is: "Business is business."

The Big Squeeze

Ted Quincy, vice-president of purchasing for Houston Tool Corporation, sat behind his desk worrying over the unpleasant duty that lay before him. On his desk were the bids for a six months' supply of components. The Harry Steckley Company bid was for $150,000, and that of the Cullen Company was $144,500. The decision had to be made, but it was not an easy one. Houston Tool had been purchasing regularly from Steckley for over 25 years. Steckley, which grossed about $500,000 a year, did almost 80 percent of its business with Houston. If Quincy gave the contract to the Cullen Company, Steckley would be in a difficult position.

Ted tried to assemble his reasons for refusing the Steckley bid because he knew he would shortly have to explain them. He remembered how the Houston board of directors had emphasized that plant purchasing currently represented the best area for cost reductions. Not only could it increase Houston's profits but it would not affect the firm's workers, management, or stockholders. Most of Houston's competitors had already announced a price cut for next year, and if Houston was to retain its share of the market they must meet competition. Ted could understand the board's reasoning and knew their idea was sound.

With this he pushed the intercom button and said, "Betty, please get Jim Goodrich from Steckley on the phone."

Ted: Hello, Jim, this is Ted Quincy. Have you got a couple of minutes?

Jim: Sure, Ted, what's on your mind?

Ted: Well, our board met yesterday and it seems our competitors have been cutting prices again and we're forced to follow. I hate to tell you this, Jim, but Cullen has given us a bid 3.5 percent lower than yours . . .

Jim: You mean you're going to tell me to drop my price again?

Ted: Hold it, Jim, you know I don't like it either. We've done business with you for a long time, but our board feels that purchasing represents the best area of cost reduction for us.

Jim: You know I can't do that. If I cut again, I won't make a cent. I'm doing 80 percent of my business with you people. If I lose your account, I wouldn't have the money to retool for other customers.

Ted: The squeeze is on all of us. We just can't afford to pay your prices next year—especially with a lower bid from another firm.

Jim: About the only squeeze I see is the one that's pushing me right out of business.

Ted: Really, Jim, I have no choice.

Jim: Look, Ted, we've given you fine service for 26 years and we both know our products are superior to anybody else's. I've built my whole business around satisfying your needs.

Ted: Quality isn't the only factor. Our selling price must drop, and we've got to reduce our costs somewhere.

Jim: Hell. You mean to tell me that 3.5 percent of one item makes that much difference after all the years we've taken care of you?

Ted: Listen, the contract doesn't come up for another 60 days. Why don't you see what you can come up with?

Jim: Sixty days for what? To knuckle under to you again?

Ted: I'm sorry, Jim. See what you can do and call me back.

Jim: Yeah, sure. (Slams down phone.)

Jim sat dumbfounded. "How can they do this to me?" he thought. "They must be able to find another way. I've met every specification they've ever asked—even done odd jobs which I wrote off as good will. It's been tough enough the last couple of years. What am I going to do from here on in?"

Pick A Bid

New Town Hospital, a private, nonprofit corporation run by a religious group, is in the process of acquiring some new equipment. Specifications are drawn up and released for competitive bids. Five companies respond, but when their bids are opened, it turns out that they have all submitted identical bids of $39,000. This is about ten percent higher than the hospital board had estimated.

The identical bids strike the board members as a bit suspicious, so they delegate a director to talk to Maynard Noble, one of the bidders, who has also been a large contributor to the hospital. Noble explains that the identical figure in the bids is the result of a standard mark-up over cost. He points out that the specifications laid down by the hospital were so detailed that only one manufacturer could supply the equipment, with the result that the costs were the same for all the distributors who had bid. During the course of the conversation, Noble drops a hint that were he to get the contract he would probably be able to make another contribution to the hospital.

The director is not happy with the result of this conversation and feels there is nothing he can do but recommend to the board that all bids be rejected and new bids requested from suppliers outside the area. The other board members, however, argue that they need the equipment soon and another round of bidding would delay the process too long. Also, they feel the contract should go to a local firm. Since all bids were identical, it rests with the board to make the award to whom they please. The final decision is to give the job to **Noble.**

What Price Pills?

The Giftig Drug Company has a policy of suggesting prices for its products. Where there are Fair Trade Laws, the company seeks to enforce them; in states which have no Fair Trade Law, the company policy is to refuse to sell to those who will not maintain suggested prices. In practice this does not mean much since most Giftig products are sold through wholesalers. Moreover, Giftig rarely refuses to sell to large retail drug chains, for two reasons: the big chains are profitable customers, and Giftig wants maximum display of its products.

The company is particularly sensitive to price cutting because it does not want its branded drugs used as loss leaders. Such practices can lead to retailers pressuring the wholesalers for lower prices, as well as to erosion of the quality image of Giftig products. If there is too much price cutting, smaller druggists may refuse to carry the drugs on the grounds that their margins on these items would be too small.

In 1966 Giftig adopted a series of measures to encourage druggists to maintain suggested list prices. Wholesalers were given lists of retailers who cut prices, and were urged to cut off all their supplies. In addition, those retailers who did *not* advertise cut-rate bargains were to be aided with cooperative advertising funds, which

136

would be denied to others. While these measures have not completely eliminated the price cutters, they have reduced the number of retailers cutting prices of Giftig products. The Company does not believe there is any question of harming the public interest as it also packages its products under private labels. These sell at prices 20 percent lower than the heavily advertised and promoted Giftig drugs.

One Hand Washes the Other

Curran Foods is a multidivisional food processor and distributor. Its supermarket division buys many products from other processors, which are then sold under Curran's private label. Curran's processing divisions sell not only to other supermarkets but in a few cases to some of Curran's suppliers.

Because it is such a complex organization, Curran has a vice-president, William Quaine, in charge of trade relations. Among other things, he is charged with getting suppliers of one division of Curran Foods to become customers of other divisions of Curran Foods. Although Quaine is somewhat reticent about his work, he describes it as a question of obtaining a favorable balance of trade, granting always that price and quality are truly competitive.

Recently Curran acquired a small company which imports and packages spices for both the wholesale and retail trade. For years before the take-over, this spice packager had supplied some of the processors with whom Curran dealt. This put Curran in the position of being a supplier to its own suppliers.

Quaine decided that the other Curran suppliers also ought to buy from the new spice subsidiary. In some cases, existing suppliers did not want to cooperate because they felt they had better arrangements elsewhere. When hints were dropped that lack of reciprocity would lead to withdrawal of business, the suppliers merely laughed. They could afford this attitude since they were not dependent on Curran for a profit. However, those firms who relied on Curran business to fill in their slack season felt compelled to agree.

Sales of the new subsidiary grew quite nicely and were reflected on the Curran profit sheet. Since the new market seemed secure for the moment, Curran's spice division even put in selective price rises. This pinched some of the suppliers, but there was no real opposition. Those who had gone along with the arrangement figured that they too had a secure market with Curran. After all, one hand washed the other.

In private, officers of the supplier companies admitted that they were not happy about the reciprocity. In the first place, Curran's spice division did charge more. Secondly, they felt that they could not get the service they were used to since complaints might lead to retaliation. There is not much that can be done, however, for Curran's supermarkets are their biggest customers.

A Declaration of War

Independent gasoline station operators typically buy gas on the open market and sell it at cut-rate prices under private brand names. In 1955 these independents had accounted for only about 15 percent of retail gas sales in the United States, but by 1961 their shares had increased to almost 30 percent. In the San Antonio market 250 of these stations accounted for almost 50 percent of retail sales.

The independents, who have been called the discounters of the trade, rely on low overhead, location, and volume to keep their prices down. Their business was helped by the advent of the compact car, which uses less expensive gas.

George Scruggs entered the highly competitive San Antonio gasoline business as the owner of an independent station in 1960. At that time, the regular brands of gasoline were selling at 30 cents a gallon. Scruggs priced his own gasoline at 27 cents a gallon in order to attract business. During the first year of operation his station was slightly profitable and the volume of business gradually increased. In the summer of 1961, a neighboring Bigg station introduced Biggtane, an economy grade gasoline and sold it for 27 cents a gallon. Almost immediately Scruggs' business started to drop off. He cut his price to 26 cents a gallon and regained the sales he had lost.

As the autumn of 1961 passed, prices were being cut all over the San Antonio area. By May, 1962 prices at the pump had been driven down to as low as 17 cents a gallon for some economy gasolines. Even the price of the regular branded gasolines had fallen to 23 cents a gallon. Scruggs was holding his price at 20 cents a gallon, but was losing business to the Bigg station again.

The price war had hit many of the independents in the area heavily. Within a year, the number of independent stations had dropped from 250 to 100, and their share of the market from 30 to 15 percent. Scruggs wondered if he could survive for another three months if his volume continued to drop.

To get enough sales, Scruggs had to sell at least a cent a gallon below the prices charged by the large gasoline company stations, which offered more services, including credit cards. Though the credit cards increased marketing costs as much as two cents a gallon, the large companies continued to use them. Scruggs could not offer an expensive service like that.

Some of his competitors, he had heard, were selling a cheap grade of gas from a pump marked with a major brand name. Others were selling rebuilt spark plugs as new. Consequently, some motorists who thought that they were gaining from the price wars were not really benefiting.

Scruggs knew that if he could hold on long enough, the large companies would raise their prices substantially in order to compensate for the profits they had given up during the past year. Then he could raise his prices and make ends meet again.

Coincidence or Conspiracy

Government procurement officials have become concerned over the increasing number of identical bids they have been receiving. Although the sealed bid system was devised to preserve free competition, in some cases the bids submitted have been identical to the fourth decimal place. The following examples given in the February 23, 1963 issue of *The Nation* illustrate the problem.

Item	Price Bid per unit	No. of Bidders at this price
Electric cable	$ 5.086	6
Asphalt	27.750	4
Microscopes	521.000	8
Calcium hypochlorite	33.850	4
Potential transformers	190.800	3
Polio vaccine	1.999	3
Hamburger rolls	0.270	3
Zinc slabs	0.1235	2
Electric meters	79.800	4
Liquid chlorine	4.080	8
Steel flange beams	0.1104	3
Power cable	0.9074	4
Hard-drawn aluminum wire	39.450	4

Since investigations and suits take a long time, the officials are debating the use of the following techniques to curb what they suspect is a real abuse.

1. Instead of drawing lots, always award the contract to the smallest firm.

2. Always award the contract to the firm that is farthest from the point of delivery so that transportation costs will cut down on the gross profit.

3. Give the contracts to the same firm again and again in the hope that the other firms will break ranks.

Some officials, however, are uneasy because they question the ethics of these methods.

The Robinson-Patman Act

[PUBLIC—No. 692—74TH CONGRESS]

[H. R. 8442]

AN ACT

To amend section 2 of the Act entitled "An Act to supplement existing laws against unlawful restraints and monopolies, and for other purposes," approved October 15, 1914, as amended (U. S. C., title 15, sec. 13), and for other purposes.

Be it enacted by the Senate and House of Representatives of the United States of America in Congress assembled, That section 2 of the Act entitled "An Act to supplement existing laws against unlawful restraints and monopolies, and for other purposes," approved October 15, 1914, as amended (U. S. C., title 15, sec. 13), is amended to read as follows:

"SEC. 2. (a) That it shall be unlawful for any person engaged in commerce, in the course of such commerce, either directly or indirectly, to discriminate in price between different purchasers of commodities of like grade and quality, where either or any of the purchases involved in such discrimination are in commerce, where such commodities are sold for use, consumption, or resale within the United States or any Territory thereof or the District of Columbia or any insular possession or other place under the jurisdiction of the United States, and where the effect of such discrimination may be

144

substantially to lessen competition or tend to create a monopoly in any line of commerce, or to injure, destroy, or prevent competition with any person who either grants or knowingly receives the benefit of such discrimination, or with customers of either of them: *Provided,* That nothing herein contained shall prevent differentials which make only due allowance for differences in the cost of manufacture, sale, or delivery resulting from the differing methods or quantities in which such commodities are to such purchasers sold or delivered: *Provided, however,* That the Federal Trade Commission may, after due investigation and hearing to all interested parties, fix and establish quantity limits, and revise the same as it finds necessary, as to particular commodities or classes of commodities, where it finds that available purchasers in greater quantities are so few as to render differentials on account thereof unjustly discriminatory or promotive of monopoly in any line of commerce; and the foregoing shall then not be construed to permit differentials based on differences in quantities greater than those so fixed and established: *And provided further,* That nothing herein contained shall prevent persons engaged in selling goods, wares, or merchandise in commerce from selecting their own customers in bona fide transactions and not in restraint of trade: *And provided further,* That nothing herein contained shall prevent price changes from time to time where in response to changing conditions affecting the market for or the marketability of the goods concerned, such as but not limited to actual or imminent deterioration of perishable goods, obsolescence of seasonal goods, distress sales under court process, or sales in good faith in discontinuance of business in the goods concerned.

"(b) Upon proof being made, at any hearing on a complaint under this section, that there has been discrimination in price of services or facilities furnished, the burden of rebutting the prima-facie case thus made by showing justification shall be upon the person charged with a violation of this section, and unless justification shall be affirmatively shown, the Commission is authorized to issue an order terminating the discrimination: *Provided, however,* That nothing herein contained shall prevent a seller rebutting the prima-facie case thus made by showing that his lower price or the furnishing of services or facilities to any purchaser or purchasers was made in good faith to meet an equally low price of a competitor, or the services or facilities furnished by a competitor.

" (c) That it shall be unlawful for any person engaged in commerce, in the course of such commerce, to pay or grant, or to receive or accept, anything of value as a commission, brokerage, or other compensation, or any allowance or discount in lieu thereof, except for services rendered in connection with the sale or purchase of goods, wares, or merchandise, either to the other party to such transaction or to an agent, representative, or other intermediary therein where such intermediary is acting in fact for or in behalf, or is subject to the direct or indirect control, of any party to such transaction other than the person by whom such compensation is so granted or paid.

"(d) That it shall be unlawful for any person engaged in commerce to pay or contract for the payment of anything of value to or for the benefit of a customer of such person in the course of such commerce as compensation or in consideration for any services or facilities furnished by or through such customer in connection with the processing, handling, sale, or offering for sale of any products or commodities manufactured, sold, or offered for sale by such person, unless such payment or consideration is available on proportionally equal terms to all other customers competing in the distribution of such products or commodities.

"(e) That it shall be unlawful for any person to discriminate in favor of one purchaser against another purchaser or purchasers of a commodity bought for resale, with or without processing, by contracting to furnish or furnishing, or by contributing to the furnishing of, any services or facilities connected with the processing, handling, sale, or offering for sale of such commodity so purchased upon terms not accorded to all purchasers on proportionally equal terms.

"(f) That it shall be unlawful for any person engaged in commerce, in the course of such commerce, knowingly to induce or receive a discrimination in price which is prohibited by this section."

SEC. 3. It shall be unlawful for any person engaged in commerce, in the course of such commerce, to be a party to, or assist in, any transaction of sale, or contract to sell, which discriminates to his knowledge against competitors of the purchaser, in that, any discount, rebate, allowance, or advertising service charge is granted to the purchaser over and above any discount, rebate, allowance, or advertising service charge available at the time of such transaction to said competitors in respect of a sale of goods of like grade, quality, and quantity to sell, or contract to sell, goods in any part of the United States at prices lower than those exacted by said person elsewhere in the United States for the purpose of destroying competition, or eliminating a competitor in such part of the United States; or, to sell, or contract to sell, goods at unreasonably low prices for the purpose of destroying competition or eliminating a competitor.

Any person violating any of the provisions of this section shall, upon conviction thereof, be fined not more than $5,000 or imprisoned not more than one year, or both.

SEC. 4. Nothing in this Act shall prevent a cooperative association from returning to its members, producers, or consumers the whole, or any part of, the net earnings or surplus resulting from its trading operations, in proportion to their purchases or sales from, to, or through the association.

Approved, June 19, 1936.

VI

Advertising

What Does List Price Mean?

Giant Food, Inc. is a supermarket chain, which sells housewares and appliances in some of its stores. Its advertising in the Washington, D.C. area sometimes appeared in the form:

Sunbeam Mixmaster $24.00—Manufacturer List Price $37.95
Regina Twin Brush Waxes $25.47—Manufacturer List $66

The advertisements also contained the following note at the bottom of each page.

The manufacturer's list prices referred to in this advertisement are inserted to assist you in identification of the products and to allow you to compare accurately the selling prices offered here and elsewhere. The use of the term manufacturer's list, or similar terminology in our advertising, is not to imply that Giant has ever sold the advertised product at such list prices, or that the products are being offered for sale generally in the area at such list prices. Many reputable national brand manufactures issue to retailers, from time to time, suggested retail list prices that are intended to afford reasonable profits to all retailers based upon their traditional costs of marketing. Giant's employment of self-service supermarket techniques enables it usually to sell below suggested list prices. Consumers, however, have come to recognize most brand merchandise by the list prices, rather than model numbers, consequently Giant includes

151

these manufacturer's list prices so that you may make simple, intelligent comparisons between our selling prices and those of others.

According to buyers from three companies in the Washington area, their stores never sold at the list prices advertised by Giant. Thus where Giant had advertised a Sunbeam appliance as selling for $13.97 with a list of $21, the three stores charged the following prices for the same item: $16.49, $14.97 and $13.49.

Giant contended that at least some stores in the Washington area had advertised the product for sale at the manufacturer's list price. Furthermore, Giant's comparison shoppers had discovered stores which actually sold the advertised products at the list price. In addition the manufacturers themselves had used these list prices in *Life, Look,* and *McCall's.*

The Federal Trade Commission claimed that despite the note inserted by Giant, the term *manufacturer's list price* meant that this was the price at which the item was usually and customarily sold in that area.

The matter was taken to the U.S. Court of Appeals of the District of Columbia, which had to decide whether the FTC has the right—when an advertisement has two meanings, one of which is deceptive—to demand the termination of such advertising. The court was also expected to rule on whether the insertion itself tended to reinforce the deception.

Encyclopedia Sales Techniques

Frank Dean, a 21-year-old college student, has been working for a week as a door-to-door salesman for a large encyclopedia company. He hopes to make enough money during the summer to pay for his last year in college. Frank, however, has misgivings about the ethical soundness of the "sales pitch" he must use in selling the encyclopedias.

The company has developed an effective presentation for inducing the prospective customer to buy its product. This involves, first of all, the use of a "qualifier." The "qualifier" serves a twofold purpose—to gain entrance to the home, and to help the salesman determine whether or not the customer is a good sales prospect. The procedure is: first, to introduce himself and the company; second, to offer a free set of the encyclopedia; third, to ask for a letter giving a frank appraisal of the set to be used by the company for advertising. Part of an actual "qualifier," which Frank was taught in training class, reads as follows:

"Right now my company is in the process of bringing out a product which would be of special interest to you: a completely new, 24-volume, pictured encyclopedia. But this set is so new that it is not on regular sale in this area, and it won't be for another five or six months—maybe even a year's time. And anything this new must be promoted and advertised. Right?

"Bearing this in mind, what we are doing is enlisting the aid of a few families in this area to help with our sales and sales-promotion program. Briefly, here is what we are prepared to do. We are going to place in the homes of a few families in each area the entire 24 volumes of this set. Of course, in exchange for this we are going to ask several things. After the family has had a chance to read, use, and enjoy the set, we ask that one adult member sit down and write us a short, one-page letter, giving us his honest opinion of this set. We, in turn, would legally reserve the right to photostat this letter and use it as part of our sales and sales-promotion campaign in this area. I am sure that you both see the value and psychology of a letter like this, don't you?

"I am not a mind reader but I think I know what you are thinking. You couldn't possibly make a decision on something like this until you knew more about it. Right? By the same token, I couldn't accept anyone into this program until I had first gotten his reaction to it. Now, I can't show you 150 pounds of books because I'm not Charlie Atlas, but if you have about ten minutes, I could show you one volume describing what the set is actually like. Okay?"

Once the prospect has agreed to look at the sample volume, the salesman goes on to the next step. Through the use of visual-aid materials and the sample volume, the prospect is shown exactly what he will get. Then the vital part of the "pitch" is given. A further stipulation is introduced to guarantee the sincerity of the prospect. ("We don't just want him to accept the set and run down to his local bookstore and sell it.") Only those families who will keep their encyclopedia up-to-date with the company will be given a set. Keeping up-to-date involves two services: a question-and-answer service and a yearbook. The service and the yearbook will cost $25 a year, and the customer must pay for the first two years in advance.

In fact, the initial $50 payment covers the company's entire cost of publishing and marketing the set and services, including a lucrative commission for the salesman, plus a slight profit for the company. Subsequent payments for the yearbook and service will yield a handsome profit to the company.

Frank is convinced that the product he is being asked to sell is first-rate. The customer gets a good item for a fair price. What worries him is the method of selling the set. It seems to involve a certain amount of misrepresentation. The prospect is more or less lured into a position where the salesman can make his "pitch." However, as Frank's boss has emphasized, the salesman is not to "hard sell" the prospect.

"Once he sees our product, it will sell itself. Your job is just to convince him that he needs it. The qualifier and sales pitch are designed mainly to get the prospect's interest and attention. You are going to use a lot of psychology in making your sales. And every firm which has a product to sell does the same thing. You are only using common sales methods to present your product. The rest is up to the customer."

Shared Responsibility

In 1956, a new, "miracle" diet pill appeared on the scene. It was marketed by the Wonder Drug Company, under the guidance of its president, Mr. John Andreadis (who also used the name André). The product was advertised and sold through the mail as an appetite depressant which enabled people to lose weight without dieting. The Better Business Bureau issued warnings about the advertising, and before the year was out, the Post Office stopped the campaign.

André then changed the product's name to Regimen, and in 1958 began to market it through drug stores, using the Drug Research Corporation as a distributor. The sales promotion was highly successful, resulting in a gross of $8 million in the first ten months of 1959. A breakdown of this figure shows that André put approximately half of it back into the advertising campaign and spent another $2 million in production of the drug. This left him with a profit on the gross in the neighborhood of $2 million. A ten-day supply, consisting of 78 pills, retailed for $3.00 but cost only 18 cents to produce.

Between 1958 and 1960 the advertising for Regimen was handled by Kastor, Hilton, Chesley, Clifford & Atherton, a medium sized agency billing close to $20 million a year. The agency's campaign consisted of one minute spot announcements in 170 markets, and newspaper advertising in 150 cities. The advertising also included the use of testimonials, such as that given by Mrs. Dorothy Brice, an actress: "Without dieting, I reduced 25 pounds in six weeks, and twelve million people saw me do it on television." In all of the copy, heavy stress was laid on the fact that clinical tests had established the effectiveness of the product. The tests were supposed to have been run by the New Drug Institute. In some cases, the advertising did carry a footnote which explained that the phrase "no diet reducing" meant reducing without a diet prescribed by a physician. This note had been added to satisfy those media which felt that the main copy was deceptive.

The government was not happy with this advertising. The Federal Trade Commission, the Federal Drug Agency, and the District Attorney of New York all investigated Regimen and its advertising claims. Moreover, the Better Business Bureau had objected to both the advertising and the research which was supposed to substantiate the claims. It would appear, however, that media men were often pressured into accepting the advertising even though they knew of the suspicions voiced by both government and the BBB. John A. Watters, chairman of *Life* magazine's copy acceptance committee, testified that the advertisements were finally accepted "partly on the basis of copy changes, continuing calls, meetings, what you might call attrition—we had a term—the squeaky wheel—all adding up to what I would characterize as pressure."

Among other things, the investigations finally revealed the following facts. The doctor who had done the research report for the New Drug Institute had been induced to change his rating. Originally, the doctor had reported that ". . . although there was a significant weight loss in a few patients, the average weight loss in most patients on the active medication (Regimen) was fair to poor . . ." When Mr. Andreadis expressed disappointment over this initial summary of findings, the doctor revised his report to read: "In taking these pills, a number of patients showed a markedly significant weight loss."

Mrs. Brice, whose weight loss was featured in the advertisements, had been involved in a strange contract. She had agreed to lose eighteen pounds in four weeks. In addition, she had been offered a bonus of $50 per pound that she lost over the basic eighteen. She managed to lose 28 pounds and thus earned a $500 bonus. The results, however, were not due to Regimen. Mrs. Brice was on a crash diet and also was given dehydration pills before her weekly weigh-in on the "Today" show. Her stage directions were to slump so that her "before" pictures would look worse. At the end of the period, she was hospitalized for malnutrition, although, of course, she was some $18,700 richer for her work during an eight month period in 1959.

There seemed little doubt that the makers of Regimen were involved in deceptive advertising. What, however, is to be said of the responsibility of the media and the advertising agency. *Advertising Age* pointed up some of the issues in an editorial on February 3, 1964.

We make no attempt to assay the facts in this case. And we recognize the untenable position in which advertising agencies as well as media might be put if they were to be held accountable for factual misstatements about products which they were in no position to check. In most instances, an advertising agency and an advertising medium must accept the authenticity of factual material about products presented to them, and if they exercise normal care and prudence in authenticating product claims, they should be protected against the possibility of deception as between them and their client or their advertiser.

Having said this, however, it should also be made clear that we see no reason why either advertising agency or medium should be held free of responsibility if the facts unmistakably make it clear that agency and/or medium was a party to a material deception with regard to a product or service. It would be sheer nonsense to maintain that either advertising agencies or advertising media are above and beyond legal responsibility for their actions if they are aware that false or fraudulent product claims are being made by an advertiser, and if they permit or abet such action through the use of their facilities.

The reaction of various agencies surveyed by *Advertising Age* cast some interesting light on this problem of agency responsibility. Some saw a problem only when there was conspiracy between agency and client; others had their own staffs to check facts; one avoided testimonial ads precisely because it was so difficult to check the claims. There appeared to be no consensus as to the exact shape and nature of the agency's responsibility.

George Bailey, the Kastor Hilton account executive for Regimen, admitted that the agency knew of the Better Business Bureau's objections to the advertising. Furthermore, Mr. King, who super-vised Mrs. Brice's appearance for the advertising agency, knew that she was on a diet, although he claimed that he was not aware of its exact nature. King not only selected Mrs. Brice for the tests but also selected her clothes ("heavy look when desired, slim look when de-sired"), checked hair styles and camera angles.

The media also knew of the BBB's warnings, but some accepted the ads after calling for only minor changes such as the footnote mentioned earlier. Some publishers and broadcasters were, of course, in no position to run a special check on validity of the claims since the cost would have been too high. The fact remains, however, that there were those who were suspicious of the ads, yet accepted them in the long run.

Media representatives, researchers, models, account executives and producers are asking themselves some probing questions. Do we have an obligation to check all statements in ads? Do we need a co-operative investigating agency which would spread out the cost of screening?

The Sandpaper Shave

The technical limitations of television pose not only artistic but also ethical problems for advertisers. As the following case shows, television may force us to redefine even such basic terms as deception. Though the case has been in and out of the courts over a number of years, the basic ethical issue is debatable. What is involved is a double evaluation: where is the line between puffery and deception; where is the line between the truth about a product and the means used to present its characteristics.

In 1959 Colgate-Palmolive Company and its advertising agent, Ted Bates Company, televised the following 60-second commercial for Palmolive Rapid Shave.

1. A famous football player appears on the screen.

2. An announcer's voice identifies the player as: "A man with a problem like yours . . . a beard as tough as sandpaper . . . a beard that needs Palmolive Rapid Shave . . . supermoisturized for the fastest, smoothest shave possible."

3. The viewer then sees Rapid Shave applied to sandpaper.

4. A hand with a razor then appears and shaves a clear swath through the sandpaper.

5. While the sandpaper is being shaved, the announcer says:

"To prove Rapid Shave's supermoisturizing power, we put it right from the can onto this tough, dry sandpaper. It is as simple as apply, soak, and off in a stroke."

6. A moment later, the screen splits. One half shows Rapid Shave being applied to sandpaper; the other half shows the football player lathering his own face.

7. Razors then shave both the sandpaper and the face with ease.

8. The commercial ends with an off-camera male group singing a jingle.

The Federal Trade Commission began to receive complaints from people who were unable to shave sandpaper in the way shown on television. A quick check showed that the "sandpaper" was actually plexiglass overlaid with sand. The FTC consulted experts on sandpaper and found that there were 37,000 different types. Experiments with some grades indicated that they could not be shaved by some people, though others succeeded. It seemed that medium coarse grades could be shaved if they were soaked for 20 to 80 minutes. Some of the finer grades could be shaved after as little as one minute of soaking. Finer grades of sandpaper were not used in the advertisement because the camera made them look like ordinary paper. The plexiglass used in the commercial was covered with sand in such a way as to give the appearance of a coarse grade of sandpaper.

The FTC claimed that this was deception since it implied properties or performance characteristics for the product which it did not possess and which are of sufficient importance to be likely to affect the decision to purchase. According to Earl Kintner, FTC Chairman at that time, this practice was to be distinguished from two other procedures which were acceptable:

1. Theatrical or technical devices to make a product seem to perform or appear on the TV screen as it actually would if viewed through the naked eye under normal conditions of use;

2. Theatrical or technical devices to make the product as attractive as possible, for example cosmetic glorification.

Both Colgate-Palmolive and Ted Bates contended that the commercial was not deceptive; at most it was puffery—an expression of enthusiasm. Furthermore, the cream did help to shave sandpaper if it was allowed to soak long enough. Eventually the company did admit that the demonstration exaggerated the moisturizing claims of the cream since sandpaper could not be shaved under the conditions shown in the advertisement. Finally, the company claimed that no person would seriously believe that the demonstration proved anything about human shaving.

The FTC countered that this last argument substantiated its claim of deception. The commercial obviously tried to imply a relationship between shaving sandpaper and human beings. The Commission admitted that mock-ups could have their place in advertising, but insisted that when attention was drawn to a product's quality, the mock-up became deceptive.

In essence, the FTC was saying that truthful television advertising must not only represent the *product* as it is, but must represent the *demonstration* as it is, if attention is called to the particular product being advertised. To put it another way, if a demonstration is intended to prove a point which is expected to motivate the buyer, not merely the claim but the demonstration itself must be truthful. The commissioners noted that if this were not possible on television, the advertisers had the option of using other media or of omitting demonstrations entirely.

The principle covering the truthfulness of the demonstrations applies to other areas as well. Thus the use of plastic ice cubes in a soft drink advertisement would probably not be deceptive since nothing was being said about the quality of the ice. The use of plastic ice cubes in an ad designed to prove that the cubes last longer would be deceptive even if the actual cubes did have a longer life.

Cigarette Advertising and
the Public Interest

The tobacco industry is deeply involved not only with the health of the public but also with the income of shopkeepers, farmers, governments, and advertising media. Tobacco advertising brings the industry into close relationship with government agencies and Congress. As a result, the problems of the tobacco industry are often as multi-dimensional as the public interest.

The report of the Advisory Committee to the Surgeon General of the Public Health Service, "Smoking and Health," appeared in 1964. Its writers admitted that there is not likely to be any simple cause and effect relationship between tobacco and a given disease. However, they did conclude that "cigarette smoking is a health hazard of sufficient importance in the United States to warrant appropriate remedial action." Among other things, the report noted: "The greater the number of cigarettes smoked daily, the higher the death rate." For coronary artery disease, the death rate is 70 percent higher for cigarette smokers; for chronic bronchitis and emphysema, the death rate of the cigarette smokers is 500 percent higher; for lung cancer, the rate is 1,000 percent higher for cigarette smokers than for nonsmokers.

The report made the health problem official. As a result, it was a threat to the tobacco industry. Even before the report, widespread rumors about its contents had caused the value of tobacco stocks to fall. Profits too were down since a good deal of money had been devoted to fighting the anti-tobacco forces. In 1955 the Federal Trade Commission had issued guides for cigarette advertising and in 1960 stopped the companies from making tar and nicotine claims. Some of the companies, such as Philip Morris, had already started to diversify into the manufacture of razor blades, flexible packaging and chemicals. Indeed, in 1962 twenty percent of Philip Morris' income came from nontobacco sources. Reynolds Tobacco too had diversified by setting up the Archer Aluminum division and Pacific Hawaiian Products, which marketed fruit juices, cake mixes, and shoe polish.

Not only the tobacco companies' profits but the income of government at all levels was involved. In 1962 tobacco sales had totaled $8 billion, two percent of disposable personal income. The federal government had taken in over $2 billion in taxes on tobacco and over $500,000 on cigarette papers and tubes. Individual states had received over a billion dollars in tobacco product taxes, and local governments had as their cut $70 million.

Tobacco sales also touch the lives of many wage earners and small businessmen. The crop value of tobacco in the United States and Puerto Rico was in the neighborhood of $1.5 billion in 1962. Approximately 95,000 people were employed in the manufacturing of tobacco products, and in one way or another 750,000 farm families depended on income from the tobacco crop. Hundreds of thousands of shopkeepers depend on tobacco sales for part of their income.

Finally, there is the obvious fact that tobacco manufacturers are heavy advertisers. In 1962, for example, they spent $119 million in television advertising. In addition, $18 million was spent on newspaper advertising and $2 million on magazines.

Despite the economic importance of tobacco, there was considerable public outcry when the Surgeon-General's report appeared. The FTC, for example, wanted every package and advertisement to carry a prominently displayed warning about the hazards of tobacco smoking. In January of 1964 the FTC proposed the following rules:

Rule 1. Either one of the following statements shall appear, clearly and prominently, in every cigarette advertisement and on every pack, box, carton and other container in which cigarettes are sold to the public:

(a) "CAUTION—CIGARETTE SMOKING IS A HEALTH HAZ-
ARD: The Surgeon General's Advisory Committee on Smoking
and Health has found that 'cigarette smoking contributes substantially to mortality from certain specific diseases and to the overall
death rate' "; or

(b) "CAUTION: Cigarette smoking is dangerous to health. It may
cause death from cancer and other diseases."

Rule 2. No cigarette advertisement* shall state or imply, by words, pictures, symbols, sounds, devices or demonstrations, or any combination
thereof, that smoking the advertised cigarettes

(a) promotes good health or physical well-being,

(b) is not a hazard to health, or

(c) is less of a hazard to health than smoking other brands, except
that a specific and factual claim respecting the health consequences
may be advertised if

    (1) the advertiser, before making the claim, has substantial and
reliable evidence to prove the accuracy and significance of
the claim, and

    (2) all facts material to the health consequences of smoking the
advertised cigarettes are clearly, prominently and intelli-
gibly disclosed in close conjunction with the claim.

Rule 3. No cigarette advertisement shall contain any statement as to the
quantity of any cigarette-smoke ingredients (e.g., tars and nicotine) which
has not been verified in accordance with a uniform and reliable testing
procedure approved by the Federal Trade Commission.

   * For the purposes of Rules 2 and 3, "advertisement" includes labeling.

The tobacco industry challenged the authority of the FTC to
make such rules. The Tobacco Institute, which, among other things,
acts as a lobby for the industry, argued that:

"1. This is a problem for Congress. Under this heading, the Institute will
contend that the Commission lacks authority to adopt substantive rules de-
fining the kinds of advertising claims that can be made for cigarettes.
In any event, the Institute will say the problem is of such magnitude that
the Commission should recognize as a matter of policy that these questions should be considered by the Congress and not by any single administrative agency.

2. The rules themselves are unnecessary. Rule 1, which requires a warning on packages and in advertising, is not needed, the Institute will say,
'particularly since the proposed rule disregards the extensive and continuing publicity given to questions of smoking and health.' "

Other groups such as the American Newspaper Publishers Association, the Advertising Federation of America, and the National Association of Broadcasters seemed to feel that the proposed regulations established dangerous precedents.

The tobacco industry mounted a many-pronged attack. Shortly after the appearance of the Surgeon General's report, the six major companies gave $10 million to the American Medical Association for research into the relationship between smoking and health. The industry announced a program of self-regulation. The question was also placed before the House Interstate and Foreign Commerce Committee. Tobacco thus became a political as well as a health and economic problem.

The House Committee asked the FTC to push back the deadline for its labeling ruling from January 1 to July 1, 1965. Lobbyists then went to work on both the House and the Senate Committee. The idea was to get a bill which put the question under the control of Congress rather than of the FTC or of the Public Health Service. The bill which Congress finally passed required that packages of cigarettes carry the warning: "Caution! Cigarette Smoking May Be Hazardous To Your Health." There was no requirement as to placement so long as it appeared in "conspicuous and legible type." In addition, the bill forbade the FTC to go ahead with plans for stricter regulations until July 1, 1969. State and local governments were also forbidden to pass measures on cigarette advertising and labeling.

The industry had proceeded with its own self-regulation measures. The major manufacturers of tobacco products agreed to abide by a new code governing cigarette advertising. Robert L. Meyner, former governor of New Jersey, was to administer the code, which sought to prohibit appeals directed primarily to those under twenty-one and to forbid health claims. Meyner's power was to be absolute, and he had power to levy fines up to $100,000. The actual scope of Meyner's job is best seen in the Code provisions governing advertising.

ARTICLE IV

Advertising Standards

SECTION 1. All cigarette advertising and promotional activities shall be subject to the following:

(a) Cigarette advertising shall not appear
   (i) On television and radio programs, or in publications, directed primarily to persons under twenty-one years of age;
   (ii) In spot announcements during any program break in, or during the program break immediately preceding or following, a television or radio program directed primarily to persons under twenty-one years of age;
   (iii) In school, college, or university media (including athletic, theatrical, and other programs);
   (iv) In comic books, or comic supplements to newspapers.
(b) Sample cigarettes shall not be distributed to persons under twenty-one years of age.
(c) No sample cigarettes shall be distributed or promotional efforts conducted on school, college, or university campuses, or in their facilities, or in fraternity or sorority houses.
(d) Cigarette advertising shall not represent that cigarette smoking is essential to social prominence, distinction, success, or sexual attraction.
(e) Natural persons depicted as smokers in cigarette advertising shall be at least twenty-five years of age and shall not be dressed or otherwise made to appear to be less than twenty-five years of age. Fictitious persons so depicted in the form of drawings, sketches or any other manner shall appear to be at least twenty-five years of age in dress and otherwise.
(f) Cigarette advertising may use attractive, healthy looking models, or illustrations of drawings of persons who appear to be attractive and healthy, provided that there is no suggestion that their attractive appearance or good health is due to cigarette smoking.
(g) No cigarette advertising shall contain a picture or an illustration of a person smoking in an exaggerated manner.
(h) Cigarette advertising shall not depict as a smoker any person well known as being, or having been, an athlete.
(i) Cigarette advertising shall not depict as a smoker any person participating in, or obviously having just participated in, physical activity requiring stamina or athletic conditioning beyond that of normal recreation.
(j) Testimonials from athletes or celebrities in the entertainment world, or testimonials from other persons who, in the judgment of the Administrator, would have special appeal to the persons under twenty-one years of age, shall not be used in cigarette advertising.

SECTION 2. No cigarette advertising which makes a representation with respect to health shall be used unless:

(a) The Administrator shall have determined that such representation is significant in terms of health and is based on adequate relevant and valid scientific data; or

(b) If the Administrator shall have determined it to be appropriate, a disclaimer as to significance in terms of health shall be set forth in such advertising in substance and form satisfactory to the Administrator; or

(c) The Administrator shall have determined that the representation with respect to health in such advertising is not material.

SECTION 3. The inclusion in cigarette advertising of reference to the presence or absence of a filter, or the description or depiction of a filter, shall not be deemed a representation with respect to health unless the advertising including such reference, description or depiction, shall be determined by the Administrator to constitute, through omission or inclusion, a representation with respect to health. If the Administrator shall have determined that such advertising constitutes a representation with respect to health, the provisions of Section 2 of this Article shall apply.

SECTION 4. No cigarette advertising shall be used which refers to the removal or the reduction of any ingredient in the mainstream smoke of a cigarette, except that it shall be permissible to make a representation as to the quantity of an ingredient present in the mainstream smoke, or as to the removal in toto of an ingredient from the mainstream smoke, or as to the absence of an ingredient normally present in the mainstream smoke, if:

(a) The Administrator shall have determined that such representation is significant in terms of health and is based on adequate relevant and valid scientific data; or

(b) A disclaimer as to significance in terms of health shall be set forth in such advertising in substance and form satisfactory to the Administrator; or

(c) The Administrator shall have determined that disclaimer is unnecessary for the reason that the representation in such advertising has no health implication or that such implication is not material; and

(d) The quantity of such ingredient is determined and expressed in accordance with uniform standards adopted by the Administrator for measuring the quantity of the ingredient present in the mainstream smoke, provided that, until such uniform standard is so adopted, the quantity of such ingredient may be determined and expressed in accordance with any recognized scientifically valid method disclosed to the Administrator without any requirement of confidential treatment.

SECTION 5. Any advertising determined by the Administrator to be in conformity with the Code may include the following legend: "This advertising (label) conforms to the standards of the Cigarette Advertising Code."

The FTC was not happy with the code, and in November 1965 it called on the cigarette companies to include provisions to prevent advertising which negated the health warning on the package. Although the FTC had been blocked from requiring each advertisement to carry the warning, it claimed that Congress had given it the responsibility "of assuring that the cigarette advertising shall not, either expressly or by implication, negate, contradict or dilute the effectiveness of the cautionary statement on the package."

Article IV of the code may not have satisfied the FTC, but it was nonetheless difficult to administer. Some executives inside the tobacco industry complained of one-man rule and of very loose interpretations. Meyner turned down commercials in which smoking was associated with big business deals, or was presented as directly promoting romance or marriage. However, the commercials were allowed to show dating couples smoking. In addition, he interpreted the code to exclude testimonials by even the fictional Marlboro man. Decisions were also complicated by the fact that study designed to determine what TV programming had distinct appeal to teenagers turned out to be inconclusive.

The problem became even more complicated when the FTC announced in March of 1966 that the producers could advertise tar and nicotine contents so long as the advertisement did not claim that the product would reduce health hazards. A month later Lorillard withdrew from the Cigarette Advertising Code. The picture became further confused when research indicated that Lorillard's True cigarettes reduced tar and nicotine most effectively. This same research also noted that no filter really protected the health of the consumer, but this did not deter the makers of True from placing a full page in the New York Times with the following copy printed in large type:

The truth is out: In the news section of this paper you read a news report that revealed new True filter cigarettes delivered less tar and nicotine than other brands tested . . .

It looked as if there would be a re-run of the tar and nicotine derby of the mid-fifties. In 1955 the FTC had issued guidelines which stated that claims for tar and nicotine could be made only if "the claim is true, and if true, that such difference or differences are significant." Both then and in 1966 there was question as to what "significant" meant. Does it mean statistically significant or physiologically significant? The question is not purely academic. Meyner, the code Administrator, noted that any discussion of tar and nicotine yields is potentially deceptive unless there is a warning that the presentation of yields does not equal a health claim. In particular, Meyner noted, "In absence of scientific information of some 'safe' limit of the ingredients measured, such collateral statements without a health disclaimer would appear to be a disservice to the public interest."

The results of some European experience raise questions about the effects of tobacco advertising. Italy banned all cigarette advertising in April 1962. However, in the fiscal year ending June 30, 1963, cigarette sales in Italy had increased by 1.7 percent, despite a price increase of 8 percent early in 1962. In 1962 a report from the Royal College of Physicians in England had caused a 12 percent drop in cigarette advertising. By January 1964, however, sales were back to prereport levels.

The problem confronting all interested parties was: What constitutes the "appropriate remedial action" mentioned in the Report of the Advisory Committee to the Surgeon-General.

VII

Dealers, Agents, and Suppliers

Is Good Business
Good Ethics?*

The cement industry is basic to our economy and well-being. As a product, cement is interwoven into many aspects of modern life—homes, buildings of all sorts, highways, and other places where construction takes place. Traditionally, at least in the Midwestern part of the country, cement producers deal directly with their customers. By virtue of the nature of the product and its uses, cement customers are widely dispersed. To preserve better control over the delivery of cement, producers have developed fairly rigid relationships in the area of transportation. Normally, where water transport is necessary, producers maintain their own fleets of boats. However, for distribution from receiving ports, the movement of cement to customers is routed by rail or motor truck. For more local distribution, cement is also moved directly from the producing plant to the customer by rail or motor truck.

Cement companies generally control the designation of the common carrier, who will deliver cement to a customer. Since the right to transport commodities over the road is granted by public regula-

* With the permission of the author, Professor Chester Evans, Wayne State University; Business Ethics Case Material.

tory bodies, the carrier must follow prescribed procedures and regulations—routes and rates are generally fixed and noncompetitive.
Most companies, then, select the carriers they use and maintain the
relationship for a variety of reasons, with good service playing an important role.

In the state of Michigan, for example, cement carriers are char-
acteristically classified as small businessmen. Most of them have built
up their businesses from one or two trucks to fleets of somewhat
larger size. As yet, cement trucking has not attracted, in this area,
any of the large interstate trucking combines. Attempts to band the
cement truckers into an effective association have thus far been of
minimal success. The suspicion between trucking firms, based in fact
on many evidences of double-dealing, coupled with cement company
resistance, has made it difficult for an effective association to be
formed. Consequently the cement trucking industry in Michigan
operates pretty much under the laws of the jungle. The following
two incidents illustrate this point.

HARDSTONE CEMENT

Hardstone Cement Company decided, for apparently
good reason, to discontinue the services of Millrock Cement Carriers
beyond a certain point in western Michigan. Millrock was an old, established business and had made some investments to provide service
from several of Hardstone's distribution points. The changeover to a
new carrier revealed the extent of expenses incurred by Millrock Carriers in setting up to do business from Hardstone's field location; a
cement silo, a terminal for trucks, trailers and equipment, operating
rights out of that point to the customer service area, and specialized
equipment on 24-hour standby to handle Hardstone's business. When
the decision had been made to change carriers, Hardstone assured
Millrock that no loss would accrue to it. They established relations
between Millrock and Newsand Cement Truckers (the new carrier),
and an orderly exchange of operating rights and terminal facilities
was accomplished. All parties benefited, with no serious damage to
anyone. Granted that Millrock suffered a loss of revenue from this
point, but it did not suffer any investment loss as a result of Hardstone's decision.

PAVERSON CEMENT

The Paverson Cement Company, in expanding its business on an interstate basis, encouraged one of its small carriers, Higrade Cement Trucking, to develop routes from Detroit into various points in Indiana. Long hauls of this sort were not profitable, so sufficient shorter hauls in the state of Michigan were promised to compensate for losses incurred on the longer hauls. State weight laws in Indiana prevented pay loads of the size allowable in Michigan, thus requiring lighter equipment with less load capacity or less utilization of load capacity. Despite a long-delayed rate increase, the Indiana business was of lesser value to the carrier, especially when the ratios of Indiana to Michigan were not maintained on an equitable basis.

An added burden was introduced when Higrade Carriers, with the encouragement of Paverson Cement, purchased $140,000 worth of specialized equipment especially designed for Indiana hauls. The new equipment was to be fully depreciated in six years on a straight-line basis. Higrade was not sure of the resale value of the equipment because it was designed especially for Indiana cement hauling. Assurances were given Higrade at the time that there would be ample opportunity to recover the investment through continued business from Paverson.

A year later, Paverson told Higrade that its trucks were no longer to be used for any cement hauling in either Michigan or Indiana. Though initially some slight interest was shown in the carrier's predicament and promises of aid were implied, no arrangement worthy of serious consideration resulted. Since Paverson provided about 90 percent of Higrade's revenues, it is obvious that Higrade was in trouble. Paverson's reaction, however, was one of disregard for the serious problems of the carrier which had for many years serviced them. Their attitude was: "That's the breaks of the business. We had too many carriers, so we cut off the one that we felt we could get along without."

Who Sold the House?

Joseph Burrows wanted to sell his house in a hurry. He had been transferred from the Boston office of Orvid Corporation to a position in Los Angeles and hoped to complete the sale before leaving Boston. His home in Boston was worth about $30,000, but since money was tight in the fall of 1966, he was not sure that the house could be sold easily. He decided that he would increase the chances of a fast sale if he listed the property with several real estate agents.

Burrows first approached the Lansdown Real Estate Agency and explained his problem. Lawrence Lansdown, the owner of the agency sympathized with his problem, but tried to convince him that an exclusive listing would prevent a great deal of trouble. Lansdown quoted Article 1 of the Code of Ethics as established by the National Association of Real Estate Boards: "The exclusive listing of property should be urged and practiced by the Realtor as a means of preventing dissension and misunderstanding and of assuring better service to the owner."

However, Lansdown agreed to handle the property despite Burrows' insistence on an "open" listing. Burrows then listed the property with Walton Real Estate. The Walton agency did not urge an exclusive listing since Lansdown had already agreed to an "open"

176

listing. Burrows made all of these arrangements within two days.

A few days later Lansdown showed the Burrows property to a prospective client, Bill Asbury. Asbury showed some interest in the property but said he wanted to look around a bit more. Asbury was not at all interested in the other properties that Lansdown showed him.

Within the week, Asbury went to Walton Real Estate. Bob Jarwell, the Walton salesman, showed him four houses but not the Burrows property, since he wanted to move some of his older listings first. Asbury recalled the Burrows property and indicated that he would like a second look at it. Since the Burrows property was also listed with Walton, Jarwell took Asbury out to the house the following day. As they went through the house room by room, Jarwell pointed out the special features of the house and some of its less obvious advantages in construction. When Asbury indicated serious interest in the house, Jarwell proposed a method of financing that appealed to Asbury.

After looking at twelve houses in a week, Asbury was becoming convinced that he could not do much better. He asked Jarwell to show the house to Mrs. Asbury and promised to give him an immediate decision. Mrs. Asbury was delighted with the house and the sale was consummated for $29,000.

When Lansdown heard of the transaction from Burrows, he contacted Walton Real Estate and asked for half of the commission in keeping with a local custom. The president of Walton refused on the ground that his salesman had done the real work. Lansdown argued that he had generated Asbury's interest, without which the sale would not have been made. Since the commission, computed according to the local custom (6 percent on the first $20,000, 5 percent thereafter), amounted to $1,650, Lansdown was in no mood for trifling.

Competition Versus Loyalty

Ward Fishwick purchased the City Filter Company in 1938, and gradually built it into a company with 125 employees, $1 million in assets and $1.5 million in annual income. City Filter sold, rented and serviced water coolers, air-conditioning equipment and similar machinery. The company had cultivated a reputation for quality, and for quick, competent service of all its equipment. For these advantages, customers paid prices slightly above those of competitors. Most business was in the form of repeat sales and rental contracts.

The company had wholesale and retail divisions. One of its coveted franchises was with the Zephyr Company, manufacturers of air-conditioning machines. Ward Fishwick had been one of the first customers of Zephyr, and had built up the reputation of Zephyr equipment in his city.

In 1957, Ward Fishwick died in an automobile accident, and his only son, Kent, became president. Kent was 29 years old at the time, having earned a bachelor of arts degree and having spent two years in the Army infantry. His five years of business experience had been divided between a bank and a large department store. As a tyro in the role of president, Kent relied heavily on the advice of his plant manager and of the company's legal counsel, who had been a close friend of Kent's father.

The only crisis of Kent's first year as president was the resignation of Arthur Felden, City Filter's sales manager. It was not difficult to find a new sales manager. Felden, however, started his own business, renting water coolers, and persuaded 120 of City Filter's customers to sign contracts with him for the following year. Kent felt that this action of Felden, which reduced City Filter's annual income by $50,000.00 was unethical.

A heavier blow fell in 1960, when the Zephyr Company notified Kent that City Filter could no longer act as both wholesaler and retailer for air-conditioning units manufactured by Zephyr. City Filter would lose heavily regardless of which operation it gave up.

The Zephyr wholesale operation, which included the franchise for the entire state, had been slightly more profitable for City Filter than had the retailing of Zephyr products. Sales of Zephyr equipment to other retailers had amounted to 16 percent of City Filter's income in 1959. Furthermore, Ward Fishwick had persuaded two other small Zephyr wholesalers to join City Filter in 1955, and Kent felt some responsibility for the job security of the two men.

On the other hand, the retail portion of the air-conditioning business which brought in 12 percent of total income in 1959, was linked with many other parts of the company's activities. One of City Filter's most valuable assets was the staff of competent salesmen and servicemen who were connected with retail operations.

Kent was irate when he reflected on the proposal of the Zephyr Company, for whom his father had been the local distributor for twenty years. Zephyr products had acquired an enviable reputation in the city because of the excellent service provided by City Filter's employees. "Because the Zephyr executives don't put a dollar figure on good will," thought Kent, "they think of City Filter as just another outlet. We built up their name, and now that customers identify it with quality, their management gives us an either-or ultimatum. They've acted just the way Arthur Felden did. We helped him learn the business from the ground up. Then when he was able to stand on his own two feet, he left us and took some of our customers with him. Loyalty is dead in the business world. Competition has killed it."

Where Does the Buck Stop?

On January 12, 1961, the directors of the Cream City National Bank of Chicago decided that, due to the bank's tremendous growth in the previous four years, it would be necessary to build a new and larger bank facility with an attached parking structure. Capital assets had grown from $50 million in 1957 to over $100 million in 1960. The bank presently occupied cramped quarters in a downtown office building with few parking spaces on the surrounding streets. The much needed new building was to be constructed apart from the congested business section but still easily accessible to public transportation and freeways.

The directors of the bank, after deciding that they had plenty of cash and available credit to go ahead with the project, solicited competing bids from ten contracting firms. The job eventually went to Learner Construction Company, a New York-based firm with affiliates in the Chicago area. Jacobus Learner, president of the company, elected to sublet various portions of the job to smaller local area firms. The J. W. Skim Construction Company won the bid to erect the parking structure. Skim, in turn, dealt with ten independent contractors in the suburban area.

Construction of the bank building and adjacent parking structure started on time and went exceptionally well until shortly before the prescribed completion date. At that time, a stretch of poor weather and a strike among the drivers of concrete mixing trucks forced costly delays in the project. However, Learner remained confident that his profit margin and built-in allowance for such eventualities was enough to absorb the loss.

Work resumed three weeks later and the job was completed in another three weeks. Learner now realized that he had miscalculated, and his losses were substantially in excess of the amount originally anticipated. Unable to meet his obligations, he went to the bank directors and requested an additional $150,000 above the original contract price. He reasoned that since the delays were obviously not his fault, and since—equally obvious—the bank was in a better position to absorb the loss, the institution had an obligation to pay the additional amount. Furthermore, Learner informed the directors that if he was not paid both the original fee and the requested increase, he would not be able to pay his sub-contractors in full.

The Cream City National Bank, represented by its president, Howard C. Burr, refused to pay the extra $150,000. Burr's response was, "We contracted for $3,500,000 and that's all we're going to pay. Learner should have allowed for such contingencies when he quoted his fee. Besides, his outfit is large enough to absorb its own losses."

Burr, however, wishing to avert a lawsuit with Learner, suggested that Learner should pay his subcontractors only 85 percent of their contract prices and take his chances with a few small lawsuits. At least, if all of them were paid the same percentage below contract, one would not have a larger deficit than the other. Moreover, the small contractors would not want to be excluded from bidding on future jobs. Learner agreed, saying, "The only way that I can maintain my company's position is to short change the other guy a little. I don't like it but it's my only alternative."

J. W. Skim felt that he could not afford a lengthy court battle with the larger company and subsequently settled for partial payment.

Regardless of this fact, Skim chose to pay his subcontractors in full. To do so he was forced to pay part of his company's obligations out of his own pocket. He later commented, "If I hadn't come up with the extra fifteen percent, I might have put several of my ten subcontractors out of business. I would hope, if the circumstances arose, they would do the same for me."

A Spy in the Shipping Room

When H. L. Moore, President of the H. L. Moore Drug Exchange in New Britain, Connecticut, gave a job to David Terpstra in July, 1965, he was getting more than a shipping clerk. Moore subsequently discovered that Terpstra's real purpose was to determine the contents of cartons shipped to and from the Moore Company and to report his findings to John Saviano, head of a Manhattan detective agency. When Terpstra's objective was discovered by Moore, he dismissed his new shipping clerk—the only course of action open to him since the agent had broken no law. Terpstra had not misrepresented himself, nor lied on his employment record, nor stolen documents or formulas; he had merely reported information.

The incident was brought to the attention of Senator Edward Long, Chairman of a Senate subcommittee studying industrial espionage. Testimony before the committee by Saviano revealed that he had been hired by the Smith, Kline & French Laboratories to plant an undercover agent on the Moore premises to determine if SK&F's suspicion of irregularities in the distribution of their drugs was founded. Terpstra was to identify SK&F franchised distributors who were selling to Moore. These distributors were entitled to certain discounts for selling directly to retailers. The distributors were claiming and getting these discounts while actually selling to Moore.

SK&F declared that although they found this type of surveillance repugnant, they felt it was necessary because of their obligation to enforce uniform wholesale distribution agreements under the Robinson-Patman Act. Moore charged that certain drug makers were "out to get me" because his company had cut prices from suggested levels. Saviano stated that although work for the drug industry accounted for 90 percent of his agency's business, he had never been asked to police price agreements or uncover price-cutters.

Hidden Costs

John Adams is president and sole owner of Adams Associates, a small advertising agency billing $5,000,000 a year. Since many of his clients do not pay promptly, Adams finds himself financing short term loans of up to 90 days. This not only affects his cash position but reduces his net profit on advertising billings by about 25 percent. In short, instead of making a net profit of four percent on billings, he makes only three percent.

Adams has found ways in which to increase his over-all profits by taking advantage of opportunities presented by other aspects of his business. He is the silent partner in a printing firm to which he forwards many orders for brochures and direct mail pieces. Joe Selva, who manages the printing firm, overprices Adams' orders so that they yield a higher profit. Adams then adds a fifteen percent agency charge when he forwards the bills to his clients. The bills have never been questioned by those clients who are slow in paying, though some of Adams' clients have suggested that he could find a less expensive printer.

The slow paying clients also pay more for photographic work done by Adams. Adams charges them approximately twenty percent more than he does other customers even before he adds his fifteen percent charge. In practice the slow payers are charged $1150 for work which other customers get for $940.

Is Enterprise Wrong?

On September 1, 1960 Robert Bartelt leased a Major Oil Company service station in a residential section in Milwaukee County. This particular station had never been much of an asset to Major, and the company had previously considered selling it to a competitor. Five years after Bartelt took over, the station had grown to the second largest retail Major outlet in Milwaukee.

1960 net profit $3,000	1960 total gallons gas 9,600
1964 net profit $11,000	1964 total gallons gas 45,000

In addition to selling gasoline Bartelt also did minor repair work: oil changes, grease jobs, wheel bearings, tires, and other small services. Consequently, with the great increase in total volume, his service area was taxed to the limit. The station had four gasoline pumps, one washing area, and two lifts; the service area was filled with cars almost every working hour of the day.

Repeated attempts to get Major Oil to expand his facilities met with no positive results, so Bartelt went looking for more working space. He found a minor company service station within two miles of his present location. The station had been vacant for about a year. It was located on a side street out of the way of business routes, but it would provide Bartelt with much-needed space for repair work.

Bartelt took a lease on the Minor station for a period of two years at a cost of $2,000. An employee of his Major location went into partnership with him.

A few months later Major executives found out about Bartelt's expansion. They were very much shocked at his move and threatened to let the lease on the Major station expire unless the Minor deal was abandoned. Since the Major station was the "bread and butter" location which enabled him to "ship" his work around, Bartelt saw no alternative to giving up his Minor lease.

Who's Bidding?

Columbine Associates is a small firm of architects which specializes in renovating homes and commercial buildings. It has a fine reputation for quality work, and over the years has built up excellent relations with several general contractors. These relationships are of considerable importance since no architect can get everything down on paper. A successful job demands that the builder translate the architect's ideas and not merely his lines and specifications. To accomplish this, there must be a certain amount of give and take based on confidence in one another's fairness and professional integrity. For this reason, Columbine prefers that only carefully selected contractors bid on its jobs.

In December of 1965 the firm was doing a renovation for Sport Clothes, Inc., a men's specialty shop. Edwin Sport wanted the names of two friends included in the list of bidders. Kyle Teckton, the senior partner in Columbine, tried to explain the advisability of dealing only with firms of established reputations, but Sport did not see why everyone should not have a chance. Teckton agreed, but was not happy, because he knew that these two contractors were troublesome to work with. They had been known to cut corners in workmanship and materials, a practice which frequently led to costly repairs and replacements later on. In most cases, they insisted on following directions literally, even when a little imaginative interpretation would show the architect's real intent. All in all, they were not the sort of builders Columbine felt would do a good job. Teckton, however, did not fight the issue since he had other ways of getting around a client.

By the time the bids arrived at the office, Teckton had already learned from a reputable source that one of Sport's friends was low bidder by $500 on the $80,000 job. Teckton then called up the three contractors with whom he preferred to work and told each of them:

"We are supposed to open the sealed bids tomorrow and I have a feeling that the bid may go to someone barely qualified to do a decent job. The word is that he is low bidder by only $500. Why don't you see whether you can give us a better price on a few individual items. If you can rework your figures and get them over here by this afternoon, we could hold things up a bit."

Samuel Elliott, a junior architect, was disturbed by this conversation and questioned Teckton about violation of professional ethics. Teckton replied: "I try to get the best job done for the client even if he seems not to want it. Look, if the current low bidder gets the job and botches it, we will get the blame and the client will not get what he wants. An architect is not like an ordinary businessman; he has to protect his client against himself at times. Experience will teach you that we are saving clients money when we do this sort of thing. Don't let appearances fool you, young man. I've done this before and never yet regretted it."

Cool-It Sales Company

In early 1966, Earl Leetz, owner of the Cool-It Sales Company, was debating whether to initiate a more aggressive marketing program than he had ever attempted. Cool-It Sales was exclusive distributor for the Hopps Brewing Company. Over the preceding five years, competition in the brewing industry had become increasingly stiff at all levels, but especially for the wholesalers. In 1960 there had been 5,500 beer wholesalers operating in the United States; at the end of 1965, there were 4,500. This was the lowest number of wholesalers since pre-prohibition days. This reduction in wholesalers took place despite an increase in beer consumption, which was due to the increase in population. The annual per capita consumption remained steady at about sixteen gallons.

Part of the wholesaler's problem was that he was caught in a squeeze between rising costs and a stable price. The brewers, who were able to dominate pricing in the industry through exclusive franchising, were reluctant to raise the price of beer because some of their patrons might turn to wine and hard liquor. While beer prices had remained constant for a decade, labor costs in the industry had risen substantially. For example, Leetz was paying his drivers $40 per week more than he had in 1955.

Cool-It had $300,000 in assets, including six trucks, refrigerated storage space, an office, and a small inventory.

Leetz had been a beer distributor for two decades, including some very profitable years. But his company's net profit after taxes was about $5,000 in 1964 and 1965, and he felt that he had to make more profit through more sales volume. Otherwise it would be more economical to put his $300,000 in a savings bank or invest it in bonds.

Leetz knew that he had to be careful about the means used to increase his volume. Since he handled nothing but Hopps beverages, all his eggs were in one basket. He knew of instances in which the Hopps management had terminated a wholesaler without warning, a practice known throughout the industry as an overnight check-out. Consequently Leetz felt that he had better not vary from the prices recommended by the brewery. Besides, he liked the idea of standard prices and standard discounts. It eliminated the need to haggle with every customer. He knew a number of ways of giving hard-to-sell retailers reduced prices without showing this fact on invoices.

For his largest accounts, Leetz felt that he might get more of their business if he extended their credit so that they wouldn't have to pay their bills for 90 days. This he could do by suggesting that they post-date their checks to him. For all accounts which made substantial increases in monthly sales, Leetz was thinking of giving a rebate of 20 cents per case in addition to the quantity discounts which were common in the industry. He could charge the rebates off to bad debts at the end of the year.

From the smaller retailers who sold a lot of packaged goods, he could secure their best floor space for his displays by paying "rent" for the space. He could also offer to pay for the retailer's advertising in neighborhood papers. These expenses could be charged against Cool-It Company costs for rent and advertising.

He knew that there was a very good chance to get Hopps beer into a downtown tavern if he would pay the bill for a new paint job. This he proposed to do. He also had heard that he could persuade the owner of another tavern to put Hopps beer into one of his two taps by giving the owner's wife a check for $500. These items could be written off as selling expenses of the Cool-It Company.

Finally, one tavern owner had promised Leetz that he would push Hopps beer if Leetz would foot the beer bill for an annual birthday party for the owner. The liquor salesmen were taking care of the party bill for liquor, but neither Leetz nor the other beer wholesaler who sold to the tavern had come through in the past.

While reading *The Brewing World,* Leetz came upon a copy of the National Beer Wholesalers Association Code of Fair Practices. He recalled endorsing the Code in 1964. Among the articles in the Code were the following:

(2) I shall extend credit only to retailers who are in compliance with the credit terms originally stipulated by agreement or applicable law.

(3) I shall provide malt beverages to retailers only at the actual list *price* applying to all accounts for purchase of comparable *quantities.*

(4) I shall charge retailers at no less than actual cost to my firm for any promotional material, merchandise or extra services provided, including electrical outside or inside brand identification signs; draft beer equipment and parts; and miscellaneous services unrelated to direct brand promotion such as painting and repairs on the retail premises . . .

(6) I shall treat all my customers on an equitable basis, not discriminating among retailers purchasing comparable quantities of malt beverages by providing any form of rebates, concessions, donations, or extra services not automatically offered to all retailers purchasing an equivalent amount of malt beverages . . .

"Too bad that the Code isn't working," thought Leetz. "The corner-cutters and chiselers are setting the standards for everybody in our industry. The lowest common denominator of ethical practices seems to prevail."

Wheel Dealers

The Los Angeles automobile market is intensely competitive. Everyone wants a "deal," and most people are willing to shop around in order to get one. As a result, some automobile dealers have evolved a series of practices to convince the buyer that he has gotten a bargain. One of these is an arrangement for setting up referrals from discount houses.

The discount houses do not purchase and resell automobiles, but they perform certain marketing functions for the dealers. In most cases, discount houses display the cars on their premises and refer potential customers to the dealers. The discounters can negotiate prices, terms, and conditions of sale as well as allowances for trade-ins. They also deliver the new automobiles to buyers. The discounters, however, have no responsibility for servicing the cars or meeting the conditions of warranty. The dealer continues to handle car insurance and registration. Originally the price negotiated by the discounters was ten percent off list price. In time, however, they began asking for a fifteen percent discount.

Dealers ordinarily provide a variety of services important to the maintenance of good will and future sales. The contracts between the manufacturer and automobile dealer called for the dealer to handle warranty claims. The dealer is reimbursed by the manufacturer for such services, though in some cases the reimbursement provided does not cover the full cost. A dealer is supposed to pre-service a car before selling it. While this usually costs from $15 to $20 a car, it can run as high as $70. Some dealers merely wash and clean the vehicle, but a quality dealer checks everything. He is, moreover, expected by the manufacturer to service such defects as rattles and leaks, which are not covered by the factory warranty. Since these services are time-consuming, a dealer who is using a discount referral system may be tempted to neglect or avoid his obligations.

The actual profit margin on a car may be very low in the case of a quality dealer. Often he loses money on the service side of his business. In 1960, for example, a typical Chevrolet dealership in the Los Angeles metropolitan area incurred an annual loss in the operation of its service and parts departments of approximately $14,000. Often, the dealer must make much of his profit through the sale of insurance and credit. Aggressive merchandising by banks, credit unions, and the financial arms of the automobile manufacturers cut into this source of profit. A marginal dealer, therefore, may be severely tempted to cut corners.

According to the automotive manufacturers, the dealer's franchise grants a nonexclusive right to purchase new cars at dealer prices and resell them in a manner which will promote sales and preserve the good will of the manufacturer. The dealer's rights and obligations are personal and not transferrable. The dealer is supposed to have the right to sell to whom he chooses and at whatever price he chooses. He cannot, however, transfer his sales and service obligations.

In the case of the Los Angeles Chevrolet dealers, each dealer's area of sales responsibility was the entire metropolitan area.

The automobile companies charge that the use of discount houses as the source of referral involves the transfer of sales obligations to a third party. Indeed, they interpret it as being the establishment of a branch office without the written permission required by the franchise. Furthermore, they argue that the increase of outlets, which results from these practices, will lead to dealer mortalities and an inadequate distribution system.

In 1960 there were 85 Chevrolet dealers in the Los Angeles metropolitan area. Over 35 percent of these dealers were small and sold 700 or fewer Chevrolet passenger cars and trucks per year. A Price

Waterhouse study conducted in 1960 looked at the prices of seven dealers who sold 96 percent of the Chevrolets that were merchandised through discount houses in the Los Angeles area. It appeared that the discount house arrangements flourished largely when automobile sales were lagging.

According to a brief filed in the Supreme Court on behalf of General Motors:

The median price at which those dealers sold directly to ordinary customers was $220 over dealer's invoice cost, while the median price at which they sold to customers through discount houses was $235 over dealer's invoice cost. Appellant asserts that Chevrolet dealers sold Chevrolets through discount houses 'often for only $165 more than dealer's invoice cost.' The fact is that in 1960 the dealers studied by Price Waterhouse & Co. sold 1461 (or 24.5 percent) of their total sales of 5970 cars to ordinary customers for $165 or less over dealer's invoice cost, whereas they sold 143 (or 10.7 percent) of their total sales of 1336 cars through discount houses at $165 or less over dealer's invoice cost.

In 1960 only 2000 out of 100,000 Chevrolets sold in Los Angeles were merchandised through discount houses. Twelve out of 85 dealers in the area were involved. Nonparticipating dealers located near the discounters began to suffer, and in June of 1960 the problem was discussed at a regular meeting of a dealers' association. When the offenders would not comply with the association officer's request to desist, the dealers agreed to ask for help from General Motors.

A G.M. executive wrote to some dealers suggesting that commerce with discounters violated the location clause of the franchise. According to General Motors, he did not consult with dealers or dealer organizations about this matter, although the action had been prompted by a large number of letters from dealers in southern California.

Early in 1961 General Motors elicited from each Los Angeles dealer a promise not to do business with the discounters. There was evidence, however, that this promise "was not obtained without reference to the ultimate power of General Motors." Private investigators were also hired to police the agreement.

In 1962 the Justice Department charged General Motors with conspiracy to prevent the sale of Chevrolets through discount houses. The United States District Court for the Central Division of the

Southern District of California was expected to answer the following questions. Had General Motors acted independently in this matter or had it conspired against the dealers who were dealing with discounters? Was the franchise contract itself legal? Did the need to protect its distribution system and the profit margins of dealers authorize the actions taken by General Motors?

VIII

Accounting

Principles Can Be Costly

Charles Simpson is the senior partner in Simpson and Richards, a small auditing firm in Davenport, Iowa. The firm employed nine people, including the two partners, until just recently, when one of its largest clients relocated in North Carolina. Because of this loss, Simpson was forced to reduce his staff to seven employees.

Last week Simpson and Richards began its annual audit for its largest client, the Morris Tractor Corporation. In analyzing the fixed assets, Charles Simpson noticed a loss of $12,000 recorded on the books due to the demolition of several buildings. When he discussed this loss with the President of Morris Tractor, James Morris, Simpson learned that the demolished buildings and the land on which they stood had been recently acquired, with the intention of demolition prior to construction of two buildings on this land some time in the future. Simpson informed Morris that the demolition costs should be capitalized rather than recorded as a loss on the building. Morris replied that he did not want these expenses capitalized since this action would cancel out the loss, and would seriously affect the company's tax liability for that year. He implied that if Simpson's firm would not prepare an unqualified report of the financial position of the firm, he was sure that he could secure the services of another accounting firm which would do so.

The decision was entirely in Simpson's lap. Morale was low in his company; Richards and two of the senior accountants were discouraged over the loss of the client who had moved. Simpson felt that if he refused to accept Morris' terms, he would lose Morris Tractor as a client. This could mean the end of the business. Yet he hesitated in his decision. He knew that if he did not qualify the opinion in his audit report, the taxes to be paid by Morris Tractor would be substantially reduced. However, in that case the report would not present the Morris Tractor Corporation's financial statements in accordance with generally accepted accounting principles. Simpson wished that Morris had never informed him of the company's intention to build.

When Is Duty Done?

Boyd Long, a recent college graduate with a degree in Accounting, had been hired by the Hevi-Duty Crane Corporation, which manufactures and markets excavation machinery used in the construction and mining industries.

One of Boyd's first assignments was the auditing of weekly expense reports. Hevi-Duty used the refunding method of expense accounting whereby the employee submits an itemized weekly report of actual expenses incurred. Upon proper approval, the employee is reimbursed or the amount of expenses is applied to an advance. As part of the audit, Boyd checked each expense report for conformity to company policies and Internal Revenue Service regulations. Except for a few arithmetical errors and lack of proper receipts, Boyd found no violations of company policies. But after a few weeks he noticed that one salesman was reporting the same amount of expenses each week. Boyd began looking for similar occurrences on the reports of other employees. To his amazement he found many reporting the same or approximately the same amount of expenses week after week.

On his own initiative Boyd made a two-month analysis of what he took to be obvious "padding" by certain employees. He then took his findings to the manager of the Accounting Department, Larry

Jackson. Jackson became quite angry and asked why he hadn't been informed of the analysis before, and whether or not Boyd had discussed his findings with anyone. After regaining his temper and apologizing for the outburst, Jackson explained that he was aware of "padding" on the expense accounts but was unable to convince his superiors that something should be done about it.

He gave several reasons for management's unwillingness to change the expense account system. One was that the "padded" amounts on the expense reports were considered part of the employee's compensation. If the company paid higher salaries, the employees would have to pay higher taxes since the "padded" amounts are nontaxable. In effect, management was doing the employees a favor. A change, therefore, would probably result in many unhappy employees. The fact that expense account "padding" has become part of the American scene was also mentioned. "Everyone is doing it, why shouldn't we?" Also, the employees knew that management was aware of the present practice and was doing nothing about it. This was taken as tacit company approval of the "padding" system. Management felt that an attempt to correct the situation would only cause the employees to develop more subtle ways of "padding." Therefore, nothing would be accomplished.

Jackson then praised Boyd for his interest and initiative in the matter, but told him to forget about it. Boyd, however, wondered whether he had an obligation to take his report higher up in the company.

Accepted Accounting Standards

When Jason Armstrong took over the presidency of Underearth Instruments in 1962, he believed that the company had tremendous potential if it could only match internal expansion with acquisitions. His vigorous action in the next four years tended to prove his point. One of his earliest acquisitions had cost the company 750,000 shares selling at $3.00 a share to acquire a firm that had only $400,000 in annual earning power. Within two years, however, 100,000 shares of Underearth Instruments, selling at $50 a share, were sufficient to purchase a company with annual earnings of $1,000,000.

Underearth's success depended, among other things, on maintaining a good picture of earnings. This in turn depended on the accounting methods used. Armstrong insisted that his accountants use the most liberal methods so long as they followed generally accepted accounting principles. His accountants, however, felt that liberal methods could be deceptive, at least for those who were not professional investors. They had serious doubts about the following entries, and did not know whether it would be ethical to make them, although it could be said that these entries complied with accepted standards.

If the accountants went along with Armstrong's suggestions, Underearth Instrument's consolidated statement would show earnings of $5,000,000 on sales of $55,000,000. Armstrong had already announced that he expected earnings to be up. Moreover, he had mentioned an increase in potential income as a result of a mineral discovery in South America. This discovery, however, would not affect earnings for several years.

In the fall of 1965, Underearth sold a subsidiary engaged in oil exploration for $2,250,000 and reported earnings of $1,700,000 on the deal. This was, of course, nonrecurring income and profit. If the subsidiary had been retained, it would have contributed only small sums to income.

In 1965, Underearth sold some of its oil and gas production payments to an insurance company. All of the income was reported in one year. As a result the net profits in 1965 were $1,250,000 higher than they would have been under a more conservative method of accounting which would have spread the income over at least five years. Armstrong also wanted the accountants to include the earnings of five new subsidiaries in the 1965 report even though these were not formally acquired until early 1966. The footnotes would indicate this consolidation, but the report would not tell how much income was to be attributed to these five subsidiaries. Actually, something like $1,500,000 in profits would be added this way. Such accounting is not illegal, and there are experts who say that the Securities and Exchange Commission regulations favor this method.

Underearth executives also insisted that the accountants use liberal methods in the handling of expenses. In the case of one subsidiary, they wanted to capitalize research and development costs and write them off over a period of five years. Armstrong was even urging the accountants to capitalize certain administrative expenses for Tubbo Oil, a subsidiary that was in trouble if these expenses were subtracted immediately from net income. Capitalizing some of Tubbo Oil's administrative costs would keep its loss for the year down to $200,000. Tubbo had become involved in a risky investment when it bought 13 percent of the stock of Southwestern Capital, which owned 50 percent of the stock of the Canadian Acceptance Corporation. When Canadian Acceptance went bankrupt, Tubbo suffered a loss of $650,000.

The accountants' doubts were magnified by a rumor which was

going around the financial community. It was said that Armstrong had not paid his brokers for 160,000 shares of Underearth which he had bought for himself and others. Was Armstrong, by use of a sharp pencil, trying to bolster the price of the stock, which had fallen when two mutual funds had sold it out? Accepted standards or not, were the accountants being asked to create a false impression?

Conflicts at Cox, Messner, and Zorach

For many years the public accounting firm of Cox, Messner, and Zorach has been the auditor for the Edgewater Stamping Company of Chicago. During the 1966 audit, Joseph Cox, the senior partner discovered that Edgewater was in serious financial trouble. Indeed, the company could very well be forced into bankruptcy within six months. Edgewater, it appeared, had invested heavily in the development and promotion of a new product for which no real market had materialized.

Cox discussed the problem with his partner, Morris Zorach, since the audit report in this case would demand unusual care. The news of Edgewater's condition disturbed Zorach greatly, for Edgewater was the major creditor of Midland Steel Warehouse, another Cox, Messner, and Zorach client currently being audited.

Midland Steel Warehouse was a new client, and Zorach was personally supervising the audit. He had discovered that Midland had an unusually large item in its accounts receivable, a note for $200,000 from Edgewater Stamping for a large shipment of steel. Cox's news about Edgewater indicated that the $200,000 might never be repaid.

Zorach found that $200,000 was the equivalent of 30 percent of all the current assets of Midland Steel, an indication that Midland had great confidence in the business future of the Edgewater Company. Indeed, when Zorach reviewed the large balance accounts with the credit manager of Midland and came to the account receivable from Edgewater, the Midland credit manager said, "Now that Edgewater note there, why that $200,000 is as good as money in the bank!"

Zorach examined all the correspondence between Midland and Edgewater and talked with key Midland executives, but found no indication that the officers of Midland were aware of the dangerous weakness of the Edgewater Stamping Company. Relations between the two companies were good and had extended over many years. But Zorach realized that if Midland pressed for payment of the $200,000, which was not due for 60 days, Edgewater would be forced into bankruptcy at once, and Midland would suffer a grave loss because of the unpaid debt.

Morris Zorach was alarmed and confused. His firm was glad to get this new account with Midland Steel Warehouse, and Zorach wanted to make a good audit. Should he tell the Midland credit manager about the bad debt from Edgewater? Wouldn't it be a good idea if Cox, Messner, and Zorach dropped Edgewater anyway? Bankrupted firms don't need auditors. If Zorach told Midland now, then Midland could perhaps get most of its money back before Edgewater's other creditors would have the chance to make claims. In this way, Midland would make the best of a bad situation. If Zorach did not inform Midland of the danger, then Midland would suffer a severe loss. Was it not the obligation of an auditor to protect the best interests of his client? Zorach's report would be read by the stockholders and creditors of Midland. Did he not have a responsibility to those people too? What was Zorach to do?

While he was debating the issues in his mind, Zorach recalled Rule 1.03 of the Code of Ethics of the American Institute of Accountants: "A member or an associate shall not violate the confidential relationship between himself and his cilent." Zorach realized that his accounting firm had a confidential relationship with its client, the Edgewater Company. He did not wish to violate this confidence. At the same time, his firm had acquired a new responsibility, the certification of Midland's accounts. Zorach knew that it would be harmful to the professional status of his firm and a discredit to the accounting profession if he were to directly and deliberately reveal to Midland the confidential information he had received about Edgewater without Edgewater's consent.

Furthermore, Zorach recalled that the Illinois accountancy law gave his firm, and all accountants, immunity from testifying in court when they would have to reveal confidences. While the public accountant-client relationship is not recognized in common law as confidential, as is the relationship between a doctor, lawyer, or priest and their confidants—and accountants debate whether it should be —Illinois law does make the accountant-client relationship confidential: "*Section 27.* A public accountant shall not be required by any court to divulge information or evidence which has been obtained by him in his confidential capacity as a public accountant."

Can You Ever Play Ball
With Bandits?

Hofbrau is a small but successful local brewery serving Lake City and its surrounding suburbs and towns. The firm was founded in the 1880's by Peter Hofmann; his grandson, Carl Hofmann, is now the president. The stock of Hofbrau is rather closely held, with 65 percent of the stock owned by five families, including the Hofmanns and their relatives. Members of these families constitute the entire board of directors. The firm has a net worth of around $5 million.

Hofbrau has done a nice local business and Hofbrau Beer is an old tradition in the community. Carl Hofmann, however, has felt that the traditions and quality of the beer deserve a wider market. In the summer of 1952 he was in the process of arranging a moderate expansion. He hoped to secure new capital for Hofbrau and, at the same time, to sell a considerable portion of the holdings of the five families which controlled the company. His treasurer had informed him that Hofbrau should prepare a registration statement for filing with the Securities and Exchange Commission and have the Hofbrau accounts audited for a three-year period. For years, Hofbrau's accounts had been audited by a small Lake City firm of accountants.

"But now," said the treasurer, "we should have the audit done by some nationally known firm. The certification of our accounts by a well-known accounting firm will help both us and our underwriters in this public financing we are to begin."

Hofmann agreed and called in Andrew Slater and Associates to do the audit. Slater and Associates is a large public accounting firm, with a national reputation for competence and integrity. Its main office is in Lake City. The Slater firm accepted Hofbrau as a client, and Andrew Slater himself directed the audit. During his examination of the accounts, Slater noticed that in 1949, the first of the three years under examination, there was a substantial increase in the expenditures for advertising. The amount spent in that year, $800,000, was greatly in excess of the amounts spent in any previous year or in the two subsequent years. Then Slater methodically examined all the underlying documents in support of those advertising charges.

The only thing that he found unusual was the fact that the entire increase in advertising expense for 1949 was cleared through an advertising agency, Williams and Johnson, that had never previously serviced Hofbrau and was no longer doing any work for them. Slater was somewhat concerned and talked the matter over with one of his partners. They decided that when Slater was finished with the field work, he should surely bring up this matter of the large advertising expenditures in 1949 with President Hofmann.

Hofmann was quite frank with Slater. He said: "Much of our advertising expense is not really for advertising at all. I want to be open with you. You see we simply cannot brew and distribute Hofbrau beer in Lake City unless we give annual payments—I guess you'd call them bribes—to certain officials or agents of Lake City.

"Three city departments are involved: the Department of Buildings, the Board of Health, and the Police Department. I don't say it's the top officials in these departments. It's the middle and the bottom representatives who demand the graft. Maybe the people at the top don't know about it. Maybe they do know and think they can't do anything about it, so they close their eyes. Maybe their hands are tied. I don't know. I just know this: When the inspector from the Zoning Division of the Department of Buildings comes around each year, if I don't see that he gets $500 in his coat pocket, we'll suddenly find that our Hofbrau plant is in violation of the zoning code. The same thing happens whenever we remodel our plant or put on some extension. Another inspector comes out to clear us so we can get a remodeling permit. That's at least $500. Then there's the factory safety inspector. He comes around more often. We try to fulfill all the safety requirements, and even to go beyond them. But no matter what we did we'd be in violation, if we did not pay off this safety inspector. Then there's the Board of Health. Their man comes out from time to time since we are classified as a food establishment. We try to be scrupulously clean here. That's my grandfather's tradition. But this health inspector costs us $500 a visit! Finally we think we have to give annual gifts to several members of the Police Department of this district. I don't know just what for. But they expect it, and we want to be on the safe side."

Slater: "Mr. Hofmann, why don't you refuse to pay such graft, and if one of the inspectors charges you unfairly with a violation of some city code, just appeal it to a higher authority?"

Hofmann: (smiling) "I don't think you understand this business, Mr. Slater. It's cheaper to pay than to appeal. Then there's always the possibility of reprisals. No, this is a kind of quick 'insurance.' "

Slater: "I see. But the kind of small bribes you say you have to pay would never explain the large increase in advertising in 1949."

Hofmann: "Correct. What we pay to the city agents is piddling, though it is constant over the years, and it does add up. But this is what happened in 1949. The 'Syndicate'—I suppose you know something about the Syndicate? It's the outgrowth of the old Capone gang. Some of its business is now quite legitimate and quite varied! For example, it operates one of our local breweries. Well anyway, the Syndicate had noticed our increasing sales and also our plans for expansion. In 1949, they demanded a payment of $240,000."

Slater: "$240,000! That is scandalous. Suppose you had refused."

Hofmann: "Frankly, if we had refused, the Lake City tavern keepers who now handle our beer would simply refuse to handle any more of it. If they did handle it, they'd find their tavern windows being broken. Or, more likely, a rash of minors would descend upon them asking for a glass of beer. A policeman or an inspector from the City Collector's office would pick up the minor, and the tavern keeper involved would lose his liquor-dispensing license; he'd be out of business for good, or something else would happen. No, he'd never take a chance on handling Hofbrau beer if we stood in bad with the

Syndicate. No matter how fine he might think our beer is—and it's the best beer you can buy around here! You see, Slater, we must make these payments. We take it for granted that we have to pay them from time to time. Everybody in our business pays the bribes. They all do it. Of course, 1949 was rather an expensive year. We had to pay more. We didn't see why such payments were not a necessary expense of doing business and therefore deductible for income tax purposes. And as you know, our federal income tax returns for 1949 were officially examined and passed by the Internal Revenue Service."

Slater: "But don't you realize, Mr. Hofmann, that the tax law courts will not allow graft or bribe payments as a deductible expense of doing business? It is true that the Internal Revenue Code does not mention graft. While it does say that a businessman may deduct from his tax 'ordinary and necessary business expenses,' the courts universally deny that graft and bribes are 'ordinary and necessary business expenses.' If you count these bribes as advertising expense, the courts could bring you up for violation of the tax laws."

Hofmann: "Yes, I was aware of the attitude of the courts. That is precisely why we set up the Williams and Johnson Advertising Agency and why *they did* pay their taxes. But quite honestly, I do not think the courts are fair. We don't like to pay graft and bribes. But we *have* to do it. It is a tribute for the privilege of doing business. Therefore, it *is* a necessary expense. If we don't pay graft, we soon go out of business. If we do pay graft, our profits will dwindle unless we can count the graft as a deduction against our income. It's only fair to count graft as advertising expense, or public relations if you prefer."

Andrew Slater thus learned that Williams and Johnson was a dummy advertising firm set up by Hofbrau only for the year 1949. All Hofbrau's bribe payments for that year, $250,000, were handled through the Williams and Johnson Agency. Williams and Johnson submitted invoices, collected the necessary cash from Hofbrau Breweries and disbursed the bribe payments to the proper channels. Total billings from the Agency ($800,000) were considerably greater than the amount of the actual bribe payments ($250,000). This was done in order to leave in the Agency the amount of cash necessary to pay the income tax of the Agency partners, Williams and Johnson roughly, $250,000; for the advertising firm filed an income tax return and did *not* claim the bribe payments as deductions. Early in 1950 the Williams and Johnson Advertising Agency was dissolved. *Hofmann:* "I feel confident, Mr. Slater, that you will understand and sympathize with the problems Hofbrau Breweries has to face. First, we have to pay this tribute money, and secondly, we are not a rich company—we simply can't afford not to deduct such expenses from our taxes. We are only a small, local brewery; if we lose our Lake City business, it would ruin us. Now the big people like Pabst, Anheuser-Busch, and so on, they sell on a nationwide scale. They can afford to lose a market here and there. We can't. We'd like to expand somewhat. But we must count on this market for many years to come."

Andrew Slater admitted to himself that he was perplexed. He was a businessman and he could understand Hofmann's point of view. At the same time he was the senior partner of an old and respected public accounting firm. What should he do? He wanted to help Carl Hofmann, whom he liked. Yet he had a responsibility to his firm, and even more, to the public. Indeed, if he were to conceal a material fact about Hofbrau's financial structure, some potential stockholder could conceivably bring suit against the Slater firm itself up to the entire amount of the new financing. Slater recalled the public letter that the American Institute of Accountants wrote in 1943 to a certain Washington senator:

The professional certified public accountant in public practice has two things to offer—one, his technical skill and knowledge based on varied experience; the other, his disinterested and objective viewpoint and his reputation for complete integrity. Others may possess equivalent technical skill and knowledge in specific fields, but only the certified public accountant in public practice may be presumed to have an independent objective and impartial viewpoint on all facts which come under his review.

This is the foundation of professional accounting practice. It is the reason why reports and opinions of professional certified public accountants are of value to banks and other credit grantors, to stockholders, prospective investors, to government agencies and to others who desire information about corporate financial affairs. When such persons see the opinion of a professional certified public accountant appended to financial statements, they know that those statements have been reviewed by an independent and impartial expert who has no axe to grind. This is undoubtedly the reason why the Securities and Exchange Commission requires audits by in-

dependent accountants of financial statements of companies registered
with the Commission.

Knowing as they do that their reputation for independence and integrity
is their principal asset, certified public accountants are impelled by enlightened self-interest, as well as by traditions of professional ethics with
which they are inculcated as a part of their training and by their own
sense of personal pride, to hew to the line and let the chips fall where
they may.

Those characteristics of the profession are well known in the business
world, and the reports of certified public accountants are generally accepted and often required by business and financial executives.

I am sure it will be clear to you on a moment's reflection that if the profession were to lose its reputation for independence, its opportunities for
service would be drastically limited.

Also, Slater thought of the American Institute of Accountants'
most important rule, Rule 2.02:

In expressing an opinion on representations in financial statements
which he has examined, a member or an associate shall be held guilty of
an act discreditable to the profession if:

(a) He fails to disclose a material fact known to him which is not disclosed in the financial statements but disclosure of which is necessary to
make the financial statements not misleading; or

(b) He fails to report any material misstatement known to him to appear in the financial statement; or

(c) He is grossly negligent in the conduct of his examination or in
making his report thereon; or

(d) He fails to acquire sufficient information to warrant expression of
an opinion, or his exceptions are sufficiently material to negative the expression of an opinion; or

(e) He fails to direct attention to any material departure from generally accepted accounting principles or to disclose any material omission
of generally accepted auditing procedure applicable in the circumstances.

IX

Finance and Stockholders

Lund Lawnmower, Incorporated

The Meehok Company was a large, southern firm that specialized in acquiring small companies, putting them on their feet financially and managerially, and then selling them at a handsome profit. Malcolm Meehok, the founder and president, had acquired the capital necessary to start the company through the discovery of oil on farm land he owned in Texas. Meehok had gradually built up his capital and a team of managers skilled at analyzing and solving the problems of small manufacturing companies.

In January, 1967, the Meehok Company was negotiating with Kenneth Lund, president of Lund Lawnmower, Inc., for purchase of his company. Lund had a good product, but he had neither the marketing outlets nor the personal motivation to make a long-run success of his company. Lund and his immediate family owned all of the company stock, and they had agreed that it would be wise to sell. There was agreement between Malcolm Meehok and Kenneth Lund about all the details of the acquisition except the price.

Meehok, who was known as a man with a sharp pencil, had offered Lund $1,100,000. Lund replied that he wanted $100,000 more, and justified his demand with the explanation: "Your price

217

is $100,000 less than the value of my company's assets and earning power. For one thing, my brother in Canada has been receiving $10,000 a year, but he has never done any work for the company. For another thing, I have been paying myself $20,000 annually for options on patents which I own in Germany, but those patents are practically worthless. So the company's expenses were really $30,000 less than the 1966 profit and loss statement shows."

Meehok nodded and said, "Of course we knew about those phony expenditures; my staff went over your entire operation very carefully. I took those facts into consideration in my original offer."

"Well," said Lund, "one thing you aren't aware of is that company income for 1966 is understated. Almost every Saturday last year I backed a truck up to the factory, filled the truck with lawnmowers and went out and sold them. I pocketed about $1,000 in cash every Saturday; that money never appeared on the company books. Knowing that, how much will you add to your offer?"

A Tip on the Stockmarket

The following discussion is taken from a statement by Edward T. McCormick, President, American Stock Exchange, during the hearings before the Committee on Banking and Currency of the U.S. Senate on Factors Affecting the Buying and Selling of Equity Securities, 84th Congress, First Session, 1955.

Senator Ives. I understand that not so many weeks ago one of our radio commentators indicated that a certain stock was very desirable to purchase. I am referring to Pantepec Oil, which opened, I believe, on the American Stock Exchange with a block of 377,000 shares, and if I am correct, has not sold as high as that particular time since. Is that correct?

Mr. McCormick. That is correct.

Senator Ives. Well, I understand you also conducted an investigation of that situation. What were the results of your investigation?

Mr. McCormick. Senator, that was not an isolated instance. The same commentator has referred to stock traded on the American Stock Exchange before, the New York Stock Exchange, the over-the-counter market in Toronto. Each time that any reference was made on a Sunday to a security traded on the American Stock Exchange, I called the Securities and Exchange Commission in New York the following morning.

To be specific now on the Pantepec situation, I happened to be listening to the program.

The Chairman (Senator J. W. Fulbright). What program was that?

Mr. McCormick. Well, I suppose there is no secret about it. It was a television program by Walter Winchell.

With reference to the Pantepec situation, I was listening to the program, and as I recall, he made reference to some 10 securities that he had mentioned over a period of a year or 18 months and pointed out the profits that had been made by all those who had bought those particular securities. I believe it ended up with U.S. Gypsum which had shown something like a 90-point rise in the interim.

He then said that he had some information concerning Pantepec Oil. As I recall the information he gave, there were three things he said. One, the company was going to have a stockholders' meeting. The purpose of the stockholders' meeting would be to increase the authorized stock. Two, the purpose of the increase in authorized stock would be to use that stock in the payment of dividends. Three, the purpose of the payment of stock dividends instead of cash was to conserve the cash of the particular company so it could expand its exploratory work. As I recall, that was the statement.

I thought that might give difficulty at the opening of the market the next day. So I called the specialist in the stock, who is Mr. David Jackson . . . I informed him that I had seen the program.

He was on the floor of the exchange early the next day. I was there. I spoke to Jim Dyer, who is chairman of our floor committee. It was just simply amazing. There were thousands of tickets, buy orders, sell orders, cancellations on the specialist's desk. We provided additional help for Mr. Jackson. We did not open the stock at 10 o'clock. It was a physical impossibility to even match the tickets.

When enough tickets had been matched so it was quite obvious that the stock was going to open substantially higher, the specialist in the stock told those in the crowd, all brokers with orders, "Now look. It is going to open substantially higher. Go back to your customer and get limits or cancellations if they don't want to go through, because it is going to open higher. And if you leave a straight market order we are going to have to execute it wherever we can get the stock."

The stock was opened. The first trade in the stock was made at

12:15 Mondays. At least by 11:30 the brokers were again told, "This stock looks like at least 8-5/8 at this point. Now, go back again to your customer and find out whether he wants to leave an unlimited market order in here."

It ended up that people wishing to buy 357,000 shares, the greatest single amount in the history of any exchange in one transaction, left their orders in, unrestricted market orders. The transaction was opened on the 357,000 shares at 8-7/8—eight dollars and seven-eighths. The close the previous Friday had been 6-3/4. An increase of $2.12-1/2.

I had called the SEC about this. I called Frank Purcell at the New York regional office. I said, "Frank, this is a rough one to handle. Have you any ideas?"

He did not have—any more than I did. I did say, "Frank, I checked back, and I see that Pantepec has been trading about 20,000 shares a week for a number of weeks." The week before this big opening it had traded some 170,000 shares. I said, "Frank, maybe we ought to find out why."

So he agreed. We agreed that at that point that was the only thing we could do. No member of my exchange was involved in the passing of the information. I had no jurisdiction over anyone else involved except the members.

That morning if you took all the public selling up to and including $15 a share you would still have come out 90,000 shares approximately short of the open-market orders at that time. That stock could have been opened at $15 with the specialist and other members on the floor providing 90,000 shares.

There was a long conference with the floor committee. As president I am an ex-officio member of all committees except admissions. I was on the floor at the opening. I know the discussions that went on before the opening. And it was the considered judgment of the floor committee that under all circumstances it would be appropriate to open that stock at 8-7/8, to permit the specialist to provide 103,000 share on round lots, 20,000 shares on odd lots, and to permit the traders to sell 21,000 shares. So the only way you could find stock was for members to step in there and keep that from opening up around $15.

What happened after that? I have here the final report which after talking to Mr. Purcell we decided we'd get. I have here the name of every individual who bought stock the previous week, where he bought, what section of the country, what he paid for it, and who his broker was. The SEC has that. We have reported what the traders did in that stock. As I say, they provided actually 21,100 shares short. On that day they started to cover. That means that at every fraction down they were buyers. So the market did not fall out of bed . . .

The specialist, as I say, provided 103,000 shares on round lots, 20,000 shares to cover the odd lots . . .

There was never any one time during the following week that the specialist did not buy stock at least every eighth.

And I want you to imagine what would have happened if that stock had been allowed to open at 15, without the specialist and the traders standing there ready to buy and in effect required to buy 144,000 shares.

Senator Ives. What is the stock selling for now?

Mr. McCormick. It closed at 7 last night, Senator. It has never seen the 8-7/8.

The Interests of Shareholders

It is an axiom of American business that management is responsible to stockholders. The problem of meeting these responsibilities is well illustrated by a speech of M. J. Rathbone, former President of Standard Oil Company (New Jersey).

Let me begin with the shareholders. There was a time when shareholders and management were pretty much one and the same. When my company was founded in 1882, it had twelve shareholders, most of them owner-managers; now it has more than 700,000 shareholders, and control of operations has moved from the owner-managers to the hands of professional managers. This is just one illustration of a fact of modern corporate life. But it brings up some important questions. How does this professional management know it is acting in the best interest of the owners? The owners now are a very broad, diverse group that includes school teachers and millionaires, Democrats and Republicans, widows and orphans, colleges and churches, investment trusts and insurance companies. How does management balance such varied interests against all the other considerations? How does it minimize the criticism and maximize the approval of all parts of this group?

An alert management nowadays will carry out many active programs to determine the interests, desires, and thoughts of its shareholder group. I know of one company that has carried out in recent years more than 50,000 interviews with shareholders. Other companies have other kinds of programs with similar objectives. In some instances, companies send out questionnaires to the owners or invite them to ask questions. Financial reports are published, and information is distributed as required by regulations of the Security and Exchange Commission and the various stock exchanges, but many companies go far beyond these requirements and issue special letters, proceedings of annual meetings, house organs, and magazines. There is a good response to such efforts.

My own company, for example, receives about 7,000 letters annually from stockholders. These are thoughtful and often provocative letters with comments and proposals about virtually every facet of our business. We also have numerous personal visits from shareholders, and phone calls from them amounting to 2,500 per year.

It is no surprise to find from all these activities that the principal interest of shareholders is profits, earnings records, and dividends. However, our antennae find that shareholders also have other interests and other standards of measuring management. They are interested in such things as good treatment of employees, civic performance, and social responsibility, aggressive research and development work, future growth possibilities of the company, good relations with customers, dealers, and suppliers. Therefore, corporate managements must also pay careful attention to these things. It is probably true that outstanding performance in some of these other areas helps a corporation greatly to minimize criticism and to build a much more attractive corporate personality.[1]

EDUCATIONAL CONTRIBUTIONS

In line with the philosophy outlined in Mr. Rathbone's speech, the Standard Oil Company of New Jersey established the ESSO Education Foundation in 1955. In the first six years after its inception, the Foundation made grants to over 400 private colleges.

Not all stockholders agreed with the philosophy or the practices of the company. In April of 1961, Mrs. Alice V. Gordon, a stockholder, asked that the company bylaws be amended to read:

No funds of this corporation shall be given away to any charitable, educational or similar organization except for purposes in direct furtherance of the business interests of this corporation.

[1] From an address entitled "The Antennae of Corporate Management," delivered by Mr. Rathbone at the annual dinner of the Wharton School Alumni Society of the University of Pennsylvania, upon receipt of the Gold Medal of Merit, October 31, 1962. Used by permission.

Mrs. Gordon explained the reason for the proposed amendment:

Your directors are giving millions of dollars of your corporation's money to charity. This seems wrong. Your company is supposedly run solely for the stockholders' benefit. It is not an eleemosynary institution. Many stockholders undoubtedly feel that charity begins at home. Others who can afford donations are certainly entitled to choose their beneficiaries. The current practice is especially reprehensible when one realizes that nearly ten million dollars have been given since 1955 to educational institutions, many of which now teach socialism and ridicule business men, savers, and investors, as recently explained in the well-documented best-seller *Keynes at Harvard*.

At the stockholders' meeting itself, Mrs. Gordon's attorney emphasized the fact that some of the educational donations had gone to colleges where "on the whole, left-wing doctrines are taught in the Economics Departments." Harvard, Yale, Princeton, Smith, Vassar, and Sarah Lawrence were specifically mentioned as examples of this.

Management explained its position as follows:

By requiring that a 'direct' benefit be shown in order to validate a particular philanthropic or educational contribution, this proposed bylaw would unduly restrict the management in the normal discharge of its responsibilities and deprive it of an effective tool in furthering corporate and shareholder interests.

As a responsible corporate citizen, any company of Standard Oil of New Jersey's stature must give financial support to philanthropic and educational institutions that rely on private sources for support. Such participation has become an integral part of the discharge of a corporation's business and civic responsibilities and, as such, been encouraged by our tax laws, sustained by our courts and legislatures, and widely endorsed by the public at large. In the directors' judgment, such contributions further the interests of the shareholders and are extremely important if the Company is to enjoy and retain the goodwill of the public, which is so essential to the company's prosperity. Quite clearly, the benefits arising from such contributions, although of real and substantial value, cannot be measured in dollars and cents.

Corporate contributions are as much the responsibility of management, and receive the same careful consideration from management as any other legitimate and necessary business expenditure. The amount of such contributions by Standard Oil of New Jersey is believed by the directors to be reasonable by any standard. In each of the last five years, the total after-tax cost to the company and its domestic and foreign affil-

iates of supporting educational and philanthropic objectives has amounted
to about 1½ cents per share. In management's opinion, the benefits derived and to be derived, although not necessarily 'direct,' fully justify this
expenditure.

Mr. Rathbone personally expanded on the deeper political and
social significance of corporate contributions:

> When you're a good corporate citizen, it is often necessary to give sup-
> port to private institutions from which you expect no direct dollars-and-
> cents benefit—hospitals, community service organizations, the Red Cross,
> colleges, universities, and so on. If good citizens, corporate and individual
> alike, did not support these institutions, they would have to turn to the
> government for support—and that, certainly is not the way to advance the
> cause of free enterprise.

> As to the merits of giving to one institution, or one type of institu-
> tion, over another, the possibilities for discussion are infinite. As we
> normally do in such a situation, we call upon a competent staff to gather
> information, to study the various facets of the problem, to appraise and
> analyze the facts, to evaluate the direct and indirect benefit to the com-
> pany and its shareholders, and to make recommendations to the board.
> Your directors are then in a position to make a sound decision, and I
> assure you that in every instance the shareholders' interests are paramount.

> Certainly I take no exception with Mr. Washburn or his principal,
> Mrs. Gordon, with respect to the undesirability of supporting anything
> unsound and improper. We try not to do that. We know that the group
> of our people studying these matters is capable, competent, and objective.
> I would be the first to agree that there is hardly a college or a university
> in the United States in which some of the faculty do not hold and express
> views which are contrary to what we, sitting as your board, might think
> was right and proper.

> And yet this goes to the heart of the Bill of Rights. We have freedom
> in this country which few other countries have to the same extent, and
> these freedoms must be protected. If we reserve judgment to any small
> group of people as to what's right and what's wrong, without the ability
> of expression, we have lost something we can't afford to lose. In effect, we
> have to take a bit of the bitter with the sweet.

A One-Knock Opportunity

Joseph Carr is president, director, and the dominant figure in the affairs of the Carr Company, which manufactures valves and industrial saw blades. Carr started the company in 1934 with an investment of $10,000. In 1966 sales totaled $900,000 and the book value of the company was $465,000.

Earnings for the past five years have averaged $45 per share, with the annual dividend pegged at $40. Carr owns 300 of the 500 shares of capital stock outstanding. The remaining shares are owned in small lots by individuals not connected with the management. None of the company stock has changed hands for eight years.

Carr, who is 66 years old, has been trying to sell the company so that he can retire and enjoy his declining years. Paul Corbitt, owner of two small manufacturing companies, has studied the Carr Company and has decided that it is worth $360,000. He feels that the book value is inflated, due in part to an unrealistic depreciation policy.

When Corbitt makes a purchase proposal to Carr, the latter replies that he is unwilling to sell his stock for less than $250,000. Since the company bears his name and he has worked hard for 32 years to make it what it is, Carr feels that $250,000 is not too much to ask. Corbitt, who is interested in acquiring all of the company stock, cannot budge Carr's asking price. However, after hearing Corbitt's plans, which include maintaining the company name, Carr enters into an agreement whereby he will get his price provided that he helps Corbitt obtain the other 200 shares at $550 per share.

Carr then writes to the other stockholders. Among other things, he tells them: "I plan to sell controlling interest in the Carr Company to Paul Corbitt. He plans a five-year expansion program, during which all earnings will be plowed back into the company. Knowing that most of our minority stockholders have held on to their stock because of our liberal dividend policy in the past, it occurred to me that you might want to sell your stock to him. He would prefer to own 100 percent of the company stock. The price Corbitt is offering for your stock is $550 per share. Please advise me if you are willing to sell to him at that price."

All of the minority shareholders sell to Corbitt at his price. A month later, one of them, James Lamb, learns that Corbitt acquired the 500 shares for $360,000. Irate, Lamb demands that Carr reimburse him $170 per share—the difference between what Lamb received and the per share cost of the company stock to Corbitt.

How Much Is a Good Man Worth?

Percy Erwin, a retired banker, has just been elected an outside director of Worldwide Broadcasting. Studying company papers in preparation for his first board meeting, he has come to realize that the executives of Worldwide are—by banking standards—overpaid. Since Erwin views himself as the representative of the stockholders, he wonders if he should take a stand on executive pay.

C. R. Lauter, the President of Worldwide, is paid a salary of $125,000. In 1965 he also received $12,000 from the company's profit sharing plan. During that year Lauter exercised his option to buy 40,000 shares of stock at the price of $8 per share. At the time of the purchase these shares, which had cost the company $16 to buy, were selling in the market at $50. Erwin figured that Lauter thus received an additional $1,680,000. Moreover, Lauter holds options on an additional 20,000 shares, which he can purchase at $25 each.

He also owns $200,000 worth of the company's six percent subordinated convertible debentures. These can be turned into shares of common stock at a rate of one share for each $20 worth of debentures. Thus Lauter can obtain another 10,000 shares and make a profit of an additional $300,000.

229

Finally, his contract calls for him to be employed as a consultant at $50,000 a year when he retires in another two years at age 65.

Erwin feels that these rewards are excessive for the president of a company which, in 1965, earned $6,000,000 on revenues of $100,000,000, and decides to investigate the situation. He learns that Lauter was responsible for bringing Worldwide from a loss in 1956 to its present healthy condition. Earnings per share have gone during that period from nothing to $3.02. People in the broadcasting business say that Lauter *is* Worldwide. Further probing indicates that Lauter bought his debentures when the company's credit was overextended and the need for cash critical.

Erwin still wonders. The Chairman of AT&T received $304,600 in salary with no additional compensation in either 1965 or 1964. William Paley, Chairman of CBS, received $150,000 in salary and $175,750 in supplementary compensation. Frank Stanton, President of CBS, received the same sums in 1965. These companies are considerably larger than Worldwide.

Erwin recognizes the significance of all these facts, but is uneasy. He wonders whether or not to bring up the matter of Lauter's compensation at the board meeting. How much is a good man really worth?

Blow Your Own Horn

When Stanley Kostka became president in 1950, the Faber Company was a pants manufacturer with sales of $85 million. By 1965 the company had diversified and was manufacturing outer apparel, underwear, and shoes. It had also acquired over a thousand retail outlets. Sales in 1965 totalled $705 million. Between 1950 and 1965, net earnings went from $4 million to $19 million, and the number of shares of common stock outstanding increased from 1.5 to 4.8 million. At the same time, earnings per share increased from $2.52 to $3.70. The market value of the stock, which had fluctuated between 15 and 20 in 1950, was in the 40 to 54 range in 1965. Working capital had increased from $25 million to $200 million and the net worth from $23 million to $146 million.

This phenomenal growth resulted from vigorous and imaginative leadership on the part of Kostka. Much of the expansion was accomplished by buying other companies with Faber stock. During a ten-year period, almost two million shares of common stock were used for this purpose. The exchanges had usually been made on terms favorable to the Faber Company because Kostka had stimulated interest in Faber stock.

Faber Company put out a bimonthly newsletter for stockholders, and Kostka gave frequent talks to small, influential groups of financial analysts. The annual report created the impression of great optimism for the company and the national economy. One report, for example, announced that the officers expected profits to rise almost 20 percent in the next six months. A five-year projection indicated an anticipated increase of 50 percent in sales volume. The company also placed newspaper ads calling attention to any increased value of its stock.

In 1950 the price earnings ratio had been 7:1. Although it was 12:1 in 1965, it had been as high as 20:1 in 1960. While this may have been attributable to financial public relations, other factors appear to have been at work. The company, and groups controlled by the company, had been buying a great deal of Faber's own stock. This was to the company's advantage in those cases where it was negotiating a merger based on an exchange of stock.

The firm bought Faber stock for its own stock option and profit sharing plans. The pension fund, whose officers were identical with those of the Faber Company, placed its funds in a pooled investment trust controlled by these officers. The pooled investment fund then traded in Faber stock. Between March of 1961 and 1965 the company, its pension fund, and profit sharing fund traded heavily in Faber Company stock. During 43 months, 25 percent of all trading in the stock was done in this way; during 19 months, the company accounted for 50 percent of the trading; and during four months these intramural transactions involved 75 percent of the volume traded.

In some cases both the company and the pooled investment fund placed orders through several brokers, and made bids at the opening of trading which were higher than the previous day's closing price. These actions tended to move the price of the stock upwards.

Once an exchange rate has been agreed on in acquisition procedures, the acquiring company does not want the price of its own stock to go up. In some cases, the Faber Company did not buy stock in the open market but purchased it from its own pension fund since this was less expensive. The price paid the pension fund was the midpoint of the stock's price on the date of the actual purchase. In one instance this involved the purchase of 150,000 shares from the pension fund for a sum of $5,250,000. This particular deal was successful since the equity acquired exceeded the cost of the purchase by $5 million. Since some of the assets of the newly acquired company were then sold and leased back, the purchase generated enough cash to cover most of the acquisition of stock needed to consummate the merger. All in all, the pooled investment fund had proved to be a handy tool for a management intent on expanding at the least possible cost.

Information Inside and Out

INTRODUCTION

In August of 1966 Federal Judge Dudley B. Bonsal ruled that two officials of the Texas Gulf Sulphur Company had violated a Security and Exchange Commission ruling. The company itself and ten other defendants were acquitted. As in so many cases, the ruling of the court leaves several ethical questions open to debate.

A MINERAL DISCOVERY

On Saturday, November 9, 1963 Texas Gulf Sulphur Company drillers in Timmins, Ontario brought up some encouraging test bores with the unmistakable glint of copper ore. Additional borings taken on Sunday morning were even more promising. Kenneth H. Darke, the field geologist, realized that he had a problem on his hands. The drilling was on a small company holding of 160 acres. If they drilled a second hole close to the first, someone might suspect that the surrounding land was valuable and make it more expensive to acquire.

After calling the New York office, Darke took down the drilling rig, concealed the hole and moved the rig. He then mailed out samples of the ore from a nearby town lest anyone in Timmins suspect a find. He gave his crew a bonus for remaining at the site until Christmas and warned them that any talk would result in firing. He then went to work getting rights to the adjoining land.

Rumors did start during the Christmas holidays, but Darke managed to proceed with the acquisition of land. By the end of March he had gotten possession of all the land he wanted. The Texas Gulf Sulphur holdings now totalled 60,000 acres. Darke moved in four more drills and began boring. Rumors started circulating in Canada and the United States.

The New York office of Texas Gulf Sulphur was disturbed. The officers knew they must make a "timely disclosure" of facts having a potential impact on the market. At the same time they did not wish to overstate the find on the basis of only a few borings. The company wanted to indicate that it had a find but was not sure of its extent. A press release was finally issued on April 12, 1964. Among other things the release said that the rumors "exaggerate the scale of operations and mention plans and statistics of size and grade of ore that are without factual basis . . . . Recent drilling on one property near Timmins had led to preliminary indications that more drilling would be required for proper evaluation of this prospect. The drilling to date has not been conclusive . . . ."

The press release was based on data available at 7:00 P.M. on April 9, 1964. Mining experts who examined these data were not in agreement. Edwin N. Pennebaker, a Scottsdale, Arizona mining geologist, felt the data indicated the existence of 5.5 million tons of proven ore and 1.1 million tons of "provable" ore. Benjamin Adelstein, chief mining engineer for the SEC, said that the evidence indicated the presence of at least 7.7 million tons worth $204,200,000. He also believed that even the initial hole drilled in November of 1963 "gave good indication, if not proof, that a large commercial rich ore body" was under the Timmins property. Others did not agree. James D. Forrester, Dean of the University of Arizona College of Mines, claimed that evidence available on April 9 was not enough to establish the existence of a commercial ore body. He did admit, however, that the early tests provided "quite an impressive indication of the existence of a potentially attractive mineral occurrence."

Since the April 12 announcement answered some questions but raised more in the minds of investors, Texas Gulf Sulphur officers were still uneasy. They followed the first announcement with a more bullish release four days later. The company now had reports from seven drills and felt that it could announce "a major discovery of zinc, copper, and silver . . . Preliminary data indicate a reserve of more than 25 million tons of ore." This announcement, made to reporters and some brokers at 10:00 A.M. on the morning of April 16, was carried by the Dow Jones News Service at around 10:45 A.M. that same day. However, the *New York Herald Tribune* had run a story on the find the previous weekend. In addition, the *Northern Miner,* a Canadian publication, carried its own story on the morning of April 16. The Canadian Press news service and Merrill Lynch had also published the company release at 10:29 A.M., about half an hour before the Dow Jones News Service.

Many stock brokers later testified that the news had been out before the company announcement. Some had heard rumors, others judged this from the volume of trading in Texas Gulf Sulphur when the New York Stock Exchange opened at 10:00 A.M. on April 16. This is not surprising, for as one broker put it, "I have seen drillers drop the drill and beat it to a brokerage office as fast as they can, even when they get a smell of something."

BUYING AND SELLING

By 10:55 A.M. on April 16, 117,000 shares of Texas Gulf Sulphur had been traded on the New York Stock Exchange. After this time the price levelled off a bit, a fact which led one broker to believe that the announcement provided nothing new to professionals. The SEC, however, was disturbed by the difference in tone between the two news releases and began investigating stock purchases. Some of the buyers were officials or employees of Texas Gulf Sulphur. The history of each purchase, however, is a little different.

David M. Crawford, Secretary of the company, who helped to prepare the April 16 press release, had called his broker late on April 15 and ordered him to buy 300 shares. In the morning Crawford had placed an order for another 300 shares. Crawford said that Charles Fogarty, the Executive Vice President, had told him that the Ontario Minister of Mines would release the announcement at 11:00 P.M. on April 15. Actually the Minister did not do so; he handed the release to reporters early on the morning of the 16th.

Thomas S. Lamont, a Director of both Texas Gulf Sulphur and Morgan Guaranty Trust Company, had hinted to the Trust Company that ticker news was going to be "pretty good." This hint appears to have been passed on after the news was given to the press in New York but ten minutes before it was published by Dow Jones. Of course, the Canadian release had been published one-half hour earlier. Lamont believed that the news was public when it had been given to the press. Morgan Guaranty bought 3,000 shares for a client just before the release appeared in the Dow Jones News Service. Later, Morgan Guaranty bought the stock for its own pension fund. Lamont himself is said to have bought 3,000 shares at 12:33 P.M. on April 16, two hours after the news was official. The Morgan employee who did the purchasing for Morgan's clients and pension fund seems to have felt the news was officially out.

Richard H. Clayton, an engineer with Texas Gulf Sulphur, later testified that he had purchased 1,260 shares between February and April of 1964. He contended that he was influenced by the Timmins project but was largely motivated by the generally improved condition of the company.

Charles F. Fogarty, Executive Vice President, purchased 3,100 shares between November 10, 1963 and April 6, 1964. He had been criticized for not holding enough shares in the company, and said his purchases were part of a regular acquisition policy. His November purchases were the result of a rumor that another company was planning a take-over. He felt that he would be more secure as both a director and executive vice president if he had larger holdings. "The Timmins project was only one factor in my purchases," he said.

On February 20, 1964 the Directors of Texas Gulf Sulphur granted President Claude Stephens, Fogarty and three other officials options for 31,000 shares at about $24 a share. It seems that at least some of the directors did not know of the discovery hole at Timmins. Stephens did not buy any stock during the period prior to the announcement of April 16, even though he held options of 12,800 shares. In April of 1965 both Stephens and Fogarty offered to cancel their options.

Some outsiders who were told that Texas Gulf Sulphur was a good bet invested in the company. An employee at the Timmins site seems to have recommended the stock to a family friend, who then passed on the information to others. It is not clear, however, whether the recommendation was general or included information about the strike itself. It should be remembered that Texas Gulf Sulphur was engaged in other exploration and diversification projects. Lehman Brothers, which bought 75,000 shares in December, 1963, said that their purchase was based on the expectation of rising prices of sulphur as well as on the company's branching out into phosphate and potash. The president of Lehman Brothers said he had not known of the first Timmins hole drilled in the previous month.

According to one account, there were other large buyers along with Lehman Brothers. The Murchisons of Dallas were supposed to have bought 100,000 shares shortly before the Timmins announcement. Pennzoil had purchased 150,000 shares before the strike.

Texas Gulf Sulphur stock had been selling for about $17 a share in November, 1963 and was in the neighborhood of $30 a share by April 12, 1964. On April 16, 1964 the stock opened at about $34 a share and closed at $37. In April, 1965, when the SEC initiated its suit against the company and its employees, the stock was selling around $71. The price moved up in 1966. Even after the market decline in the summer of 1966, it was selling as high as $88 on September 16, 1966.

OPINIONS, CODES, AND PROBLEMS

Although the SEC won its case against only two of the defendants, it raised some interesting legal-ethical questions. The Commission's pre-trial brief stated: "It is the Commission's position that even after corporate information has been published in the news media, insiders still are under a duty to refrain from securities transactions until there has elapsed a reasonable amount of time in which the securities industry, the shareholders and the investing public can evaluate the development and make informed investment choices."

The SEC also contended that though the results in November, 1963 did not establish the existence of a commercial mine, they should have constituted a block to trading by officials of the company until the results had been announced to the sellers of the shares. The SEC felt that Rule 10b-5 under the Securities Exchange Act of 1934 had been violated. Rule 10b-5 reads as follows:

It shall be unlawful for any person, directly or indirectly, by the use of any means or instrumentality of interstate commerce, or of the mails, or of any facility of any national securities exchange,

(1) to employ any device, scheme, or artifice to defraud,

(2) to make any untrue statement of a material fact or to omit to state a material fact necessary in order to make the statements made, in the light of the circumstances under which they were made, not misleading, or

(3) to engage in any act, practice, or course of business which operates or would operate as a fraud or deceit upon any person, in connection with the purchase or sale of any security.

Orison S. Marden, who represented the company and ten of the defendants, argued that no official could ever purchase stock in his own company if *any* inside information constituted a block.

The following paragraphs from *An Official Interpretation of the Public Relations Society of America Code of Professional Standards for Practice of Public Relations As It Applies to Financial Public Relations* suggest other important problems.

2. It shall be the objective of such member to follow the policy of full disclosure of corporate information, except in such instances where such information is of a confidential nature. The purpose of this objective is to enable an accurate evaluation of the company by the investing public and not to influence the price of securities. Such information should be accurate, clear, understandable. . . .

4. Such member shall disclose or release information promptly so as to avoid the possibility of any use of the information by an insider for personal gain. In general, such member should make every effort to comply with the spirit and intent of the "Timely Disclosure" provisions of the New York Stock Exchange Company Manual. Information deemed not confidential but which is not subject to a formal release shall be available to all on an equal basis. . . .

5. Such member shall exercise reasonable care to ascertain the facts correctly and to disseminate only information which he believes to be accurate and adequate. Such member shall use reasonable care to avoid the issuance or release of predictions or projections of financial or other matters lacking adequate basis in fact. . . .

6. Such member shall act promptly to corect false or misleading information or rumors concerning his client's or employer's securities or

business whenever he has reason to believe such information or rumors exist. . . .

8. Such member shall not exploit the information he has gained as an insider for personal gain. However, this is not intended to prohibit a member from making bona fide investments in his company's or client's securities in accordance with normal investment practices. . . .

The Teamsters' Pension Fund

INTRODUCTION

Jimmy Hoffa is a controversial, many-sided character. He is also an imaginative and creative man in the areas of labor negotiations and union management. It has been suggested that he knows as much about trucking as any man in the United States. His knowledge and ability account for his success in creating a situation where truckers rely on him even though they may resent his tough bargaining. Ralph and Estelle James have described him:

He possesses a brilliant mind, but one which in many respects is non-intellectual. He has built a well-deserved reputation for ruthlessness, but beneath the tough exterior is a genuine concern for others. He is a devoted family man, although his life centers about his work. He sees enemies and spies all around him, yet is unnecessarily trusting of a new acquaintance. He views the world in terms of power relationships rather than in terms of what is right and wrong, yet he is motivated by a deeply instilled sense of morality; his behavior seems unethical and uncouth to some, while in others his personal drive and magnetism arouse an unswerving loyalty.[1]

[1] From James and James' *Hoffa and the Teamsters*. Copyright 1965, D. Van Nostrand Company, Inc., Princeton, N.J. We have drawn heavily on this book since it is by far the most balanced and best researched of those available. The reader may want to look at other treatments such as: Robert F. Kennedy, *The Enemy Within* (New York, Harper & Row, 1960); Clark R. Mollenhoff, *Tentacles of Power: The Story of Jimmy Hoffa* (Cleveland, World Publishing, 1965).

Controversy about Hoffa and his ethics is heated because some of his activities would be impossible without the cooperation of businessmen. Moreover, in the operation of the Teamsters' Pension Fund, Hoffa and the associated businessmen often act on concepts which are unusual; for example, it seems that the trustees use the Fund to benefit both union and industry on the grounds that in the long run this will benefit those who receive pensions. This is quite different from the usual objective of operating such a fund, which is to increase income to the fund directly.

There is also question about which norms should be used to judge the activities of self-administered, self-insured funds. Some observers may be tempted to prejudge issues because Hoffa is involved, but fairness demands that the underlying assumptions be examined and the facts weighed before passing judgment.

PENSIONS AND POWER

The Central States Drivers Council negotiated its first pension fund under the leadership of Jimmy Hoffa in January, 1955. The plan, which covered 100,000 workers, required each employer to pay $2 per worker per week into the Central States Pension Fund. The contract made no specifications as to administration, level of benefits, or composition of the board of trustees. The Taft-Hartley Act, however, required that the number of union trustees equal the number of employer trustees.

Ben Miller of the American Trucking Association wanted five employer trustees. Hoffa wanted six because he felt that the larger the number was, the easier it would be for him to divide and conquer. Hoffa also wanted to be sure that the independent truckers would be represented on the board. When opposed, Hoffa argued that law required that the independents be recognized, and also threatened to file grievances against every carrier.

Threats of grievances, strikes, and selective shutdowns were very real to the truckers. Many teamster contracts have an open-end grievance procedure which does not provide for arbitration but leaves the union the right to strike. As a result the teamsters can strike even between negotiations. Open-end grievance procedures are not governed by fixed rules or codified decisions so that the carriers cannot be sure of their position in a given case.

Hoffa's view prevailed: the board was composed of six representatives from each side, including a representative of the independent truckers. In time the board of trustees was composed of eight union and eight employer representatives. No alternates were allowed for trustees who could not attend a meeting. Decisions were to be made by a majority vote, although in most plans that are jointly administered, the unit bloc rule prevails. This rule requires each group to vote as a bloc, submitting ties to arbitration. The simple majority rule permitted either side to carry the day by maintaining solidarity and winning one vote from the other group.

The board chose to adopt a self-insured plan rather than turn the funds over to an insurance company for investment and administration. At first, funds were deposited in the La Salle National Bank of Chicago, which invested them. By January, 1956 the funds totalled $10 million and had a rate of return of about 3.5 percent. Later it was decided to disperse the money in banks that were located in cities important to Hoffa, the Teamsters and some truckers. In the next three years $20 million were deposited in seventeen trust accounts in banks in addition to the La Salle. Since banks use a sliding fee for the administration of larger amounts, this dispersion of funds reduced the net income from the Fund by as much as $150,000 annually.

The trustees had set broad policy rules for the banks which administered the trusts. The banks, however, were irritated by broad guidelines which specified: 30 percent in U.S. Government Bonds, 30 percent for high grade corporate bonds, 15 percent for FHA-guaranteed mortgages, 10 percent for preferred stock, and 15 percent for common stock. The banks wanted to patronize their local investment houses in order to promote the banks' images in the local communities. With only 15 percent allotted to common stock, there was not much commission money to be gained by local investment houses. Later the banks were allowed to invest 50 percent in stocks, but by then the banks were handling only a small and diminishing share of the Fund's reserves.

In December, 1956 Hoffa urged the trustees to change from a bank trustee plan to a self-administered plan. Such arrangements were not unusual in plans administered jointly by employers and unions.

For a pension fund to be tax exempt, the Internal Revenue Service requires that there be an actuarially determinable benefit formula. The IRS does not check the standards used but does require an actuary's statement, and one from the trustees saying that they are satisfied with the actuary's calculations. Several employer trustees wanted to choose an insurance company or broker as an actuary, but Hoffa did not want an actuary who would demand that they use conservative actuarial standards.

Hoffa nominated an actuary amenable to his proposals, Maxwell Kunis, of Union Casualty. This company carried the health and welfare insurance for the Central States Drivers Council. Moreover, the Michigan Conference of the Teamsters had $250,000 invested in Union Casualty. This made it a major stockholder.

At first Hoffa's nomination of Kunis was not even seconded. There was opposition from both teamsters and employer representatives. The two groups were deadlocked over other proposals, and it was finally decided to submit the question to the Advisory Board, which consisted of 36 union and management representatives. The teamsters on the Advisory Board backed Hoffa; the employers disagreed and suggested using an arbitrator. Hoffa was sure that an outside arbitrator would pick a national firm with conservative standards. The matter was set aside. The trustees reconvened; forty-five minutes later Hoffa had convinced the opposition to follow his ideas, and Kunis was unanimously chosen actuary.

SOME LAWS AFFECTING PENSION FUNDS

Before studying the activities of the Fund trustees, it will be useful to glance at a few laws concerned with pension funds. Under the Internal Revenue Code of 1954, contributions made by an employer to welfare and pension funds are tax deductible. The fund itself may be tax exempt if it meets the following qualifications. First, the plan must be "established and maintained by an employer primarily to provide systematically for the payment of definitely determinable benefits to his employees over a period of years . . ." Secondly, the plan must be such that "the determination of retirement benefits and the contributions to provide such benefits are not dependent upon profits." The plan must be permanent and provide benefits for employees in general, though it need not provide benefits for all employees. The Code does not set down limitations as to specific types of investments. Tilove[2] notes that Section 401 (a) of the Internal Revenue Code ". . . interferes only if a tax-exempt trust engages in one of the following transactions in favor of the creator of the trust: (1) makes a loan without adequate security and a reasonable rate of interest, (2) pays unreasonable compensation, (3) provides services preferentially, (4) buys securities or property for more than an adequate price, (5) sells securities or property for less than an adequate price, or (6) engages in any other transaction which results in substantial diversion of its income or corpus." The tax exemption can be lost if substantial amounts are diverted to the creator of the trust or related persons. In addition, there are disclosure provisions covering those who might be able to profit from management of the trust, which might cause conflicts of interest.

One of the most important provisions of the Internal Revenue Code provides that the funds in the trust may not be used except for the exclusive benefit of employees or their beneficiaries.

The Taft-Hartley Act, Section 302, forbids employers to pay funds to employee representatives except when these will be used in employee benefit programs. This Act also provides that the employers and employees are to be equally represented in the administration of the fund, which must be audited. The law, however, contains no provisions requiring efficient management, or limiting compensation and expenses of those who administer it.

The problems posed by Taft-Hartley are complicated by the fact that the National Labor Relations Board has refused to admit responsibility for the enforcement of Section 302. In addition, some have doubts as to whether or not the Federal government has preempted this area completely. It is reasonable, however, to assume that states can pass laws which cover areas not touched by the Taft-Hartley Act.

Those funds which are administered by banks as trustees come under regulations of the Federal Reserve Board when the bank is a member of the Federal Reserve. State laws are also applicable in many cases.

Some departments of the government collect data on pension funds. They do not, however, have much to do with the actual ad-

[2] Robert Tilove, *Pension Funds and Economic Freedom*, copyright 1959, without restriction, by The Fund for the Republic, Inc., pp. 64, 65.

ministration of pension plans. The Securities and Exchange Commission, for example, is hesitant about involving itself in the regulation of pension funds except where they issue securities. The Federal Welfare and Pension Plans Disclosure Act, which went into effect in January, 1959, requires that pension plans be filed with the Department of Labor. This Act also requires trustees to make available a report telling any participating employee about all investments in or loans to the employer's business.

In 1956 there was little if any state regulation of pension programs. By the end of 1958 six states had statutes covering the area. A few provisions of these laws are pertinent since they indicate the thinking of good minds about the problems of pension funds. The California law, for example, requires that retirement funds must create and maintain reserves to cover liabilities. Moreover, the experience tables are subject to the approval of the State Commissioner of Corporations. The Massachusetts law of 1956, amended in 1958, sets up a board which, among other duties, can bring action for beneficiaries when any trust fund has been depleted by negligence. Furthermore, all fund documents must be submitted for the approval of the board.

The regulation of pension funds is being studied seriously. For example, in the report, *Public Policy and Private Pension Funds,* a presidential committee made important recommendations in January of 1965. Among other items, the committee suggested these minimum standards for funding:

(1) As a minimum standard of funding for *stated benefit* plans, the plan should be required to fund fully all current service liabilities and to amortize fully all accrued liabilities over a period that roughly approximates the average work life of employees but not more than 30 years.

(2) As a minimum standard for funding of *fixed contribution* plans, the contribution commitments of the plan should be realistically related to benefits promised and actually paid.

(3) The funding process of every qualified plan should be certified at the inception of the plan and periodically thereafter by an actuary with acceptable professional qualifications.

(4) The funding process should be subject to review by the Internal Revenue Service on the basis of guidelines or ranges of standards with respect to such actuarial assumptions. The guides should be specified by the Internal Revenue Service with the advice and consultation of a public advisory body of actuaries and other interested parties.

(5) Concurrent with actuarial certification, a determination should be made by a professionally qualified public accountant with respect to the value of pension fund assets.

NEW INVESTMENT POLICIES

In December, 1956 Hoffa proposed several methods of granting long term mortgages or purchasing property and leasing it back to the present owners. Although the trustees postponed and ultimately discarded the proposal to buy the Sands Hotel in Las Vegas and to lease it back to the owner, they did lend money to Hank Greenspun, editor of the *Las Vegas Sun,* who was deeply involved in Nevada politics. This loan to finance a golf course was made at six percent, although one trustee objected that this was too low an interest rate for a risky loan of this type. The first loan of $250,000 was increased to $500,000 in 1959. Within three years, Greenspun was finding it hard to meet his payments. Before the Greenspun loan, the Central States Pension Fund trustees had made a $1 million mortgage loan to Cleveland Raceways. The terms were ten years at six percent interest. When Robert Kennedy challenged this loan two years later, racetrack officials paid it back immediately since they did not want to be mixed up in a questionable operation.

Year	Value of Mortgages and Collateral Loans	Percent of Total Investment
1956	$ 1,002,000	10.0
1957	1,699,000	7.2
1958	6,270,000	16.1
1959	15,760,000	25.7
1960	47,202,000	53.4
1961	72,575,000	57.6
1962	117,559,000	69.4

After granting $3.7 million for five other mortgages in the first six months of 1957, the trustees rejected applicants for mortgages for awhile. As the cash flowed in, it was put into banks or used to purchase highly liquid assets. At this period, the trustees were unable to make up their minds about investment policy and so avoided long term investments. This indecisiveness resulted from the fact that Hoffa was under investigation and liable to fall from power.

However, as Hoffa's position became stronger, employer trustee opposition diminished, and in the summer and early fall of 1958 the trend to mortgage commitments increased rapidly.

This trend was highly unusual, as Max Kunis, the actuary, pointed out. The following chart, Table 1, prepared by the Securities and Exchange Commission shows that during the period 1954-1964 private noninsured pension funds tended to increase their allotment of funds for the purchase of common stock. Mortgages, included under "other" assets, were not popular with most funds. Max Kunis, who was aware of these trends, pointed out that the purchase of common stock would give some protection against inflation. Hoffa's preference prevailed, and the policy was not changed. In the meanwhile, the trustees decreased the funds held by bank trustees, and refused to let the banks go beyond the 50 percent limit on the purchase of common stocks.

The *geographic distribution* of investments was noteworthy. Over 40 percent of the funds invested by May, 1962 had gone into Florida real estate, even though advisors had warned against this. The warnings ultimately had some effect, and new investments in Florida were reduced. At this time (1962-1963) the trustees were making arrangements to invest $16 million, or 22 percent of the 1962-63 funds, in Nevada. In addition they voted to loan $5 million to Harold's Club in Nevada. Such loans are considered by many to be risky since the prosperity of the state depends on gambling, and a change in law or fashion might cause a sudden decline in the value of real estate.

Not merely the location but the nature of the collateral was risky. The Central States Pension Fund bought mortgages of income-producing property rather than of residential housing. They stayed away from insured Federal Housing Authority mortgages. In 1962, 31.5 percent of the actual mortgages were in hotels and motels. These can be particularly risky since new highways might divert traffic, and the continual growth of new facilities tends to depreciate old ones rather rapidly. Hotels, of course, must attract considerable convention business if they are to succeed. In 1962-63 the Fund was going to jump investment in hotels and motels to 60 percent of their actual mortgages.

The most hazardous of all investments are probably in land development, and the Fund had invested $17 million in such proj-

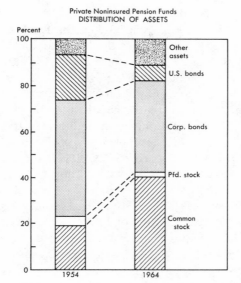

Private Noninsured Pension Funds
DISTRIBUTION OF ASSETS

ects between 1957 and 1962. This represented 13.1 percent of actual mortgages held in 1962. Those of the loans made during the tight money market of 1959-60 could easily have carried higher interest charges; the charges were between 5 and 7 percent, with the 6 and 6-½ percent type predominating. This, despite the fact that the Fund sometimes accepted collateral that other institutional holders would not accept. In at least one case the Fund accepted interest ½ percent lower than the borrower was willing to pay, at a time when money was very tight.

In May, 1960 the Fund adopted the policy of not loaning more than 60 percent of the appraised value of the property that was mortgaged. However, this policy was not always followed. In the case of one motel, this rule would have provided $200,000 less than the amount the borrower needed, and the Fund raised the loan to two-thirds of the appraised value. A similar procedure was followed in the case of a proposed discount house in St. Louis in 1962.

In some cases where the appraised value would not justify the loan required, the appraiser was seemingly asked to move his figures upwards. In other cases the Fund loaned two-thirds of total construction cost even when costs did not seem to relate properly to anticipated income.

The law requires that pension funds be operated in the best interest of those who are to benefit from the fund. Ordinarily this would be interpreted to mean that the funds should be managed so as to maximize the return to the beneficiaries without becoming so speculative that the whole venture might be lost. Hoffa and some trustees felt that the Fund should also be used to further the interests of Hoffa and the teamsters rather than merely to maximize the Fund itself. Hoffa himself admits that he has used the Fund to win powerful friends. He could not have done this without the cooperation of the employer representatives. Although the records indicate periodic opposition from employers, on the whole they appear to have gone along with Hoffa.

Ralph and Estelle James believe that Hoffa would not have been convicted for fraud in July of 1964 if he had given a true picture of the Central States Pension Fund investment policies. They reason that all of his acts in handling the Fund appear to have been approved by the trustees as well. While it may be true that Hoffa deceived the trustees as to the condition of some properties, this does not absolve the board of all culpability. Perhaps the trustees did not know all the facts about several loan applicants.

PENSION BENEFITS

In 1956–57 the trustees lowered the retirement age of members of the Teamsters' Union to 60. It was argued that older drivers are not as safe on the roads as younger men and not worth the high wages they were receiving. The retired drivers were to receive benefits according to this schedule:

Year	*Payments Per Month*	
	Age 60 to 65	*Over age 65*
1957	$ 90.00	$ 22.50
1958	135.00	90.00
1961	200.00	90.00
	Age 57 to 62	*Over age 62*
1964	$250.00	$110.00

In 1957 a teamster, in order to qualify, had to have 20 years of experience and have been under the collective bargaining contract for three years. In 1962 the retirement age was lowered to 57, and the reduction in payments took place at age 62. Of course, Old Age and Survivors Insurance benefits taken at age 62 are lower than those taken at age 65.

The Teamsters' Pension Fund makes little allowance for disability. The pension, moreover, is not vested so that a driver who leaves the industry loses all his rights. There is no provision for reciprocity with other unions. Thus a driver who transferred from the central states to the West Coast lost his pension rights. As a result, younger workers, who have a higher turnover, were not receiving the benefits.

The report, *Public Policy and Private Pension Funds,* recommended:

A vesting requirement is necessary if private pension plans are to serve the broad social purpose justifying their favored status. The Internal Revenue Code should be amended to require that a private pension plan, in order to qualify for favored tax treatment, must provide some reasonable measure of vesting for the protection of employees.

In 1959 the Central States Pension Fund admitted St. Louis Warehouse Local 688 and granted full past service credits. Local 688 soon had more retired members than any other local since it had a large number of older members. Max Kunis, the actuary for the Fund, objected to bringing in locals without their paying the amount which would have accumulated between the time the Fund was started and the date of their admission. Kunis, however, was voted down unanimously by the trustees.

As the ratio of retired members to working members continues to increase, it will probably be necessary to increase member contributions. The necessity for such increases will of course depend on the soundness of investments made by the Fund and on the number of workers involved in trucking.

X

Government and Community Relations

The Manager as Citizen

John Foreman was manager of the Northeastern Electric plant at Wattsville. He was a man who was aware of his duty and did not avoid doing it. Right now he was not happy about the reports he had heard about Joe Livio, his assistant plant manager. He called Livio to his office.

"Joe, I don't know any diplomatic way to put this so I'll come right to the point. You have to stop agitating for reform in the local school board. You have only been here a short time and so you probably don't realize it, but you are playing with political dynamite. A lot of people are disturbed, and I've been getting hints that the company will suffer if we don't get you out of this political involvement."

Joe Livio listened politely to all of this, but he wondered. The Northeastern Electric plant of which Foreman was the manager was the largest employer in Wattsville. The town needed Northeastern more than Northeastern needed the town. Indeed, Joe knew that the firm had made a preliminary study about the feasibility of moving the plant since it was getting a bit outmoded. He said nothing about this. He did, however, ask for a clarification of company policy.

Mr. Foreman explained that while it was company policy to encourage managers and workers to participate in community affairs, no employee had ever dabbled in politics. Political activity was not forbidden, but in the present situation common sense would dictate to stay out of it.

Joe nodded his head but made no definite stand. He wanted time to think over his position.

Joe had been with Northeastern Electric for five years when he was transferred to Wattsville, a small town in northeastern Pennsylvania, to become an assistant plant manager. He liked the new town, especially since his children had only a short walk to school, and his wife enjoyed being out of the big city bustle. His transfer was another step up the ladder, and the pay increase had eased his financial burdens. All in all, life seemed good.

After about three months, however, Joe found that the schools were not up to the standards he was used to in bigger cities. A little investigation unearthed the reasons for this. There had been no pay increase in years, with the result that younger teachers could not be attracted. The teachers, therefore, tended to be older and out of touch with new developments. Unfortunately, many of these teachers had been appointed in the days when political pull rather than competence was the criterion.

Joe decided that he ought to become involved in local school board affairs and, if necessary, run for election. Indeed, since his boss had been urging him to participate in the local Community Chest work as a part of corporate public relations, Joe felt that involvement might help him advance in the company. In December, he attended some school board meetings that were open to the public and raised the questions which were bothering him. He felt that his questions were not answered but fobbed off.

Conversations with teachers were almost equally unsatisfactory. Most of them did not want to talk at all. Finally a younger teacher, who had remained in the area because his mother was sick, spoke up. It seemed that the school board had been in power for a long time. It had not only done nothing about increasing salaries, but was also fighting a state law which would force it to consolidate with other districts in order to improve the quality of the school. Four years ago, the board had failed to pay teachers' salaries for over six months due to financial mismanagement. Teachers had been forced to borrow money in order to live. The school board, moreover, was a prize political possession since it controlled expenditures for supplies and promotions in the school system. Recently it had instituted a $1,000 a year bonus for merit pay. This was given to only two teachers annually, but had proved to be an effective political tool since it went to those who had played ball.

The more he heard, the more Joe became convinced that he could protect his children and those of his neighbors only by running for the school board. He would not be eligible for some time, but he decided to start working towards this goal. He even went to a local college to study education and to see if he could not interest the professors in his crusade.

It was at this point that Foreman, the manager, laid down the law. Joe Livio trusted Foreman's sense of fairness, but he was pretty sure that if he did not play ball his chances for promotion could be hurt. At the same time, he felt strongly about the local school situation. He wondered, too, whether or not giving in on this occasion would really solve the problem in the long run. He could easily get another job, but wouldn't he face the same sort of situation elsewhere?

Joe talked his problem over with one of the professors at the University, who was quite indignant about the conduct of both the school board and Mr. Foreman. The professor, however, did not have any concrete advice to give Joe.

Almad Realty *

BACKGROUND OF ALMAD REALTY
AND ITS OPERATIONS

Almad Realty was incorporated in 1961 to engage in general real estate business, including commercial and residential property brokerage, management of commercial, industrial and residential properties for their owners, and buying and selling real estate on its own behalf. Mr. Daniel Archer, former manager of the mortgage department of a local lending institution, was retained as its manager; he became one-third owner and a member of the three-man board of directors. The other two stockholders, Archer's close friends, are an attorney whose business law practice includes handling Almad's legal affairs, and a construction company president whose firm does a major share of Almad's construction work and helps arrange financing. Archer is the only one of the three actually employed by the corporation. Each invested $7,500 in the business at its incorporation.

The business' income is composed about equally of brokerage fees and management fees. It employs a staff of 16 persons to manage property and run its sales office, including maintenance workers and

* With the permission of the copyright holder, NATIONAL CONFERENCE OF CHRISTIAN EMPLOYERS AND MANAGERS. This case was prepared by Alfred A. Albert for NCCEM's Program Publication Center. Copyright 1966.

office personnel on salaries, and salesmen on drawing accounts applied against commissions. All Almad employees are married with dependents, and rely upon the corporation for their livelihood.

The corporation set up its business in a northern U.S. community with a population of 90,000; immediately adjoining communities had an additional 150,000. The Negro population in the combined areas was about 3500, mostly living in sub-standard housing.

As a broker, the corporation, through its sales agents, listed various single residences for sale and rental throughout the area. It placed a number of multiple-residence units in all-white areas under management contract for their owners. During the course of its business it also acquired, as owner, a number of similar properties in white neighborhoods.

At the time of Almad's incorporation, the law of the state in which it was incorporated required all realty brokers to be licensed. As a condition of this license, no broker was permitted to discriminate because of race, color, religion or national origin in the showing of any real property, whether for sale or rental. The law also prohibited any owner of property from such discrimination when making a public offering of property, whether for sale or rental. Penalties were imposed for violation.

THE DEVELOPING PROBLEM

About a year after the Almad Corporation commenced business, its real estate brokerage operations began to receive inquiries from Negroes for rentals and home purchases. Other brokers in the same all-white area were known to discourage their employees from showing rentals or sales to Negroes. Instead, they tried to locate the Negroes in areas that were at least racially mixed. But Almad, at the direction of Archer, accepted the inquiries and sent Negro clients out with their salesmen. When they were sent to inspect single homes, they found that most owners, especially in all-white residential areas, refused to show their homes to Negroes. These owners withdrew their home listings from the corporation. Archer learned that word was being spread to prospective customers not to list property with Almad because it would attempt to show and sell to Negroes. Archer phoned and called on Almad's clients, making a considerable effort to explain the law to them, but failed to win their cooperation. Listings and sales for Almad fell off sharply.

At the same time Almad started to show rentals on its own property to Negroes. Tenants objected to the practice, and threatened to move if Almad rented to a Negro. Here, too, Archer called on all the tenants who complained, explaining in detail what the law requires as well as what he deemed to be his and the corporation's moral obligation. Some tenants saw the reasonableness of Almad's position and acquiesced; others said they definitely would move if he persisted. In spite of this, Almad did rent one unit in a four-plex to a Negro family. When the Negroes moved in, the three white families moved out. Since then, Almad has been unable to rent the vacant apartments; most white couples who looked at the units made it clear they didn't care to move into a building with a Negro family.

The only tenants to whom Almad could then rent were Negroes and thus the building became all Negro. The effect of this was merely to create a new ghetto replacing the old. This in no way helped the over-all public policy of integration.

Threats to move then came concerning properties which Almad managed for others. In one case, an owner withdrew his property from Almad management because of a rental to a Negro family.

Almad's problems were further complicated by phone calls from owners of property adjacent to rental units it owned and managed. In substance, these owners requested Almad not to continue renting to Negroes because of their fear of depreciating values, as well as just plain prejudice. Several said they would discourage others from doing business with Almad unless there was a change of policy. The corporation has been informed that many landlords will not permit it to manage their property because of its policy of non-discrimination.

Of course, Almad's experience was not all bad. In several cases, a sale to a Negro in an all-white residential neighborhood brought no reaction and these Negro families have been accepted. In these cases, Almad's management had exercised great care in screening the Negro family, paying particular attention to financial stability and educational background. In other instances of rentals to Negroes in all-white areas, there was relatively no difficulty.

But Almad hit other snags. The firm tried to refinance one property it had rented to a Negro family. It applied for mortgages with two local banks, but neither bank would approve an amount sufficient to meet Almad's needs. Later, Archer was told in strict confidence by a bank employee that the mortgage officers were "discouraged because of a change in the character of the tenancy."

THE BOARD OF DIRECTORS' ACTION

As the problem developed, Almad's Board of Directors became concerned about its drop in sales and profits. Recently, after a thorough examination of the corporation's records and procedures, it determined that to continue a broad policy of nondiscrimination would result in severe financial loss. The board thereupon called a special meeting and privately instructed Archer as its manager "to exercise extreme care" in sales and rentals, both of its own property and that which it managed for others, emphasizing that he should normally seek to locate Negroes in areas that were already at least racially mixed. Both other board members, who personally approve of the principle of nondiscrimination, had implicitly gone along with Archer's policy in the past, hoping—though somewhat skeptically—that with some ingenuity he could find an adequately profitable way of continuing his policy.

While Archer was willing to continue experimentation, the other two felt that recent experience had proven conclusively that such a risky approach could not be reconciled with the firm's goal of long-term profit maximization. They were convinced that an immediate and significant change in policy was mandatory.

Archer, while disagreeing with this policy, felt bound in conscience to preserve the best interests of the corporation and carry out the board's policy directives. It was incumbent on him either to accept the board's directive and carry it out, or make some response. He debated what to do.

APPENDIX

As a member of the local board of realtors, which in turn is an affiliate of the National Association of Real Estate Boards,

Almad has accepted some obligation to subscribe to the national association's code of ethics. Parts of the code relating to this question read as follows:

From the Preamble:

The Realtor is a creator of homes, both urban and rural, and by his activities helps mold the form of his future community, not only in the living of its people, but in its commercial and industrial aspects.

Such functions impose obligations beyond those of ordinary business; they impose grave social responsibilities which the Realtor can meet only by diligent preparation and by dedicating himself as a civic duty to their fulfillment.

Accepting this standard as his own, every Realtor pledges himself to observe its spirit in all his dealings and to conduct his business in accordance with the following Code of Ethics, adopted by the National Association of Real Estate Boards.

From Part I, Relations to the Public:

ARTICLE 3. It is the duty of the Realtor to protect the public against fraud, misrepresentation or unethical practices in the real estate field. He should endeavor to help stamp out, or prevent arising in his community, any practices which could be damaging to the public or to the dignity and integrity of the real estate profession. If there be a board or commission in the state, charged with the duty of regulating the practices of brokers and salesmen, the Realtor should lend every help to such body, cooperate with it, and report violations of proper practice. . .

ARTICLE 5. The Realtor should not be instrumental in introducing into a neighborhood a character of property or use which will clearly be detrimental to property values in that neighborhood.

From Part II, Relations to the Client:

ARTICLE 11. In accepting employment as an agent, the Realtor pledges himself to protect and promote the interests of the client. This obligation of absolute fidelity to the client's interest is primary, and does not relieve the Realtor from the obligation of dealing fairly with all parties to the transaction.

ARTICLE 12. In justice to those who place their interests in his hands, the Realtor should endeavor always to be informed regarding the law, proposed legislation, legal orders issued and other essential facts and public policies which affect those interests.

Furthermore, NAREB's Board of Directors has issued a policy statement regarding the real estate broker's role in minority housing matters, which contains the following guidelines:

1. Being agents, Realtors individually and collectively, in performing their agency functions, have no right or responsibility to determine the racial, creedal, or ethnic composition of any area or neighborhood or any part thereof.

2. No Realtor should assume to determine the suitability or eligibility on racial, creedal, or ethnic grounds of any prospective mortgagor, tenant, or purchaser, and the Realtor should invariably submit to the client all written offers made by any prospect in connection with the transaction at hand . . .

4. The property owner whom the Realtor represents should have the right to specify in the contract of agency the terms and conditions thereof, and correspondingly, the Realtor should have the right and duty to represent such owner by faithfully observing the terms and conditions of such agency free from penalty or sanction for so doing . . .

8. Realtors may properly oppose any attempt by force of law to withdraw from property owners the right freely to determine with whom they will deal with respect to their property, irrespective of the reason therefor, and any law or regulation which would operate to prevent a real estate broker from representing any property owner or faithfully abiding by the terms and conditions of any agency stipulated by the property owner . . .

10. Realtors should endeavor to inform the public, religious, and civic groups that enhanced opportunity for the acquisition of private housing by minority groups must of necessity depend upon the attitudes of private property owners and not upon the real estate brokers, who are the marketing media; that the right of property owners freely to determine with whom they will deal is a right fundamental in the American tradition; that the real estate broker cannot fairly be utilized in his agency function as a means for accomplishing the withdrawal of the right of free decision from the property owner; that the broker fully performs his legal and social responsibilities when he faithfully engages to find a purchaser acceptable to his principal; and that real estate brokers should not be expected to inhibit or promote "open occupancy" housing, this being a matter to be resolved between prospective buyers and sellers of private residential real property and not by real estate brokers functioning as the marketing intermediary.

The GSA Is Knocked
on Wood*

Lumber mills and distributors are complaining bitterly that they were left holding a $300,000 bag when the Government backed out of a tentative order for $1,500,000 of plywood.

On May 17, about two weeks before a strike deadline in the lumber and plywood industry, the General Services Administration, the Government's supply agency, invited bids on about 20 million square feet of plywood. Normally, any such invitation carries a clause that allows the Government 20 days in which to decide whether it wants to make a firm order.

Mills and distributors were faced with the fairly substantial order in the face of a possible strike; labor negotiations still were in progress, and the outlook was uncertain. The upshot: Many mills committed production facilities, and some plywood was loaded on rail cars and moved out to packaging plants, in case a strike would be called.

On June 3, however, producers settled with the unions. Three days later, the 20-day period ended without a Government order, and distributors were left with large plywood stocks. In the mean-

* *The Wall Street Journal.* June 23, 1966. Used by permission.

time, plywood prices had declined. Moreover, mills and distributors claim they could have sold the plywood to private purchasers at better prices than they can get at present if they hadn't been reserving the wood for the Government. The total loss to the industry is estimated by one distributor at about $300,000.

"It was a pure case of the GSA playing a game," says Erling Thompson, vice president of North Robins Plywood, Inc., Seattle, one of the two main distributors for the bid. "I had placed about 95 percent of our business with 13 mills. We had to get immediate coverage because of the possible strike. All the raw materials had been ordered and the groundwork had been laid."

Mr. Thompson figures the Government move will cost him about $12,000, as he had already paid the mills for the plywood and was holding it in inventory. What will he do with the plywood? "We'll have to eat it," says Mr. Thompson.

Collins Lloyd, president of Lloyd Plywood Co., Seattle, another distributor, says: "We'll lose about $20,000 here. I had 19 cars of plywood en route. Right now they're still sitting in the packaging plant. We don't know what to do with it."

Says a sales manager for an Oregon plywood company that made commitments on 35 cars of plywood: "The Government has never cancelled out before, so we figured we'd go ahead. We could have taken a lot of solid civilian business. If the Government isn't capable of speculating a couple of weeks ahead in the market, it shouldn't be buying."

A spokesman for the GSA in Washington, D.C., claims there was no connection between the decision against awarding the contract and the labor settlement. "It was just a case of prices being too high," he says.

At the time the 20-day period expired, plywood prices on the market were in a sharp decline. In the two weeks from May 26 to June 9, mill prices for quarter-inch sanded interior-grade plywood dropped about $12, to $62 a thousand square feet. Prices this week are still near the $62 level.

Competition or War?*

       The legal limit of over-all weight of a truck is of considerable economic importance. The higher the limit, the better the chance of distributing the cost of driver and fuel over a bigger pay load. This influences the cost of shipping a cargo and, so, the ability of the trucker to compete with other forms of transportation. The cost of drivers and helpers is the largest single operating cost for truckers.

       If weight limits in contiguous states are not close together, the trucker may be forced to support extra charges for transfer and re-shipment when entering a state with a lower limit. In other cases, he may have to waste space by sending a truck out with less than a full load. In short, the relationships of limits in adjacent states influence the trucker's ability to utilize full capacity.

       In 1943 the legal over-all weight limits for Pennsylvania and the contiguous states were as follows:

---

   * The legal aspects of this case were decided in favor of Carl Byoir and the railroads by the Supreme Court of the United States. Those interested in this facet should read Andrew Hacker, "Pressure Politics in Pennsylvania: The Truckers vs. the Railroads" in Alan F. Westin, ed., *The Uses of Power* (New York, Harcourt Brace and World, 1962) pp. 323-376.

Pennsylvania	43,000 lbs.
West Virginia	60,000
New Jersey	60,000
Delaware	60,000
New York	61,000
Maryland	65,000
District of Columbia	65,400
Ohio	67,000

The truckers in Pennsylvania clearly had an interest in having the limit raised to at least 60,000 lbs. They tried unsuccessfully in 1949 but were determined to try again in 1951. The Pennsylvania Railroads, of course, were interested in maintaining the existing limit, which gave them a competitive edge. In Pennsylvania the railroads had great legislative influence, so it was sure to be a hard fight. Interestingly, the Pennsylvania Railroad, which had operated a fleet of long-haul trucks between 1930 and 1940, discontinued this business largely because weight restrictions in Pennsylvania made it difficult to operate at a profit.

The truckers started lobbying through the Pennsylvania Motor Truck Association (PMTA). In this they were helped by the fact that the Association was composed of individuals who lived in a variety of communities. Association members, then, were in a position to have frequent contacts with local politicians. In addition, the Association encouraged members to contribute to the campaigns of local representatives. The PMTA itself collected funds, and in 1950 gave $37,000 to the Republicans and $39,000 to the Democrats. As a result of its efforts, the bill raising the weight limit was passed in both the House and the Senate by December, 1951. The bill, however, still had to be signed by Governor John S. Fine.

The railroads had not been idle, but they did operate under some disadvantages. They did not have owners or officials in a large number of small towns, nor could the corporations legally give money to be passed on to politicians. Realizing their need for help, the Eastern Railroads Presidents Conference (ERPC) decided to retain Carl Byoir and Associates.

In August of 1949, Byoir accepted the account for an annual fee of $75,000 and reimbursement of operating expenses, including the salaries of those who worked on the account.

CARL BYOIR AND ASSOCIATES

Carl Byoir and Associates was one of the largest public relations firms in the country. In 1936 it had been employed by the Freeport Sulphur Company to fight a Louisiana tax on sulphur. As a result of Byoir's work the tax had been reduced and the Louisiana Constitution amended so that a change in the tax required a two-thirds majority of both houses. The Great Atlantic and Pacific Tea Company became a client in 1937, and Byoir helped it to fight a tax on chain stores in the State of New York as well as a proposed Federal tax. By 1949 Carl Byoir and Associates had been involved in several hundred fights against various chain store bills.

Once hired by the ERPC, Byoir was to take over completely and quietly. The railroads would foot the bills, but were not to appear on the scene. Even Byoir was to remain as hidden as possible. The campaign was to have several prongs. Media were to be induced to use material which would put the truckers in an unfavorable light. Organizations were to be recruited to bring pressure to bear on the legislature and the governor. In general, the idea was to create an impression of massive opposition to the proposed bill.

THE MEDIA CAMPAIGN

Like any professional public relations firm, Byoir gathered a vast mass of material on trucks and road problems. This collection included pictures, statistics, and reports on road tests and accidents. The firm then acted as a recruiting agent for writers, and as a broker for magazines and newspapers. Byoir made its files available to writers who might be interested in doing an article or a book on the truckers. Byoir would also approach a magazine editor and inform him that a certain writer might be available for an interesting article on trucking. This is fairly common practice in public relations. Byoir was successful in getting articles into mass circulation magazines such as the *Saturday Evening Post, Reader's Digest,* and *Newsweek,* as well as the Sunday supplement *Parade.* Articles favorable to the railroads, or at least unfavorable to truckers, also appeared in *Country Gentleman, Harper's, Argosy,* and *Everybody's Digest*. In some cases the Byoir organization helped the writer draft his story and tailor it to particular editors. In addition, an effort was made to persuade radio and television writers to portray truckers as tough guys.

The titles of a few articles will illustrate the tone of the campaign: "The Giants Wreck Highways," "What Bad Roads Are Costing Us," "Hell on Wheels," "The Rape of Our Roads."

THE MARYLAND ROAD TEST

Many of the articles relied heavily on information that was supposedly based on a Maryland Road Test conducted by the Highway Research Board. According to the Opinion of Judge Thomas Clary, given in the United States District Court for the Eastern District of Pennsylvania:

The principal object of the test was to determine the relative effects on a particular concrete pavement of four different axle loadings on two vehicle types. The loads employed were 18,000 and 22,400 pounds for single axle, and 32,000 and 44,800 pounds per tandem axle. The tests were conducted in a 1.1-mile section of Portland-cement-concrete pavement constructed in 1941 on U.S. 301 approximately 9 miles south of La Plata, Maryland. The pavement consisted of two 12 ft. lanes, each having a 9-7-9 in. cross-section and reinforced with wire mesh. The road at the beginning of the test was in fairly good condition and insofar as the records of the Maryland Road Commission could determine, the entire length of the test site was constructed on good granular subbase material.

There were four separate test sections. The first, which was the west lane of the southern half mile of the pavement under test, was subject to 18,000 lbs. single axle load; the second, which was the east lane of the southern half mile, was subject to 22,400 lbs. single axle load; the third, which was the west lane of the northern 0.6 mile, was subject to 32,000 lbs. tandem axle load; and the fourth, which was the east lane of the northern 0.6 mile, was subject to 44,800 lbs. tandem axle load.

The final report, which had nineteen technical findings, was given in engineering language. Judge Clary summarized them as follows:

Briefly stated with respect to the point under discussion in this case that big trucks break roads, they are as follows: (1) That where the road was built on granular soil, very little damage occurred no matter what type of vehicle was used; (2) That where the test road was built on fine grain soil, there was no damage until the fine grain soil became permeated with water; (3) That in the presence of water, the subsoil was pumped from under the concrete slab through joints in the road; (4) That the degree of pumping was faster and the amount greater upon the application of the heavier vehicles; (5) That with the subsoil removed, the concrete would and did crack, with the heavier vehicles doing the greater and quicker damage.

These conclusions were not particularly damaging to the truckers, but they were not always reported with the same regard for the purpose of the tests and the limits of the results. Byoir, it appears from the court records, knew Clinton H. Johnson, Director of Publicity for the Maryland Roads Commission, who became an employee of the ERPC in December of 1952. While it is not clear how he did it, Byoir got information about the test as it progressed. While nothing should have been released before the official report, Byoir's organization put out releases indicating that big trucks, in the sense of gross weights rather than axle loads, were the chief villains in destroying roads.

Byoir also used a cut-down version of a film produced by the Bureau of Public Roads. The Byoir version, for example, omitted such important commentary as the following:

The Test shows conclusively that a concrete pavement, of the strength and dimensions of the test road, will support indefinitely, without structural failure, single-axle loads as great as 22,400 pounds—*if* there is a subgrade, of adequate thickness, of nonplastic, granular soil. The equivalent of such support must be supplied by the design of roads *in the future*.

The language of the actual report and original film was restrained and even technical. Fairness required this, for, during the short test period, the road in question was being subject to wear that was estimated to equal 40 years of normal use. In addition, only minimal and not normal maintenance was used during the test period. Such facts had to be considered if the meaning of the test was to appear clearly.

According to Judge Clary the information made available by Byoir and printed in *Newsweek* "completely distorted the purpose and results of the test and attributed all road damage to big trucks. . . ."

GRASS ROOTS CAMPAIGN

Byoir, like any first-class public relations firm, did not rely on media alone. In attempting to mobilize public opinion for or against anything, it is wise to seek the aid of existing groups who already agree with you or are disposed to do so. In the present case, the Pennsylvania State Association of Township Supervisors could be expected to oppose anything that might increase the cost of road maintenance. In addition, the Pennsylvania State Grange, which had been interested in the railroad system, was brought into the Byoir camp. In some of these cases the railroad, through the agency of Byoir, provided funds for advertisements and news releases. Although the officers of these organizations may have been quite sincere in their opposition to the truckers, the rank and file members do not appear to have known of their connection with Byoir and the railroads.

Existing organizations are not always adequate for public relations purposes. Byoir helped in the formation of new groups such as the New Jersey Citizens Tax Study Foundation and the Empire State Transport League. This second organization, to which many prominent people lent their names, was used as another source of anti-truck literature. The purpose of all this was obviously to create the impression that opposition to the bill was widespread.

RESULTS

Byoir had started operations on behalf of the railroads in August, 1949. The bill favorable to the truckers had been passed but not signed by December, 1951. In January of 1952, Governor John S. Fine held hearings on the subject and vetoed the bill on January 21, 1952. In his veto message the Governor argued that the legislature had not had all the information available. It would seem, however, that the Governor was referring to the results of the Maryland Road Test, of which the legislature was very much aware. It appears that to some extent the Governor acted on the basis of a version of the tests supplied by his own experts but containing an anti-truck bias. Judge Clary noted that the Chief Engineer of the State Department of Highways was against the bill on the basis of statistics drafted by his department. The statistics, however, had originated with a desk space organization (the Empire State Transport League) created by Byoir.

In the spring of 1952 the truckers hired their own public relations firm to create the impression of public support for their position. This firm, Allied Public Relations Associates, organized the Pennsylvania Motor Safety League and the Citizens Committee for Highway Safety. These organizations had little success since they recruited few members and were opposed by the rank and file truckers, who did not like the idea of a front organization. Furthermore, the truckers did not want to play up the sins of the railroads so much as their own virtues. The Pennsylvania Motor Transport Association, however, was successful in raising money from the oil companies and in obtaining support from the United Rubber Workers. The Grange changed its anti-truck position.

The truckers found a disgruntled Byoir employee who agreed to give details of the campaign on behalf of the railroads. In January, 1953 the PMTA and 37 trucking firms brought suit against the railroads and Carl Byoir for conspiracy. A federal district court in Philadelphia enjoined Byoir from his activities. Within a year and a half a new bill favorable to the truckers was passed and signed into law by the new Governor, George M. Leader. The Governor had supported the original bill when he was a State Senator. Moreover, the railroads had not supported his campaign for governor.

The suit against the railroads, begun in 1953, was not settled finally until February 20, 1961, when the Supreme Court unanimously overruled the verdict of two lower courts and decided that the railroads and Byoir were not guilty of conspiracy nor of violating the anti-trust laws, The Supreme Court pointed out that the Sherman and Clayton Acts covered economic and not political activity.

Private Gain and Public Power

David Peterson is the owner and manager of a medium-sized paint company which ten years ago established itself in a young suburban town. Since that time sales have grown tremendously, and the business today cannot efficiently keep up with all of its orders due to lack of productive capacity.

Peterson definitely wants to expand his thriving company, but his efforts are being thwarted. He cannot expand to the right of the present building because this area is occupied by a relatively new one level warehouse. To the left of his site is a stretch of land occupied by an old, vacant farmhouse in a state of disrepair.

The house and property are owned by Mrs. Julia Moran, an eighty-year-old widow. Mrs. Moran lives in a small apartment building close to the heart of the town. Peterson has seen her many times to discuss buying the land from her. He has offered her a fair price for the property, but—seemingly without any reason—she flatly refuses to sell the property. The last time Mrs. Moran lived in the house was fifteen years ago, when her husband was still alive and they farmed the land together. On occasion, employees of the company have noticed her walking through the empty fields.

Peterson believes that Mrs. Moran will be more likely to sell if he can induce the town to condemn the farm building and force her to tear it down. He plans to present his case to the town officials. In his favor is the fact that this area was specifically zoned for industry, although the Morans were there before anyone had conceived the idea of establishing a township in the area. Peterson claims that the area is an eyesore. Furthermore, his paint company provides quite a bit of tax revenue for the town. If the company could expand and increase its income, taxes to the town would increase, thereby benefiting the entire population.

A friend suggested that Peterson build the new plant in another part of the town. Peterson has thought about this but has concluded that added transportation costs would make such a move uneconomical.

Is the Government
Always Ethical?

On May 31, 1962 the Board of Directors of the DuPont Company authorized distribution of one-half share of General Motors common stock for each DuPont common share, to be made July 9, 1962 to stockholders on record June 8, 1962. This was the first of three steps in the divesting of the DuPont Company's 63 million shares of General Motors stock, in compliance with the final judgment entered March 1 in the U.S. District Court in Chicago by Judge Walter J. LaBuy. The judgment provided that the divesting must commence by July 30, 1962 and be completed by February 28, 1965. The distribution of July 9, 1962 involved nearly 23 million shares of General Motors stock with a market value in the neighborhood of a billion and a quarter dollars.

When the three-step divesting process was completed, a stockholder with 100 shares of DuPont stock on June 8, 1962, had received a dividend in the form of 136 shares of General Motors stock. Of course, the value of the stockholder's investment in DuPont had decreased by approximately the same amount as the value of the General Motors stock he had acquired.

A HISTORY OF DUPONT'S
INVESTMENT IN GENERAL MOTORS

DuPont's Executive and Finance Committees authorized the initial investment in General Motors on December 21, 1917. By 1919, DuPont had bought shares of General Motors and Chevrolet (later exchanged for General Motors shares) equivalent to about 29 percent of General Motors outstanding stock. From 1935 to the beginning of divestiture in 1962, DuPont's holding of General Motors shares amounted to about 23 percent of General Motors common stock outstanding. Immediately preceding the initial distribution, the 63 million shares were carried on DuPont's books at a value of $1,266,300,000, an amount which closely corresponded to the equity indicated by the consolidated balance sheet of General Motors Corporation at December 31, 1961. The market value, at $55 a share, was $3,465,000,000.

The action was the result of a complaint brought under Sections 1 and 2 of the Sherman Act, and Section 7 of the Clayton Act. The Antitrust Division of the Department of Justice filed its complaint June 30, 1949, naming as defendants and conspirators the DuPont Company, General Motors Corporation, United States Rubber Company, Christiana Securities Company, Delaware Realty and Investment Company, and more than 180 individual members of the DuPont family, including many minor children ranging in age down to eight months. The complaint charged that stock ownership had been used to obtain and perpetuate control not only of DuPont, but also of General Motors and U.S. Rubber, with the effect of dividing fields of activity among the companies and requiring the companies to purchase goods from one another. All defendants denied the charges. DuPont's defense was based on the contention that each of the three manufacturing corporations purchased from the others only such products, and only in such quantities, as each considered appropriate to the efficient conduct of its own business; that the full history of dealings among the three corporations disclosed neither restraint of trade nor monopolization, but free and open competition. The government did not produce any witness to testify that he had been excluded from General Motors markets or that he had been injured in any way by DuPont's investment in General Motors.

In the District Court Decision, Judge LaBuy ruled on December 3, 1954 that the government's complaint should be dismissed, saying, "When read as a whole the record supports a finding, and the Court so finds, that there has not been, nor is there at present, a conspiracy to restrain upon General Motors' freedom to deal freely and fully with competitors of DuPont and U.S. Rubber, no limitation or restraint upon the freedom of General Motors to deal with its chemical discoveries, no restraint or monopolization of the General Motors market, no restraint or monopolization of the trade and commerce between DuPont and United States Rubber . . .

"It may be that a violation of the Clayton Act can be made out in the absence of an actual restraint of trade where it is established that there is a reasonable probability that a condemned restraint will result from an acquisition of stock. The acquisition challenged by the government—DuPont's investment in General Motors—took place over 30 years ago. In those many intervening years, the record disclosed that no restraint of trade has resulted. Accordingly, the Court is of the opinion that there is not, nor has there been, any basis for a finding that there is or has been reasonable probability of such a restraint within the meaning of the Clayton Act.

"The government has failed to prove conspiracy, monopolization, a restraint of trade, or any reasonable probability of restraint, and for these reasons the Amended Complaint should be dismissed."

The Department of Justice, on February 4, 1955 filed notice of appeal to the Supreme Court of the United States. The appeal was argued before the Supreme Court on November 15, 1956. The government did not challenge the District Court's findings. It contended, rather, that DuPont's stock relationship with General Motors constituted a "combination" which exerted an influence whereby some purchases by General Motors were channelled to DuPont.

DuPont contended that the record amply supported the District Court's findings that DuPont did not control General Motors; that General Motors made its own purchasing decisions and bought from DuPont and others on the basis of quality, service, and price; that General Motors did not buy from DuPont when they did not want to and had good business reasons for buying when they did.

The Supreme Court handed down on June 3, 1957 a 4 to 2 reversal of the District Court's dismissal of the complaint, and remanded the case to the District Court "for a determination after further hearing of the equitable relief necessary and appropriate in the public interest."

The Supreme Court found that "all concerned in high executive posts in both companies acted honorably and fairly, each in the honest conviction that his actions were in the best interests of his own company and without any design to overreach anyone, including DuPont's competitors." Nevertheless, the Court, by-passing the Sherman Act question, ruled that Section 7 of the Clayton Act had been violated because DuPont's acquisition and ownership of 23 percent of the outstanding stock of General Motors was sufficient to create a "reasonable probability" that DuPont would receive a preference in supplying General Motors' requirements for automotive fabrics and finishes.

Justice Burton, in his dissent, pointed out that the four-judge majority "disregards the language and purpose of the statute, 40 years of administrative practice, and all the precedents except one District Court decision," and that "to make its case the Court requires no showing of any misuse of a stock interest—either at the time of acquisition or subsequently—to gain preferential treatment from the acquired corporation."

The Department of Justice plan, filed on October 25, 1957, asked that DuPont be compelled to divest itself of its 63 million shares of General Motors stock. Under this proposal, the stock would be deposited with a trustee who would distribute it pro rata over a ten-year period to all holders of DuPont common stock. However, shares allocable to certain stockholders (Christiana Securities Company, Delaware Realty and Investment Company, and stockholders of Delaware Realty who are also stockholders of DuPont), aggregating about one-third of the total, would be sold for their account by the trustee over a ten-year period.

DuPont's objections to the government were filed on May 14, 1958 in a memorandum. It pointed out that the government plan would require the trustee to sell about 2,000,000 shares of General Motors stock annually for ten consecutive years, and that each offering would be an unprecedented financial effort in the industrial common stock market. Furthermore, the trustee would be required to distribute more than 4,000,000 General Motors shares each year for ten consecutive years to DuPont stockholders. Many stockholders would sell their DuPont stock before receiving the General Motors stock in order to avoid paying taxes on this dividend. Others, who retained their DuPont stock, might lack the cash needed to pay the tax on the stock dividend.

DuPont's memorandum of May 14, 1958 said:

These staggering losses, coupled with the immeasurable effect of such forced selling and market depreciation on industrial stocks generally, the handicap on General Motors and DuPont in raising equity funds, and the resulting peril to the stability of the economy could have far-reaching effects beyond the sheet dollar figures. No General Motors or DuPont shareholder—whether an individual investor or corporation or one of the thousands of educational institutions, trustees, labor unions, or charitable organizations that own either stock—would be spared from the adverse effects, nor would the general economy escape the impact of such a decree. . . . In essence, this is the harsh, unreasonable and wholly unnecessary penalty which would be inflicted on shareholders and others having no responsibility for the actions adjudged to have violated the Clayton Act.

Together with its memorandum, DuPont filed a plan which, the company said, "prevents DuPont's stock interest from being used to influence General Motors to deal with DuPont, but without a compulsory sale and distribution which will necessarily result in confiscatory taxes and wide destruction of property values."

Under this plan, the General Motors stock held by DuPont would no longer be voted by DuPont, but would be voted pro rata by DuPont's common stockholders, who then numbered more than 185,000. Christiana Securities Company and Delaware Realty and Investment Company also would pass the right to vote their shares pro rata to their more than 4,000 stockholders.

DuPont would be prohibited from acquiring additional General Motors stock. No General Motors officer or employee would be permitted to be a director, officer, or employee of DuPont, and no DuPont director, officer, or employee could become a director of General Motors without Court approval. Even if so approved, he would be forbidden to take part in any matter involved General Motors-DuPont relationships.

"What would then remain in DuPont . . . would be an investment, pure and simple," the company told the Court. "Section 7 (of the Clayton Act) is expressly applicable to stock held 'solely for investment'—stock which is not used 'by voting or otherwise' to lessen competition. The General Motors stock could not be so used because the power so to use it would be gone."

Judge LaBuy's judgment, entered on November 17 and effective November 18, 1959, provided that the right to vote the General Motors stock held by DuPont should be transferred pro rata to DuPont stockholders, except that no General Motors stock should be voted by Christiana, Delaware Realty, nor by anyone who is a director or officer of DuPont, Christiana, or Delaware Realty, nor by a member of the family of a director or officer resident in the same household.

On January 14, 1960 the Department of Justice filed notice of appeal from Judge LaBuy's judgment on divestment. The appeal was argued before the Supreme Court on February 20 and 21, 1961.

The Department of Justice contended that divestiture of DuPont's General Motors stock was necessary; first, as a matter of law, and second, because as long as DuPont held bare legal title to the stock, it would have the means and the motive to influence General Motors to purchase from DuPont. The Department of Justice suggested several methods by which, it said, divestiture could be accomplished without "undue" hardship on stockholders. It urged that "the impact of federal taxes is not a pertinent factor in ordering relief in an antitrust proceeding," and dismissed the financial losses which might be caused by divestment as "no excuse" for rejecting its demand for divestiture.

DuPont told the Court that there is nothing in the law to make divestiture mandatory; that Judge LaBuy's judgment was fully effective, depriving DuPont of every attribute of power that might be used to influence or control General Motors, leaving in DuPont "a most sterile kind of investment." DuPont said that the methods of divestiture suggested by the Department of Justice would involve sale or distribution of the General Motors stock and would impose unnecessary injury on approximately one million DuPont and General Motors stockholders.

On May 22, 1961 the Supreme Court, by a vote of 4-3, directed "complete divestiture" of DuPont's 63 million shares of General Motors stock. The Court sent the case back to the District Court for formulation of a final judgment which would provide for complete divestiture.

Judge LaBuy's final judgment, effective May 1, 1962, provided: DuPont must dispose of its 63 million shares of General Motors stock by distribution to its stockholders or by such other methods or combination of methods as it may select. The divestiture must commence within 90 days from May 1, 1962 and must be completed within 34 months from that date.

Aluminum Prices and
Presidential Power

On October 19, 1965 the Olin Mathieson Chemical Corporation announced a price rise of ½ cent a pound for primary aluminum. Olin Mathieson, the fourth largest producer of primary metal in the United States, accounted for only six percent of the market, but its move was followed by Reynolds, the second largest, and Kaiser, the third. Alcoa, the leading producer, was expected to follow suit. This was the first price rise in a year on primary aluminum or ingots, and the industry was waiting to see how the government would react.

President Johnson requested a cabinet-level meeting to discuss the possible disposal of the government's aluminum stockpile. At first government spokesmen said they did not know if there were any connection between the price increase and the cabinet-level meeting. Within a few days, however, they issued a statement that there was no connection between the two events. At this point, Alcoa too raised its prices by ½ cent a pound.

Representatives of the aluminum industry had been meeting with government officials to discuss the orderly disposal of 200,000 tons of the 1,400,000-ton stockpile. When Alcoa announced its price rise, a number of things happened. The government announced that the discussions had failed and that it would not dispose of the 200,000 tons at "market prices." One of the President's economic advisors denounced the price rise as inflationary. Industry spokesmen said that they were threatened with antitrust investigations, tax audits, and a review of the rates the companies paid for electric power purchased from the government. Subsequently the industry rescinded its price increases and quickly reached an agreement with the government about the stockpiled aluminum.

Many businessmen voiced the opinion that the government was trying to repeal the law of supply and demand. It was also argued, however, that the government was using that very law to control prices. Secretary of Defense McNamara noted, "I'm the largest buyer of aluminum in the country." The government, indeed, expected to buy ten to fifteen percent of domestic production in 1966. Secretary McNamara also explained that "it simply does not make sense for the government to spend the taxpayers' money to buy increasingly large amounts of aluminum (in defense goods) when it holds 1.4 million tons which are surplus to any conceivable defense requirement."

The meaning of the government's moves was not clear. According to the *Wall Street Journal* on November 2, 1965 many businessmen interpreted the attack as a dramatic means of warning all businessmen that the government was serious about the danger of inflation. On the other hand, there were denials that there was any connection between the disposal of the stockpile and the price increases.

There was even debate as to whether or not the sale of government aluminum could really depress the price. Government officials noted that the aluminum was to be sold at domestic market prices and that the stockpiled aluminum might not be attractive since it needed some reprocessing. Moreover, if only a part of the stockpile was dumped, the big processors could buy it up and take it off the market. The government had, after all, announced that it would sell the first 100,000 tons by competitive bid in order to test market prices. Some industry spokesmen admitted that the disposal of even 200,000 tons would not affect the market in an orderly way. Here and there fabricators noted that they would look for foreign aluminum if prices went up. This, of course, concerned officials who were already worried about the balance of payments problem.

INDUSTRY STRUCTURE

There are eight domestic producers of primary aluminum, but the big three—Alcoa, Reynolds, and Kaiser—account for 85 percent of primary production. In addition there are six foreign companies which sell aluminum in the United States. On the whole, however, the primary aluminum field is oligopolistic.

The competition in the aluminum industry takes place among the 200 independent, domestic fabricating companies which produce extrusions, sheet, plate forgings, rolled bar, and tube aluminum. Alcoa, Reynolds, and Kaiser are important in fabricating as well as production, which means that in many areas they are competing with their own customers for primary aluminum. If it were not for fear of the antitrust laws, the big, vertically integrated companies could raise ingot prices and squeeze the independent fabricators out of business. In practice, however, this is not done. In the first place, some producer is nearly always willing to discount the price of basic aluminum. In the second place, it is useful to have an active group of fabricators selling aluminum against competing metals. However, in September, 1965 Kaiser was sued on the grounds that price fixing had forced two fabricators to sell their companies.

In the years before 1965 the higher profits were in the production of ingots rather than in fabrication. Aggressive price cutting had even led to a situation where the integrated companies sometimes lost money on their fabricated products. The fabricating divisions of the integrated companies, however, were the largest customers for ingot. Alcoa used about 85 percent of its ingot production in its own fabricating plants; Kaiser and Reynolds, in the neighborhood of 70 percent.

Independent fabricators are extremely important in some lines. Between 1950 and 1965, for example, the independents increased their share of the market for extrusions from 35 to 61 percent. The independents also sell 26 percent of the sheet and plate aluminum.

ALUMINUM PRICES

In the late 1950's there had been excess aluminum ingot capacity. In addition Alcoa, the largest producer, had inadvertently introduced price instability with its system of commodity pricing. Under this system, certain finished products had a special low price so that aluminum might break into potentially large volume markets. In those cases where basically the same product was sold at two different prices in two different markets, the lower price tended to spread. The effects of the company's own policy would have been more serious except for the fact that the government's purchases for its stockpile had acted as a cushion. Until 1961 the government stockpiling effort had tended to support ingot prices so that the effect of over-capacity and commodity pricing may have been mitigated. Between 1951 and 1963 the government, through the General Services Administration, bought nearly two million tons of primary aluminum. This represented almost $926 million in sales revenues. Stockpiling eased off after 1959, and in 1963 the GSA was authorized to start selling off some of the ingot supply. While this hurt prices somewhat, increasing demand in 1964-65 helped prices to rise.

As early as 1962 Reynolds and Kaiser had offered to start buying back the excess stock of aluminum at current market prices. The idea was to avoid dumping by gradually reintroducing the ingots into the market over a period of fifteen-to-twenty years. In order to obtain this result, the companies were willing to absorb the cost of resmelting the older and less pure oxidized stock. In 1963 Kaiser, Reynolds, and Alcoa did start buying back 106,000 tons on the basis of a short term agreement. The Office of Emergency Planning, however, said that it did not have the authority for long-term agreements. In addition there was then—and now—considerable debate as to the requirements which the stockpile should meet.

PROFITS AND EXPANSION

In 1965 the primary aluminum industry was operating close to full rated capacity. Profits, however, had not increased proportionately to sales and the return on invested capital was below the return for all manufacturing firms. As a result of these factors, the "big three" found themselves in a position where it might be difficult to get the capital needed to expand productive facilities. Assuming that the market for aluminum would grow at an annual rate of six percent, one estimate said the industry would need to

invest $1 billion in primary production facilities and an additional
$3 billion in fabricating plants within the next five years.

During the decade 1956-1966 the production of aluminum increased 63 percent. However, the *combined sales* of Alcoa, Reynolds
and Kaiser increased only 42 percent ($1,531 million to $2,173 million). Their *combined net income* varied as follows:

1956	$173,200,000
1960	88,500,000
1964	126,100,000
1965	162,000,000

Since their capital investment had increased greatly, the *combined
return on net worth* had gone down as follows:

1955	17.7 percent
1960	5.9 percent
1964	7.3 percent

These returns do not compare favorably with the average 12.1 percent return of the 500 top industrials. The *return on total invested
capital* (total assets less current liabilities) was also decreasing for the
aluminum industry as a whole:

1955	10.6 percent
1960	3.9 percent
1964	4.9 percent

Alcoa was in a much better position than the other companies
in 1965, for it had 125,000 tons of unfinished capacity at its Warwick
plant and a low debt ratio. This may explain why Alcoa was not so
anxious about the price rise as some other companies.

GOVERNMENT RELATIONS

Not only stockpiling, but other government actions
placed the aluminum industry in a very special relationship to the
government. In 1947 the government had finally won its antitrust
suit against Alcoa, insofar as the court held that the company had
in fact monopolized the market for primary aluminum.

As recently as October, 1964 six fabricators of aluminum electrical cable (Alcoa, Kaiser, Reynolds, Olin Mathieson, Anaconda Wire

& Cable, and General Cable) had pleaded no contest in a price fixing case. Each was fined $50,000. The consent decree gave the Justice Department access to the companies' books as a means of checking compliance.

Kaiser had bought many of its plants from the government, while Reynolds had received loans from the Reconstruction Finance Corporation. Kaiser and Olin Mathieson are, moreover, among the 100 biggest suppliers to the government. The government is one of the biggest customers of the aircraft industry, which in its turn is a major customer for the aluminum fabricating companies. Finally, in some cases the aluminum producing companies depend on power purchased from the government for the refining of ore. All of this makes the industry particularly vulnerable to government action. Close association with any large customer or supplier, whether these be private companies or the United States government, can be troublesome.

GUIDELINES

Labor costs in the aluminum industry had gone up when labor won a four percent increase in early 1965. The increase had annoyed the government since it went beyond the guidelines suggested by the Council of Economic Advisors. The October 19 price increase of ½ cent a pound also seemed to violate guidelines. There was, however, debate as to the applicability of the guidelines to the case of the aluminum industry.

According to the guidelines theory, prices should be reduced if the industry's rate of productivity exceeds the over-all rate of 3.2 percent a year. On the other hand, prices should be increased if the opposite is true. In theory, such pricing is supposed to prevent inflationary behavior. The Council of Economic Advisors did add that these general rules could be modified in certain cases. Prices, for example, should be allowed to rise where earnings were not high enough to attract the capital needed for expansion or where wage increase were needed to attract workers.

Some experts estimate that the aluminum industry's rate of increase in productivity was more than five percent. This rate would seem to call for a price decrease rather than an increase. However, in the last decade, aluminum prices had fallen. As a result, the earnings on invested capital were not satisfactory in the eyes of the industry leaders, who felt that a higher return was necessary to attract capital. Moreover, labor costs were rising. In May of 1965, for example, it was estimated that the Alcoa collective bargaining agreement raised labor costs by 4.1 percent a year, well beyond the guideposts' 3.2 percent. However, when the aluminum companies raised their prices, the Council of Economic Advisors reinterpreted their figures so as to take away the justification based on a rise in wages. The reinterpreted figure said that labor costs had only gone up 3.5 percent.

In April of 1966 the *Wall Street Journal* announced that aluminum prices had been rising since January and, indeed, were in many cases higher than the proposed increase which the government had beaten down. The companies did not raise list prices after the rollback; they merely stopped discounting, and negotiated contracts at prices which were closer to the real list prices. Theoretically, then, prices were not being raised but restored. Therefore, no government protest was expected. The companies felt that when they had gotten all they could by firming up prices, they would then follow the pattern of the steel industry and increase prices selectively. Such a tactic, since it was less visible, seemed unlikely to arouse the ire of the government.

Company Social Responsibility
— Too Much or Not Enough?*

PANEL PARTICIPANTS

Chairman
H. Bruce Palmer, President
    National Industrial Conference Board

Members
Adolf A. Berle, Senior Partner
    Berle, Berle & Brunner
Gilbert W. Fitzhugh, President
    Metropolitan Life Insurance Company
Arnold H. Maremont, President
    Maremont Corporation
J. Irwin Miller, Chairman of the Board
    Cummins Engine Company, Inc.
Thomas R. Reid, Director
    Civic and Governmental Affairs Office
    Ford Motor Company

* The National Industrial Conference Board, *The Conference Board Record*, April, 1964. Used by permission.

Chairman Palmer: For better or for worse, large segments of our business community have embraced a series of social responsibilities.

The involvement of some companies grew from their feelings that a void existed that had to be filled. In other companies, it has represented a general desire to be responsible citizens of their community. Of course, some segments of the business community have refused this role entirely.

As a result, business has been charged, on some occasions, with becoming overly social conscious to the detriment of the profit-making motive of the corporation itself. On the other hand, we still hear the charge that business is an unfeeling force which is concerned only with the means of making bigger and better profits.

Obviously, this is a controversial issue. We hope this session will clarify some of the controversy.

Fundamental to any discussion of social responsibility is the definition of the term. Let me try to draw a definition from our panel members by posing several questions.

What does the phrase social responsibility mean to each of you? Who defines a company's social responsibility? Government? Society? Or top management within your company? Is this a role that business has sought or has business found itself pushed into this role? Is this a comfortable or uncomfortable role for business?

Thomas R. Reid: There are two main viewpoints. The first is that corporate management's sole responsibility is to the stockholders to work toward maximizing their long-term return on investments.

The second holds, in effect, that corporation management has a number of allegiances or at least a number of interests to which it must respond.

Realistically, if management must regard the stockholder as just one of several interests to satisfy, it is cast in the role of an arbitrator among the various interest groups. My own feeling is that corporation management cannot suggest it has responsibility to any group other than its stockholders. But in carrying out its obligations to the stockholders, intelligent company management will give due weight to the interests of other elements in our society as they bear on the task of representing the stockholders' equity.

The basic responsibility of the businessman is to earn a profit for his company by responding swiftly and efficiently to consumer wants as expressed in the market place. Like all other citizens, he is well advised to stick to his knitting, mind his store, and guard his interests. But as with other citizens, this is not the whole of his relationship to his fellow men. If he is wise and foresighted, he will see that his own best interests are served by doing unto others as he would have others do unto him. He will not turn his company into a charitable agency, but he will encourage and support those organizations that serve the needs of his fellow men, within reasonable limits.

Primarily, the social function of the business system is to produce sufficiently what people want. This goal is best served when businesses compete with each other to maximize long-run profits. If we should have a platform as business, I suggest it might be this: a consistent, thorough-going defense, not of profit as such, but of freedom and incentive to compete for maximum profit throughout the economy. This means being opposed to restraint on competition from whatever source.

There are some businessmen who seem to want to bury their heads in the sand, ostrich-like, and say business has no influence on society. This is ridiculous. Obviously, the corporation and businessmen do have a profound influence. But they are only one of many interest groups which have such influence.

The management of a corporation has neither the responsibility nor the right to seek to impose its own views upon the lives of other people. It has no right to tell its employees how they should live or behave off the job, and it has no such right with respect to citizens of the communities where it has facilities. For a corporation, by virtue of its economic position in the community, to assume such functions would be inconsistent with its own nature and with the principles of democratic society.

J. Irwin Miller: Of those three words "Company Social Responsibility," two give us very little trouble. We know what we mean today by a corporation or a company; we also know what we mean by the word social—it's the society in which a corporation or a business finds itself conducting its affairs. It might refer to a local community, or to a regional area; it might mean the whole nation.

This word "responsibility" is the one that gives me trouble.

The English dictionary says it means being answerable or accountable to somebody for something. The closest I came to it in a Latin dictionary I found was a verb meaning to promise or offer something in return for another thing. Any place I turned, this word "responsibility" had the idea of some kind of contract implicit in it; that someone is supposed to give something of value because he receives something of value.

Now how do we make any sensible application of this to the relations between a corporation and society? The only legal contractual relation I know of is the legal obligation to pay taxes and to pay attention to existing ordinances. We must mean something more than that.

Perhaps we are referring to a contractual obligation of some sort other than legal. Let's ask ourselves a few questions. Suppose you are responsible for choosing a new plant location. After you have found that the various natural resources are there, do you simply pick the one with the lowest taxes and the cheapest utility rates, and look no further? Do you ever also say something like, "This is a good community, that is a bad community?"

You look for a first-class community—good schools, good recreational facilities, few slums, little crime—because you will have a great deal of difficulty operating a first-class plant, staffed by able people, in a rundown community. You look for what you call a good town— and by that I also mean a good state or a good nation or trade area.

Isn't a good town one whose citizens have a habit of voluntarily working for its welfare? Their spirit puts the interest of the whole community first; private interests come second. This kind of spirit is the result of the free and voluntary labors of past generations of concerned citizens.

The work of these past generations produced a good community —the kind you want to put your plant in. This benefit is a major asset to the business. It comes at no charge—for free.

There is an interesting sentence in Scripture which says, "Other men labored and you are entering into their labors," and this is what happens when we locate in a good town. As a businessman you say: "Fine. But why should I have to pay for it?"

Legally there is no debt. There is no payment required for this asset. Morally there might be some kind of obligation. If there is, that obligation might consist of making a return toward the good of the community or society, a contribution in work or thought or money that is somehow comparable to the value of the asset which the corporation freely enjoys.

Two dominant characteristics of this free society are found in two phrases that we use a lot; one is individual liberty, another we call private property. Well, if individual liberty is intended to mean a single-minded concern for my own liberty, and to heck with everybody else's; if private property is intended to mean exclusive concern for my own property and things, then what we have is no different from the jungle. In a jungle, lives and property are constantly threatened; you really don't have very much liberty.

But if, in our society, individual liberty means a fierce concern for the liberty and rights of the other fellow; if our definition of private property means a dominating concern for the property rights of the other fellow, then everybody in that society enjoys the maximum of freedom. He can move around in safety. He can have opportunities that are known no other way.

A loss of freedom or an impairment of right or property for any man diminishes my freedom and my rights. This is the lesson of the free society about which we are so concerned.

For its own freedom, for the maximum pursuit of its own true property interests, the corporation, like the individual, must make a free response to the society of its time. Its response must be aimed at the good and the improvement of that society. It is, therefore, in our desire for a free society that we begin to find the reason for the social responsibility of a corporation.

Arnold H. Maremont: Fifty years ago this very month,[1] the Ford Motor Company increased its wages to $5 a day. At the same time, the company reduced the work day from 9 hours to 8 hours a day. At that time, the *Wall Street Journal* made the following comment, "This is on a high biblical or spiritual principle where they do not belong."

If we substitute the word social responsibility for biblical or spiritual principle, aren't we just updating the question?

Today we know that Henry Ford was shrewd enough to realize that higher wages would attract the best workers, obtain higher productivity, and lower unit costs including overhead. What the Ford Motor Company did was just good business.

When we use the term social responsibility, couldn't we agree that we are talking about acts that tend to assist men to live together more compatibly? Let's take an example. A paved road in front of a

[1] January, 1964.

plant makes driving easier than does a corduroy. But the company receives all its supplies and all shipments by rail. The question arises, should the company pave the roadway? My answer is no—not unless it adds to the profits of the shareholders. That is what a corporation exists for.

The corporation is a statutory privilege that allows folks with savings to invest money for profit with a limited liability. The corporation is a legal entity, not a person. It is a property right, not a human right. It has no conscience. (For this discussion, let's forget public utilities. In my judgment they are a special breed of corporations.)

Let's not confuse the company managers in their role as managers with their role as individuals. A company man, in a social responsibility sense, is not a man at all. He is just two dimensional, and he is not human. Since a corporation has no conscience and is not a person, it cannot be charitable. It cannot take shareholders' profits to help mankind, womankind, or even the animal world.

Following this philosophy through, corporation foundations have no justification. A legal entity created to earn money cannot be distorted into becoming a funnel for a philanthropy. The managers of the company were not elected to the office because they had competence as philanthropists. I admit it is a heady experience for a manager to participate in doling out large sums of money for education, particularly if it is to his Alma Mater, but that doesn't make it profitable. (The Maremont Corporation has a foundation. I don't mean to be hypocritical in my statements, but there would be a disadvantage if we didn't follow the system.)

Can I think of areas where the corporation has a measure of social responsibility? Of course I can, but they all relate to corporate profits.

Suppose a fire threatens the entire town in which the corporation is located. It would have the social responsibility to close and let the employees go out and save their homes—and incidentally to stop the fire before the company's plant is destroyed.

Regarding the racial question, a corporation might well participate in a program to relieve tensions before its work force is impaired.

Suppose television shows are unspeakably vulgar and offensive. The only question the corporation need ask itself is whether the pro-

gram sells its products at a lower cost than newspapers and magazines—unless sponsorship of it engenders attitudes that will be adverse to the corporation.

Should a corporation encourage its employees to devote company
time to community activities? Should it, in fact, go so far as to train
employees to be active in such nonbusiness affairs? My answer is a
big no! I would add that this goes for unions, too.

The ultimate abdication of all social responsibility is typified
by the usual business argument that all taxes are inimical to business
interests. It is argued that the higher the taxes, the more objection-
able they are. Since businesses pay taxes, they are justified in pressing
for honesty and efficiency in their administration. But no executives
are elected by the shareholders to decide whether the high schools
need more money for education or whether urban renewal is a valuable aid in better living.

I believe we have permitted an establishment of corporation
executives to flourish who are less interested in the stockholder's
benefit than in their own vanities. I think a total ventilation of the
subject is long past due.

Gilbert W. Fitzhugh: I work for a large mutual life insurance company with no stockholders. But I don't think that makes our responsibility any different from anybody else's. Our job is to provide insurance at as economic a cost as possible and to pay larger dividends
to our policyholders—which, although in fact quite different from
dividends paid to stockholders, may be considered in a broad sense
for our purpose here as analogous to making a profit for stockholders.

We cannot distinguish and extricate the function of making
such a profit from the other responsibilities that the company has
as a company and not as individual managers. The management of
the corporation is the only group that can speak for the corporation.
They are fallible, like everybody else, and they will make mistakes.
But it is their responsibility to do their best in the name of the corporation to improve the world they live in. That responsibility is
not incompatible with making the most profits possible.

Social responsibility is a many-faceted thing. Our first responsibility is to make a good product and provide as good a service as we
can at an economical price so that the public will buy from us.

We have a second responsibility to be a good employer to the people that work for us. And we have a third responsibility to the community in which the corporation lives, the town, the state, the country, or the trading area, as was mentioned. This might be considered public affairs. But these other responsibilities lead back to the first one.

Does the corporation seek these responsibilities or are they thrust upon it? Actually, it's neither one. They are there. They are inescapable. They are part of the warp and woof of the society in which we live.

Is the corporation comfortable with these responsibilities? This is irrelevant. We have got them whether they are comfortable or not. We must do our best to measure up to them if we are to do our job for our stockholders or policyholders as well as for our country. After all it is really the same thing.

If everyone of us does his best for his company and does what he thinks best for the community, that collective decision is going to be much better than one that any one person or government can make for them. We will make mistakes, but it is better to have a lot of small mistakes than one big mistake made by an all-powerful government.

Let's be practical about this. Some may say that labor unions or others shouldn't take stands or make decisions, but they are doing it. Well, if we don't speak up for the things we believe in as businessmen, as people representing our companies, who will? Who is going to speak up for the private enterprise system, for a sound dollar, and a sound economy if businessmen don't? We cannot possibly avoid it —and I don't think that it is inconsistent with maximizing our profits to the stockholders or dividends to the policyholders.

Adolf A. Berle: I'd like to put a slightly angular twist on this subject. In the first place, I don't think any of your companies are private enterprises in any conventional sense. Second, I am not sure that you know whether you are productive or not. You have a particular niche in an integrated system, the American Economy, which you try to enlarge and should. You make money, yes. But you don't know what your efforts cost the community around you. If those costs were added to your costs, it might be that businesses very much in the black now would find themselves in the red—and vice versa.

This means in substance that we all are cogs in a vast machine. Sometimes the cogs are very big—but big or little there is no escape from your being in the machine.

And third, when it comes to social responsibility, I agree with Mr. Fitzhugh: you have got it, because you have got it. This is not a responsibility perhaps that anyone sought. It is there because of the fact that social thinking is an essential of business thinking. Over a longer period of time, the best social thinking will be the best business thinking—as the Henry Ford case shows. In citing the Henry Ford experiment, however, we are considering the situation quite frankly rather than concealing the premises on which we act.

There are two forms of social responsibility. One is the fringe benefits of being the good citizen through community chests, etc. This is minor. The major responsibility is handling the job of running your business with a certain degree of enlightenment. Now this is where I bring in my twist. You are the principal users and suppliers of capital. How you apply the capital influences the country. To bring it down to brass tacks, in the current application of the capital, you are the greatest experts in creating unemployment in the world. I participate in making such decisions, so I appreciate their necessity. But, every voucher you sign for a new piece of machinery puts a finish to, we might say, the labors of 10, 15, or 20 men. As a result, even with the expansion and vigorous upturn projected for the next year, the percentage of unemployed at the end of the year is expected to be greater than before.

Here we have a real question of business and social responsibility.

Let me draw an analogy. The bankers of 1925 didn't interest themselves in public affairs. The ensuing smash in 1929-30 passed the most terrible verdict ever cast on the financial community. It wasn't that the bankers were wicked or bad. It was that they failed. The power went to Washington, and most of it didn't come back.

In the unemployment situation, business faces the same sort of thing. There are several alternatives for business. You can meet the situation yourself. If you can't meet it, you can support necessary government or combined government and private arrangements designed to solve it. Or, you can let loose the most explosive force conceivable in the country—a group of unemployed young men, who in some places are further driven by race problems. Their explosive force could blow you all out of the water.

We have what is probably the best productive organization in the world, the American economic organization. It is far from perfect, of course, but it is a superb way to get things done. Here we sit with our undreamed-of resources and our power of organization. Do we have a responsibility to meet this problem or not?

While it is true, as Mr. Maremont says, that maximizing profits for the shareholders is a major job of management, another of its jobs is maintaining institutions capable of making profits. Some are still talking of the American economic system in terms of the classical analysis of 50 years ago. The modern fact is that you now are all part of one machine. You have this social responsibility because what happens evolves out of what you do.

Chairman Palmer: Each of you has given us a concept of social responsibility. There is, I think, one basic area where there may be disagreement.

Mr. Maremont stresses that when he speaks out on matters of "social responsibility" he is not speaking as a corporate executive, he is doing it as an individual. . . .

Mr. Reid: Can in fact the businessman who is prominent in the corporation and is respected in the community in truth simply say, "I am speaking entirely as a private citizen"? Will the public really believe that?

Mr. Miller: Mr. Maremont, don't you think the reception of your words is different because people know you are the head of a corporation? Would the reception be the same if you were a union leader or an active member of the Communist party?

Mr. Maremont: There's really no categorical answer. Obviously people would also be influenced if my hair were some freakish color or if I came here with a sport shirt with an open collar. But I think we are oversimplifying the issue.

I don't think the fundamental question here is what a man says so much as what he does.

I believe profoundly that everyone of us as a human being living in this society has an obligation to participate actively in every element of our society. This is a personal responsibility. We are not just businessmen, we are fathers, we are husbands, we are highway users, we are church members. We aren't just single-faceted people, we are people of multiple interests. I strongly believe that we should stand up and say what we think in the light of all our responsibilities and all our relationships.

But I don't think that is what we are talking about here. Let's take the question of whether or not a certain kind of educational system or a certain curriculum for the high school in your city is proper. You can stand up and say anything you want to say as an individual. But to give corporate money to change the curriculum of the high schools is completely outside of your province and your responsibilities as a corporate executive. We don't have the competence, knowledge, or expertise required to bring any influence to bear on what kind of curriculum the high school should have.

Mr. Miller: Up to a point, I would agree. But suppose this high school offers no college preparatory work at all. Suppose the sons and daughters of the people you hope to hire would have no chance to get into any good college. Has the corporation any business questioning the action of the local school board?

Mr. Maremont: Not as a corporation.

Mr. Miller: Wait a minute—this affects profits. Say I have a laboratory there, and have to hire some Ph.D.'s. They won't come if their children have little chance to go to college. This affects my operations. Knowing that, do I get involved in curriculum as a corporation?

Mr. Maremont: The risks of opening this door and permitting a corporation to get involved in curriculum are much more serious and dangerous than not allowing it in. Once you open the door, the next question you could ask me is, "Suppose we need more machinists or computer experts?" Before you know it, the high school isn't a high school at all, it simply becomes some kind of a vocational training base. I think that path is too dangerous.

Chairman Palmer: You have indicated that, as a corporate president, you have no right to articulate a corporate position on matters of public affairs even though that opinion might be the consensus of the management group. Does that also imply that, as a corporate president, you should not attempt to get others of your management group involved in undertaking either their individual citizen's responsibility or a total corporate responsibility? Does it imply that you should not take advantage of the corporate structure to train individuals to undertake and exercise their responsibilities as individual citizens?

Mr. Maremont: Yes, I think you have paraphrased my philosophy quite clearly. By way of further delineating it let's take the fair employment practice legislation. In my judgment the fair employment practice legislation has nothing to do with corporations; it doesn't

make corporations any richer or any poorer. Corporations as such
and corporate associations as such should stay out of this area.

As a human being, as a citizen, I am under a real commitment
to have a feeling about fair employment practice legislation and I
should go out and work vigorously for my point of view. But this is
not within the area of corporate responsibility. Furthermore, this is
the kind of business opposition that injures the image of business
vis-à-vis the public and legislatures.

Mr. Miller: Arnold, you insist that the responsibility of the president
of a corporation is single mindedly to make as much money for his
shareholders as he can. Is this a general statement to which there
may be numerous exceptions or is this a single matter unqualified?

Mr. Maremont: In his role as the president of the corporation, it is
his responsibility to make as much money as he can make for the
corporation with due recognition to the implications of elements
that may or may not affect the corporation.

For example, I think that if a corporate executive believes profoundly that the tariff or tax policy of the country directly affects
the business, he obviously has to take a position on this.

Mr. Miller: Let me ask a silly question just to dramatize your point.
Why, as president of a corporation, are you here at this meeting
instead of out calling on customers?

Mr. Maremont: Where, in a man's work, he has the opportunity to
do this kind of service without impairing the effectiveness of his
job, he should be given the opportunity to do it. If I were to spend
my time going around and propagandizing and propagating this
point of view to the exclusion of my work and to the risk of the
corporation's welfare, then I think my action would be highly reprehensible.

Mr. Berle: I find Mr. Maremont's statement extremely refreshing.
Two men made similar statements quite a few years ago. One was
John Stuart Mill, who described the duties of a manager of an enterprise under classic economic theory. The other who used similar
phrases was Karl Marx, who concluded that because their potential
power was so dangerous, all entrepreneurs ought to be killed in the
class war. Mr. Maremont insists that as a business you do one thing,
and as a man you do another. Obviously, whether anyone pays attention to the man turns on many elements. But can you as a corporate
executive stay apart from these things? If you accept my theory that

the Maremont Corporation or any other business is one cog in an elaborate machine are you not working in public affairs simply when you are working at your desk? Can you escape it in any way?

Mr. Maremont: Suppose I try to answer that by asking a question. A report has just been released on cigarettes and health. Suppose tomorrow morning one of the large cigarette companies walks into a banking institution seeking a loan to expand production of cigarettes. The balance sheet is perfectly good, the company is willing to pay the going rate, and by any standard their credit is excellent. How many institutions do we know of whose profound sense of social responsibility would cause them to say: "We are very sorry. From now on we don't make loans to build plants to make cigarettes, because we think cigarettes are injurious to the entire community."

Mr. Fitzhugh: It so happens that I've just been writing something on this subject—not about cigarette companies, but basic objectives of our company—which could be applied to the general question you raise. One of our objectives and responsibilities in maximizing earnings for our policyholders is to follow a sound investment policy determined by the highest qualities of stewardship.

If we were to take a very narrow-minded view, and if we had two loan applications of equal security but one had a half of one percent more yield than the other, we might pay no attention to what we thought was good for the country and community and take the higher yield. But I don't think that is really in the interest of our policyholders or stockholders, even in terms of maximizing earnings.

We can maximize our short-run earnings, but we might not have any customers or country—and what good does that do us over the long run. If we do act as a good corporate citizen, if we take into account what is good for the country, we maximize the earnings of our corporations over the long run. If you like, it is being selfish—or call it enlightened self-interest.

So, Arnold, answering your question generally, we would not loan to a company that we thought was doing something that was not in the public interest.

Mr. Miller: In our small town, I am a part-time banker. One of our customers has become pretty wealthy through his holdings of slum property. It's a remarkable circumstance that with slum property, you get the same rent as with good property. Economically, slum property may be the best real estate in the country.

Actually, this would be a good loan. You might even pick up half a point on the interest rate making it an extremely profitable one. But we won't loan him.

Mr. Fitzhugh: Neither will we.

Mr. Miller: I could cite other examples—but the principle would be the same. None of us can get along in this society unless we practice self-restraint. As crowded as this world is, all of us can exist only if there is a large amount of restraint. In a free society the best kind of restraint is voluntary restraint. If there isn't voluntary restraint, there is going to be imposed restraint, and then we are all going to be considerably less than free.

Can a man really have an escape hatch? Can he avoid responsible behavior merely by associating himself with a group of other men for a purpose? I don't think so. The idea of splitting up your personality to behave one way in the family and another when you go out and work in a corporation—this produces catastrophe. It is a form of national suicide. There is a monstrous job of national kidding if we think there is some way to escape responsibility.

Mr. Reid: I support that view.

In this question of business deals, we can assume that people are going to be guided by conscience. If not, there will be restraints. Just as Gil Fitzhugh has pointed out, business really has no choice on this question of its place in society. It is there.

Business is not the only power center; it is one of many power centers. The businessman has been too timid about this; he is behind the parade. It is high time he recognizes the fact that just as he makes decisions on purchasing and production and marketing, he must make some decisions and take some stands and express business positions with respect to public policy.

Until he accepts the responsibility to pull up a chair at the table where these decisions are being made in public affairs, he in effect is defaulting. Labor unions do it, the educators do it, people with all kinds of interests have something to say. The businessman should have something to say too.

Mr. Berle: I wonder whether the question we're really aiming at isn't a little more complex. What Mr. Maremont said before is that a lot of things that are in the public affairs sector are beyond the competence of corporate executives. For example, telling the humanities department of a university what it ought to teach would be so far out of bounds as to be ridiculous.

When Mr. Reid talks about pulling up a chair at the table and being heard, I believe he has in mind issues that are within the competence of businessmen.

If there is anything you do not want, it is setting up the business community as a kind of arbitrator of social aesthetics and other values of life which they don't know any more about than anyone else. Their individual opinions on these matters are worth no more, just because they are executives or presidents of big companies, than those of any other employee.

This is the point I would want to stress by way of clarification: Business has the duty to participate in those matters in which its experience and knowledge give it some expertise and where the issues have a direct impact on the work of the company. But business should try to separate itself from other types of issues or it will find itself monkeying with affairs that it doesn't know anything about—where it ought to keep off the grass.

Chairman Palmer: One of the more controversial forms that business involvement in public affairs has taken is its activities regarding politics. Some companies have encouraged political responsiveness on the part of their individual employees and participation in the political parties of their individual choice.

The business community has noted the Ford Motor Company's work, for example, in the field of government. Tom Reid's title reflects his responsibility for civic and governmental affairs.

In this work, Tom, where do you start and where do you end?

Mr. Reid: In our view, the corporation should express itself on those public issues which, in general management's opinion, affect its business.

The corporation should not bring pressure or inject itself into matters which affect primarily the lives of people, but which do not directly affect the corporation.

The corporation has no business in politics. It should take no stands for or against any parties or any candidates as a corporation. But it does have an obligation and a responsibility to encourage its employees as private citizens to become interested in the subject of government and public affairs.

In addition, we solicit employees once a year to make contributions to the political party of their choice in order to help finance the high cost of political campaigns.

This latter practice is simply an extension of the accepted form of encouraging participation in the charitable campaigns run in every city and village of this country. The Community Chest and the United Foundations, for example, couldn't raise the money they need for health and welfare unless the corporation contributed money, and also unless they solicited employee contributions to these fund drives through the corporate mechanism.

It is incumbent on us to give the same encouragement to employees' participation in the shaping of governmental policies as we have to their participation in charitable activities. In so doing, we are trying to get across a very simple but fundamental idea: there is nothing sordid or dirty about government, or politics, or participation in them.

Mr. Berle: If I may comment, the program seems a little restricted in its objectives. When you see private or governmental conditions emerging which will affect the state of business or of the corporation itself, your economic departments or analysts should be mobilized to start work on solutions. There is some duty in a corporation to foresee the difficulties before they emerge, and take an active part in drafting remedies.

Mr. Palmer: Moving on to another type of specific activity, over a long period of time the Metropolitan Life Insurance Company has taken a great interest in the health of our citizenry. Gil Fitzhugh, has this been done as an expression of social responsibility or have you done it with the thought that better health means lower mortality, which means higher dividends to your policyholders?

Mr. Fitzhugh: I don't think Metropolitan's welfare program was started just for missionary reasons or because it was a wonderful thing to do. I don't think you can really distinguish between what is done for public relations reasons, what is done for the profitability of your company, or what is done in the public interest. They are all the same. Certainly, in our company, they are.

When we started our demonstration in Framingham, Massachusetts, tuberculosis was one of the principal causes of death. Through our community demonstrations, we helped reduce tubercular death rates in a few years to a fraction of what they had been.

In the Province of Quebec in Canada, infant mortality was very high. Again with a community demonstration we showed that education, proper sanitation, proper care of the mother during pregnancy, and proper clinics could reduce infant death rates very markedly. That idea spread.

Then we started a nursing service. The bulk of our policyholders were blue-collar workers who had nobody to come in and take care of them when they were sick. That service has been taken over by various voluntary nursing associations.

Our objective in this effort is to close the gap between the development of new medical concepts that help reduce mortality and the public's knowledge and acceptance of them. We have distributed millions of booklets on overweight and heart care to name just a couple.

What is our motive? It is a mixed motive. We probably would be wrong if we did this purely out of the goodness of our hearts.

We have people in our own company saying we shouldn't be spending this money, it is a waste of money. It may look like that to some, but most of us think that it is a good investment. It is a social concept, but we think it helps the return to our policyholders; it helps Metropolitan in the community; it helps us write more business. It is a mixture of all these things. Now, are we wrong?

Mr. Maremont: If you were president of the United States Steel Corporation rather than the Metropolitan Life Insurance Company, would you be equally enthusiastic about a program of health and a reduction of mortality?

Mr. Fitzhugh: You espouse that we should stick to our knitting, and I agree that we should. But the broadness of the concept of what your knitting is depends upon your company. I think the health of our policyholders is part of our knitting. It may not be in the case of the United States Steel Company. But United States Steel or any other company does other things which are not narrowly involved in making more money but still do help make more money for the company. Each has its public works, so to speak, in areas for which there is some reason or rationale in terms of the company's objectives.

Floor Question: Back in history, what a corporation chose to do or chose not to do by way of expressing its social responsibility reflected the owner-manager. It was his company. Now, our giant corporations are in the hands of hired management who may have little ownership stake. What bearing does this change in accountability play? What can we do to satisfy hundreds of thousands of shareholders or policyholders that our public affairs activities are a reasonable or proper use of corporate funds?

Mr. Reid: As corporations get more and more into public affairs matters and governmental and legislative issues, it is incumbent upon them to develop the right kind of organizational mechanism to make sure the positions they take are appropriately researched, that the decisions are sound, and that when they are made public they are not done so lightly. With that in mind, we have taken the point of view that public affairs issues are to be dealt with in the same way that we make other major decisions in management.

Floor Question: We sort of passed the fair employment practice issue along as one that didn't affect profits. I come from a part of the country where it does affect profits.

Personally, I happen to believe that it is an abomination to discriminate against any individual or group because of descent or birth. But this is not a unanimous view. The issue I am trying to get at is this. First, any question, no matter how technical it may seem to be initially, if pressed far enough, ultimately becomes a moral question. Secondly, every moral question ultimately becomes an effective force on profits. I question whether there is any area of management activity where a fully developed scale of moral values is not needed.

Mr. Miller: I would like to enthusiastically associate myself with the tenor of those remarks. The idea that there is some place where principles of right action or good behavior are to be locked out fascinates me. This is a great thing if we can pull it off. But this is about like saying that there is some area in which the law of gravity does not apply or where two and two may equal five.

The tenor of all the major religions of the world, and of all of the great philosophers is that the rules of behavior are about as inexorable as the laws of mathematics or physics. You violate them at your peril. I would strongly support the idea, especially in these times, that the most critical and perplexing problems in any association of human beings—whether for profit or anything else—are in essence truly moral problems.

Chairman Palmer: It would be very difficult to summarize adequately the points you gentlemen have made. From what you have said, there are evidently no exact perimeters to corporate social responsibility. Social responsibility involves economic well-being of individuals, business, and the nation. Social responsibility entails political responsiveness and participation. Social responsibility includes broad social concerns such as health, charity, culture, and morality.

The consensus seems to be that to assure continuing profitable production of goods and services under the free enterprise system, the business community has the responsibility to nurture and enhance this environment by fulfilling to the greatest possible extent the role of good company citizenship. It has this role, not because it asked for it, but because it can't escape it. As several of you have stressed: "It is there."

XI

Business Policy and Philosophy

Both Sides Benefit

Gardner University is a privately endowed institution located in the Midwestern United States, with a full-time, coeducational student enrollment in excess of 10,000. At present the University is in the midst of a vigorous program to solicit funds and pledges for future growth.

Like many universities, Gardner indulges in the practice of storing all material despite its age or usefulness. Years later, when there is no longer any space for storage, the decision is made to sell or scrap these items for the best possible price. At Gardner this was the task of Samuel Jones, the University Business Manager. After carefully scrutinizing the material, Jones decided that certain items were useless and should be discarded. The remainder he assembled into one huge pile. He then called three used-equipment dealers, inviting them to inspect and bid on these materials. William Kearns of the Kearns Equipment Salvage Company was usually the high bidder.

In the course of conversation one day, Kearns said to Jones, "Why, you're sitting on a gold mine, and you don't realize it. Since Gardner is a nonprofit institution, it can accept donations of pieces of equipment from manufacturing concerns in this area. The rapid advancement in technology and production has resulted in inflated

311

book values on manufacturers' equipment; in reality, the equipment
is worth much less and sometimes nothing at all. The corporate tax
structure makes it beneficial for the manufacturing concerns to do-
nate this equipment to the University. The company can then write
the equipment off at its appraisal value. You, in turn, could sell it
for whatever it is worth. Both sides would benefit."

Kearns went on to state that if Gardner University would be
interested in doing this, he would make the necessary arrangements
to have Jones meet with some company executives who were looking
for a recipient of their donated equipment. They felt that these donations not only made for tax benefits but fostered good will and a
sound corporate image. Kearns had read a newspaper article which
estimated that such gifts accounted for $40 million of the $250 million that corporations parcelled out in one year to institutions of
higher learning.

Jones knew from other sources the story of the handsome, four-
teen-year-old Benton Aircraft plant. Benton had been stuck with a
large and relatively new plant in the Midwest when it decided to
move its operations to the West Coast. Other companies could have
used the plant, but refused to pay the price demanded by Benton.
After the plant had been idle and vacant for two years, it was given
to a local college. Benton wrote off the gift at the lowest price they
would have been willing to accept from a business concern. This
covered the undepreciated part of the initial cost of the plant.

The college which had received the gift sold the property within
a short time and applied the money to construction of a needed addition to its student union building. The addition was named Benton
Annex. While the college's selling price was much lower than the
amount the company had written off its books, the proceeds from
the sale still amounted to over one million dollars.

Jones, after receiving this information, consulted with Orson
Smith, the Director of Corporate Donations for the University.
Smith felt that this idea was completely acceptable as long as it was
clearly understood that these donations would in no way affect the
present amount of money pledged to the University by the corporations. He further commented that this type of program was being
conducted on a large scale in another Midwestern university with
very successful results.

Jones had a decision to make. Should he encourage or reject a program designed to seek out donations of equipment for subsequent resale by the University? He estimated that acceptance of this program would result in an income in excess of $60,000 annually for the University, without adversely affecting the present endowment program.

Enough Said?

John Paul Jones is a systems manager responsible to the treasurer of the B & L Manufacturing Company, which employs more than 3000 people. Jones was hired two years ago because of his experience, knowledge, and success in installing automated management information systems utilizing large computers.

Jones and his staff have worked diligently to prepare a comprehensive study of total company operations and have come up with a five-year plan for an online computer information system. Pilot operations have been attempted and appear to be most successful. Benefits to be achieved after installation of the complete system are expected to allow the company to remain competitive.

Although some reluctance has been encountered because of initial expenditures, top management approval has been obtained for the entire project. Recently, management has been pressuring Jones for personnel reduction statistics. Originally he received approval for the entire project based upon ability to reduce inventory and the time required to fill orders. He has known that substantial reductions of salaried office personnel can eventually take place. He has attempted to avoid basing a project of this scope only on clerical reductions because, during the critical period of conversion, more clerical personnel may actually be needed for audit and parallel operations.

314

Word of possible personnel cuts has filtered throughout the office and plant. As a result, Jones and his staff find themselves receiving less and less cooperation from operating personnel. Whereas at one time most personnel had enthusiastically cooperated with the pilot operations, Jones now finds passive resistance and a negative attitude. He has become greatly concerned because several deadlines have not been met, and the entire project is approximately two months behind schedule. Some fairly extensive and expensive computer systems are due for delivery in the near future. Rumors of starting an office union have been heard. Morale, not only of Jones' staff, but also of the operating personnel with whom the staff works, has hit an all-time low. Jones has consistently recommended that the President of B & L Mfg. Co. issue a policy statement indicating objectives and goals for the complete project. Although Jones did not base his own planning merely on reductions of personnel, he has evidence to predict that over 50 percent of personnel reductions can ultimately be effectively accounted for through retirement, pregnancies, and normal attrition. He, together with the industrial relations manager, has submitted a program detailing how such reductions can take place.

At a recent meeting, Jones was told he must meet the deadlines originally established. He countered with the following statements. The system as planned was well suited for company operations and would produce the greatest benefits and savings over the long haul for B & L Mfg. Co. This was sufficiently demonstrated in the pilot models. He also insisted that unless some statement was issued by top management with respect to this project, morale problems would continue to exist and that the entire project would be in jeopardy. Also, he emphasized his fear that key operating personnel would leave of their own accord thinking their jobs were being threatened, when in fact they were sorely needed. He concluded by mentioning that members of his staff were thinking seriously of leaving because of the frustration encountered in not being able to work with the operating people.

Jones was told by the president that "the company always took care of its own and would continue such a policy in the future." The president stated that he would discuss the matter with the board and advise Jones of the decision.

Beer and Stumbling Blocks

In September, 1966 W. R. Grace & Company purchased controlling interest in the Miller Brewing Company from Mrs. Lorraine John Mulberger. Mrs. Mulberger, a granddaughter of the founder of the Miller Brewing Company, sold 53 percent of the Miller Stock for $36 million. She said that religious motivation prompted her to sell the stock.

The Miller Brewing Company is one of the giants of the United States brewing industry. Producers of Miller High Life and Gettleman beers, the company sold 3,667,000 barrels of beer and ale in 1965. Frederick A. Miller founded the company in 1855, and the Miller family has always had large stock holdings.

Mrs. Mulberger is the daughter of Mrs. Elise Miller John, president of the company from 1938 to 1946. Mrs. Mulberger, 52, has been actively engaged in company affairs, having at various times held the posts of vice president, treasurer, director, and honorary chairman of the board of directors.

On September 21, 1966 the *Milwaukee Sentinel*[1] gave this account of an interview:

Mrs. Mulberger, of Oconomowoc Lake, told a reporter that she realized that 'the brewery was not the will of God for me.' She said that she

[1] Used by permission.

put the matter 'in His hands' and that she felt that the sale was 'the will of God.' . . .

Born a Roman Catholic, Mrs. Mulberger said she attends the Waukesha Bible Church of which the Reverend William Pederson is pastor. Mrs. Mulberger said the religious motivation that prompted her to sell her interest in the brewery began about five years ago. . . .

Mrs. Mulberger said she did not want to 'put a stumbling block' in the way of others, and quoted Romans 14:13: 'Let us not therefore judge one another any more; but judge this rather, that no man put a stumbling block or an occasion to fall in his brother's way.' 'That's the reason I sold,' she said.

Pastor Pederson said that Mrs. Mulberger had advised him of 'the step she was taking.' The pastor said there was nothing in the church constitution against drinking. He said that Mrs. Mulberger made her decision 'based upon her understandings of the teachings of the Scriptures and her personal convictions.' Pastor Pederson said that Mrs. Mulberger has been attending his church for five years, but has not joined. . . . Formed fifteen years ago, the Waukesha Bible church is an independent church in association with the Independent Fundamental Churches of America, a fellowship of 1,200 churches.

In the October, 1966 issue of the *Brewers Digest*,[2] monthly publication of the brewing industry, the editor and publisher, Bernard O. Erf, editorialized:

Assuming that the temptation of which Mrs. Mulberger was talking was beer, the brewing industry could be inclined to react with disgust to Mrs. Mulberger's seeming disdain of a product from which she has benefited in the amount of 36 million dollars in stock sale alone. Inclined as the brewing industry is—and as are many other industries—to push 'under the rug' the seeming negatives with which it is confronted and to be content to settle for mere plausibilities, we believe the industry should take the time to understand Mrs. Mulberger's remarks and to benefit from them.

Obviously, no one can fully understand another person's motivations and particularly this is true with regard to another's religious motivations. While there is a meaningful sense in which a person's relation with God is a private affair, this does not mean that religion or one's relation with God is a merely subjective matter, devoid of the application of intellectual analysis and the application of rational principles. Nor does it mean that the establishment of one's relation with God is a once and for all

2 Used by permission.

time matter. Rather, as broadened experience and greater intellectual understanding are brought to bear on the relation, we should expect a constant refinement of the relation. This implies that changes over time in one's religious outlook will occur and that our worldly involvements will change in varying degrees in accordance with that changing religious outlook. We presume that something of this sort has occurred for Mrs. Mulberger who was originally of one Christian denomination and is now influenced by another. We wish her well in her religious 'journey'—certainly it is the most important of human undertakings—and we commend her for her humility. In saying that 'the brewery was not the will of God *for me*' (emphasis added), she does nothing to lend comfort to the Prohibitionists, *to whom* we would commend a similar humility. . . .

For Mrs. Mulberger's motivations, to the extent that we understand them, we have only respect, but some further clarification is in order relative to Romans 14:13. Indeed, the next passage (Romans 14:14) says 'I know and am persuaded in the Lord Jesus that nothing is unclean in itself; but it is unclean for anyone who thinks it unclean.' It should be understood at the outset, then, that anything that can be improperly used is a potential 'stumbling block' on the road to personal fulfillment or salvation. This is true of beer, but it is equally true of money, of automobiles, of food, of 'status,' of one's home and the like. More importantly, this is true—if somewhat more subtly—of ideas, persuasive contentions, emotional appeals and religious convictions. The seriousness of this is compounded by the fact that excessive indulgence with regard to any one of these can lead to a condition wherein the individual loses balance and perspective. In short, one can become 'hooked' on automobiles, on money, on particular ideas, on status, on a religious conviction, etc., etc. . . .

It has not been infrequent that we have found people within the brewing and allied industries (usually at the executive level) to have quasi guilty consciences about their involvement in the brewing industry. We have heard this attributed to the social stigma of prohibition that the industry suffered many years ago, but where relevant at all we think it to be an excuse rather than a cause. We think the cause is otherwise and we expressed it this way in an article 'Responsibility and the Brewing Industry' in the April, 1965, issue of this magazine. We said then in part:

> '. . . society has failed and is failing to gain all of the benefit that it
> can and should from beer and the brewing industry because too many
> members of the industry, and too many of the most influential members at that,
>
> (1) fail to have developed a clear and comprehensive idea of the role
>   of beer in a meaningful human life, and
> (2) fail to have reflectively determined for themselves the nature, ex-

tent and limitation of the industry's responsibility relative to the use of its product.'

'A result has been that beer has too often been identified with the superficialities of life, and the *breadth* of the potential market for beer has been consequently restricted—not because of legal restrictions, but because of the industry's own self-imposed roadblock: the failure to relate the product to the very essence of meaningful human life, or, if you will, the failure to afford beer cultural credence.'

To be sure, the individual self-examination suggested herein may lose for the industry some capable talent (just as we have already failed on occasion to attract capable talent as a result of our often negative self-image with its resultant extremes of assertive or submissive defensiveness), but the sense of moral—as distinct from legal—justification that we would achieve for our product, our industry and our own involvement in the industry would well be worth such loss.

J. W. Stern & Son, Incorporated*

As of May, 1956 Gilbert Stern, President and General Manager of J. W. Stern & Son, Inc., plumbing contractors, was convinced that the firm was losing money. He believed that the loss was largely a function of the firm's objectives and method of operation.

J. W. Stern & Son, located in a large midwestern city, was a family-owned corporation controlled by J. W. Stern, who had begun to taper off his part in actual operations. The general management function was devolving on his son, Gilbert, a man in his late thirties. A younger son, Morris, was reaching a level of experience which would enable him to take over field supervision of the plumbers occasionally employed by the firm. Both sons were licensed journeymen plumbers but an attack of poliomyelitis had forced Gilbert to give up working in the field.

J. W. Stern had emigrated from Russia at the age of 16, settling in the city in 1901. Seeking a trade, he had become an apprentice plumber and secured his journeyman license in 1908. Two years later, he accepted an offer from his employer to become a partner by contributing $250 in cash, equal to the value of the firm's assets at that time.

The partners developed a reputation for high-quality work and were able to draw living expenses and still divide substantial profits every year. During the early part of World War I, however, they agreed to dissolve the partnership. Stern, taking one-half of the cash, tools, materials, and other assets, set up his own business as a licensed master plumber, engaged principally in "jobbing" work, i.e., repair or maintenance work on old plumbing.

By 1928, Stern had built up a volume of more than $100,000 per year, employing 25 plumbers, and had moved out of the field of jobbing into contracting on new installations. During this period he did all of his own office work, acted as his own field superintendent, did some of the actual work as a Master Plumber, and set up his own layouts and specifications as needed.

The depression years and the decrease in new building hit the business hard, with an estimated loss of over $100,000 in the period from 1929 through 1931. Stern attempted to carry out all his contracts in full even though the chances were poor that the client would be able to make full payment. Some completed work was never paid for. In spite of his losses, however, Stern refused to take refuge in bankruptcy, and, over the next few years, succeeded in paying off all debts in full. Throughout his career, he has never been refused any desired amount of credit by any of his suppliers.

Losses and lack of capital resulting from the depression made it difficult to rebuild the firm. However, by cutting costs to the limit, working very long hours, and doing only the highest-quality work, Stern was able to recover to a considerable extent. By the beginning of World War II, he had developed a volume which returned a comfortable income.

The years following World War II saw a basic change in plumbing contracting. Whereas Stern had formerly been able to estimate jobs with great rapidity due to their similarity, it was now necessary to work largely from architect's drawings and engineering specifications. This required analysis of plans to determine the number and size required of each piece of piping, each fitting, and each fixture to complete the job, and determination of the contractor's cost for this material. It was then necessary to estimate the amount and cost of labor required to install all of the materials plus the cost of testing to be sure specifications were met (see Table 3 for a partial estimation sheet).

When his illness forced Gilbert out of field work, he took over the duties of estimator. As more complex jobs came up, it sometimes required three days to a week of paper work to estimate a $25,000 job in order to bid on it. Although J. W. Stern realized the necessity of this, he still tended to resent the idea of what seemed to him to be "nonproductive" work. He also felt that such office fixtures as filing cabinets were unnecessary. He consented to purchase an adding machine only after a fatigue-induced error of $1,000 was discovered in an estimate.

In addition, the late 1940's and early 1950's saw a proliferation of small plumbing firms consisting of nonunion partnerships who took over many of the smaller jobs at greatly reduced prices. Development of mass building operations by general contractors sharpened competition among the larger plumbing firms. The net result was a decline in gross margins for all small and medium-size firms.

"This puts us in a real bind," Gilbert Stern pointed out. "You'd think these men would have more sense than to cut their own throats. I suppose some of them don't know their real costs well enough for accurate estimating. Then, too, some of them are real 'dogs' who bid on first-class work and expect to do the poorest job they can get away with. But the ethical firms still have to meet those bids, if they want the jobs."

According to Gilbert, plumbing firms fall into five general categories:

1. The very large contractor, often owned or directed by expert managers who know nothing of plumbing work. They have staffs of engineers and operate in the area of consulting, engineering, and contracting on a national or international scale. Experimental and cost-plus jobs are common. Few of these firms do less than a million dollars a year with some running into tens of millions.

2. Highly selective companies doing a volume of around one million dollars yearly on a bid basis. Usually well-managed and with plenty of capital, they seek contracts for hospitals, laboratories,

skyscrapers, large industrial plants and similar projects. Many of them engage in high-grade jobbing or maintenance work on a contract basis. Commonly, they have staff engineers for their own work.

3. A group of firms in the range of $250,000-$500,000 per year, with one or two well above that figure. These companies do not offer engineering service and work from plans or specifications. Contracts in the $25,000-$50,000 range are the standard for these firms and very keen competition exists for the plumbing in single stores, small plants, government installations, blocks of residential housing, and similar projects. Practically all the volume of such firms is done within a single metropolitan area.

4. A group classified by Gilbert as "robber" or "dog" firms using legal but unethical methods. Usually small in size, they bid on any kind of piping or sheet-metal work, including heating, plumbing, sewers, and other relatively small jobs. Using nonunion workers, they operate in "hit-and-run" fashion, trying only to be sure that the work will hold for the standard one-year guarantee period. It is this group which does most damage to reputable firms by low bids which leave practically no margin on first-class work.

5. The local or neighborhood plumber, usually skilled in heating, plumbing, and air conditioning, who rarely works on a contract basis for other than service contracts. About the only member of the plumbing fraternity who has contact with the ultimate user, he depends heavily on fast-service jobbing, with occasional new construction in dwellings or small buildings. Commonly, he operates from a retail store carrying fixtures and appliances. His location is of great importance and is usually in a shopping center in metropolitan areas.

"All of these groups differ widely in personality of the ownership or management people, the tools and equipment they use, their operating methods, and the type of work they look for," said Gilbert Stern. "We don't feel that the first and fifth of these categories offer us any competition. We're not interested in the little guy's jobs, and we couldn't possibly swing the kind of contract the big firms handle. We'd like to move into the second group because their jobs really pay off but we don't have the capital for it.

"At the moment, we're trying to straddle the third group, although it offers the keenest competition. One of our problems in moving into it is capital (see Tables 1 and 2). We try to operate on an average gross margin of around ten percent, but we run into the 'fifteen percent rule.' In this business, fifteen percent of a contract price is withheld for 45 to 90 days after the job is completed to see whether the work is satisfactory. With high volume, that wouldn't be so bad because we'd have a string of withheld payments coming in all the time. At our volume, it's a real headache.

"Sometimes, too, we get a call from a general contractor who finds a low bidder was a 'dog' that he doesn't want on his job," Gilbert added. "He offers us the job because of our reputation, but only if we meet the other price. We call it shopping. It's all very nice that people have so much confidence in us, but it sure doesn't do much for our profit ratio.

"We've got a mighty good reputation in the city and the surrounding area," said J. W. Stern, "principally because I've always insisted that we must do a first-class job regardless of the price. The trouble is that nowadays most people don't know a good job of plumbing when they see it, and a lot of those who do know just don't care. Still, there are some general contractors who want a good job. We often get calls asking us to bid on a particular job that we'd like to do, and we have to refuse it because Gilbert doesn't have the time to estimate it. As he gets more experience, I'm hoping to see him fast enough to estimate a job in half the time he needs now. That way, we can bid on twice as many jobs and get our volume up to carry this overhead."

"As far as I can see right now, we're on the ragged edge," Gilbert summarized. "We've got to establish ourselves firmly in that third category I mentioned, or we're going to wind up in the 'dog' class. To move up, we've got to do our estimating faster, bid on more jobs, and give better and faster service. That means increasing our overhead. We've got to have more capital to carry the overhead and, on a ten percent gross, capital doesn't grow on trees. As it stands now, we're losing money every month. We're too big to compete with the little outfits and too little to compete with the big ones. I'm beginning to wonder, seriously, if our only solution isn't to drop into the 'dog' class deliberately and start cutting every corner we can. With the pride we've always had in our work and our reputation, I'm not sure we'll be able to live with ourselves but, in a cutthroat business like this, what the hell can you do?"

Table 1

J. W. STERN & SON, INC.

Comparative Balance Sheets for Fiscal Years
Ending June 30, 1953–1955

ASSETS	*1953*	*1954*	*1955*
Current assets:			
Cash in bank	$ 5,235.63	$10,416.52	$ 5,761.04
Accounts receivable	7,420.24	4,203.46	10,961.76
Inventories	1,717.59	1,689.55	2,293.39
Bond deposits		201.00	
Total current assets	$14,373.46	$16,518.53	$19,016.19
Fixed assets:			
Land	$ 1,000.00	$ 1,000.00	$ 1,000.00
Building	5,000.00	5,000.00	5,000.00
Trucks and equipment	4,427.55	4,761.86	4,761.86
Furniture and fixtures	330.00	330.00	330.00
Total fixed assets	$10,757.55	$11,091.86	$11,091.86
TOTAL ASSETS	$25,131.01	$27,610.39	$30,108.05
LIABILITIES AND NET WORTH			
Current liabilities:			
Accounts payable	$ 1,685.56	$ 1,825.93	$ 5,885.28
Accrued payroll taxes	254.38	266.68	331.78
Accrued taxes (other)	157.83		
*Loans from offiers	14,844.44	16,704.34	15,128.64
Total current liabilities	$16,942.21	$18,796.95	$21,345.70
Capital and net worth:			
Reserve for depreciation	$ 2,395.86	$ 3,004.22	$ 4,239.58
Capital stock (common)	5,000.00	5,000.00	5,000.00
Earned surplus	792.94	809.22	477.23(d)
Total capital and net worth	$ 8,188.80	$ 8,813.44	$ 8,762.35
TOTAL LIABILITIES AND NET WORTH	$25,131.01	$27,610.39	$30,108.05

* Consists principally of unpaid officers' salaries and loans made from personal funds of Mr. Stern.

(d) Deficit.

Note: *All figures contained in this statement have been altered by introduction of a common factor.*

Table 2

J. W. STERN & SON, INC.

Comparative Profit and Loss Statements for Fiscal Years
Ending June 30, 1953–1955

	1953	1954	1955
Total Sales Billed	$ 70,062.68	52,676.10	52,367.15
Cost of Sales Billed	30,663.90	20,246.49	20,949.32
Gross Profit on Operations	39,398.79	32,429.61	31,417.83

OPERATING EXPENSES

	1953	1954	1955
Salaries and Wages	31,106.02	25,046.78	21,641.78
Truck Expense	1,759.75	1,554.99	1,070.74
Permits	187.39	65.45	129.92
Rentals	223.17	99.00	132.00
Advertising		22.00	55.00
Insurance	1,162.31	1,107.05	1,044.78
Telephone and Telegraph	601.37	783.62	850.08
Union Dues & Health Fund	900.20	902.23	1,515.60
Sub-Contract Payments	172.08		2,521.20
Payroll Taxes	474.33	410.26	599.43
Other Taxes	389.70	382.88	339.71
Legal and Audit Expense	330.00	181.50	247.50
Office Expense (General)	132.88	266.42	365.24
Heat and Light	370.93	294.50	400.44
Depreciation Expense			
Trucks and Tools	885.50	885.50	952.36
Building	250.00	250.00	250.00
Furniture & Fixtures	33.00	33.00	33.00
Total Operating Expenses	39,068.65	32,285.18	32,159.78
Net Profit on Operations	230.14	144.43	741.95(d)
Interest Expense	150.00	128.15	544.50
NET PROFIT FOR PERIOD	$ 80.14	16.28	1,286.45(d)

(d) Deficit

Note: *All figures contained in this statement have been altered by introduction of a common factor.*

Table 3

J. W. STERN & SON, INC.

*Job Estimate–Master Sheet

No.	Item	Page Ref.	Our Cost
1.	Fixtures	2	4,224.00
2.	Soil Pipe (Rainwater-1205; Sanitary-2110.	4	3,315.00
3.	Water Pipe	6	2,000.00
4.	Hangers, sleeves	Est.	275.00
5.	Insulation (Bid by Wilmuth Bros.)	–	1,530.00
6.	Staging—None needed—	Est.	—.—
7.	Permit	2	83.00
8.	Hot Water Tank, delivered w/saddles (205 gal)	Bid	1,128.00
9.	Hot Water Tank trim	Est.	35.00
10.	Street Water Conn.—to prop. line only	8	750.00
11.	Extend Wat. Serv. to Bldg. w/hydrant	8	1,895.00
12.	Street Gas Conn. & ext. into bldg.	8	150.00
13.	Extend Gas Serv. to Bldg. (included Item 12)	–	—.—
14.	Interior Gas Piping	Est.	50.00
15.	Floor Drains (11 @ $38.00) (including labor)	7	418.00
16.	8″ vent flashings (13 @ $4.00)	Est.	52.00
17.	Paint unfin. surf. of enam. fixt. (incl. in labor)		—.—
18.	Valve tags and frames	Est.	10.00
19.	Gas Hot Water Heater, delivered	Bid	633.00
20.	Flue piping for heater	Est.	15.00
21.	Hot Water Circl. Pump & acquastat	Est.	75.00
22.	Sump pump	Bid	190.00
23.	Thermostatic Mixing Valve	Bid	231.00
24.	Wall Hydrants (4 @ $18.25)	Est.	73.00
25.	Pressure reduction valve	3	95.00
26.	Hot Water Tank Stand	Est.	30.00
27.	Access Panels (for conductors) (9 @ $5.00)	Est.	45.00
28.	Excavation for water line	Bid	550.00

Materials and sub-contract work	$17,852.00
Labor to install and test	7,750.00
Travel	500.00
Payroll Tax	450.00
Total cost	$26,552.00
Plus 10% overhead charge	2,655.00
Total Estimate	$29,207.00
Actual Figure Quoted on Bid	$28,900.00

* This exhibit shows the master sheet and one sub-sheet of an 8-page estimate.

NOTE: *"Bid" in the column headed "Page Ref." indicates a bid by a supplier to furnish the item at the price noted.*

Table 3 (continued)

J. W. STERN & SON, INC.

SUB-SHEET # 2   PROJECT

ESTIMATE FOR   Fixtures (Dalton-Ingersoll)

Item	No. Req.	Cost Each	Total Cost
Floor Toilet	2	$ 46.50	$ 93.00
Floor Toilet (w/9500 seat)	4	48.00	192.00
Lavatories	7	39.60	277.20
Lavatory w/wrist fitting	1	52.65	52.65
Bradley Fountain (washing)	4	89.25	357.00
Urinal	8	64.00	512.00
Slop Sink—enameled	4	76.00	304.00
Drinking Fountain	1	63.00	63.00
Classroom sink	14	54.25	759.50
Slop Sink—v.c.	1	91.00	91.00
Wall Toilet (blow-out)	7	97.00	679.00
Wall Toilet (siphon)	5	103.00	515.00
Stainless Sink	1	55.00	55.00
Electric Cooler	1	273.75	273.75

Total Fixture Cost $4,224.10

ESTIMATE FOR   Permit

    60 fixtures @ $1.00 . . . . $60.00
    11 Floor Drains @ $1.00 . . . . . .   11.00
    10 Roof Drains @ $1.00 . . . . . .   10.00
    H.W. Tank & Htr. 2.00

        Total Permit Cost $83.00

Does the End Justify
the Means?

A group of 100 businessmen were asked to comment on the following paragraph:

The first responsibility of a businessman is to keep his business solvent, for if his business is bankrupt it will no longer provide a living for himself and jobs for others. Therefore, it is ethical for a businessman, in time of financial distress or severe competition, to make decisions directly opposed to those which his conscience dictates. Do you agree or disagree?[1]

Eleven agreed, 87 disagreed, and two declined to answer. Here are some of their ideas.

"It's better to be financially bankrupt than to be ethically bankrupt."

"Either a guy has ethics or he hasn't. If he agrees with that statement, he hasn't got ethics in my opinion."

"I disagree. The businessman's first responsibility is to himself, to keep his principles unblemished. That's a hell of a lot more important than staying solvent."

[1] The statement is a paraphrase of a paragraph in *Ethics in a Business Society* by Marquis Childs and Douglass Cater (New York, Harper & Row, Mentor Book, 1954), p. 173.

"If you agree with that statement, you make solvency the norm of conduct and I see no sense in that."

"If this statement is so, we are a lost society."

Some of the men asked for an example of conduct like that described on the card. Each was told a true story of small merchandising company whose top management acted on the belief that staying in business justified, temporarily at least, lying to customers about merchandise and billing a supplier for advertising that was never done. The reaction of most who heard the story was unfavorable to the small company's management:

"That's like taking the first pipeful of opium."

"Are they still in business?"

"They are inherently bad; they won't change."

"To do something like that would open the door to panic. The management certainly wouldn't stop at one or two unethical actions."

Some businessmen rejected the statement for economic reasons:

"If this man cannot make money by operating a legitimate business, then there is either no market for his product or he is a poor manager. If this is true, regardless of his short-run decisions, he will go broke sooner or later."

"Unethical behavior won't save such a man. His troubles are usually long range. Fellows like that are either in the wrong business or they don't know how to run a business."

"A company that reaches a crisis like this probably should not be in business. If it reaches this stage, the operation is probably not economical and should be ended. Such a company is not contributing to the economy. By making solvency the norm, inefficient companies would go on and on, and that's no good."

The minority who agreed with the statement gave these reasons:

"In a small degree, decisions such as these are necessary to keep the business going. This necessity to compromise whittles away at your ideals."

"I would feel that I must keep the business going and this would perhaps justify some of my unethical actions."

"You have got to keep your business solvent. This is your first responsibility. If you are soft and a patsy, you deserve to go broke."

"Conscience is the policeman of ethical principles, but you do not always have to follow your conscience. . . . If you want to be a success, you have to give up some of your ethics."

Controversy, Profits, and Policy*

The Ajax Soap Company is one of three sponsors of a half hour TV dramatic series entitled, "The Lawmakers." Axel Adams, the advertising director of Ajax Soap, has just been informed by the network of a show planned for next month which deals with a doctor who crusades for legalized abortion. The show has already been filmed by the syndicating agency and the network time has been cleared.

Adams does not feel that his company should enter into the question of program content, and ordinarily he does not concern himself with this matter. But he has learned that the Pepper Company, one of the other sponsors, has flatly refused to be associated with the show because of the subject matter and has withdrawn its sponsorship for that week. So Adams has approached Pepper's senior vice-president in order to be sure of his ground on a possibly controversial issue. Adams explained the issues involved. Then the vice-president said:

"We don't supervise the networks or tell them how to do their

* With the permission of the author, William C. McInnes, S.J., Fairfield University; Business Ethics Case Material.

business. But we do have a moral obligation to turn down anything which might embarrass our viewers. Complaints in such cases rarely get to the networks; the advertiser bears the brunt of such reaction when it comes.

"This is an extreme case. Abortion has been covered on the air before, but in each case the abortionist was a 'heavy.' In the present drama he is a sympathetic character, who makes no bones about crusading for legalized abortion. Abortion is illegal in every state, and it's against a lot of religious beliefs. We just don't think this is the kind of drama to be introduced into the living room for the entire family in the early evening when teenagers as well as adults may be there.

"This show was turned down in script form, but shooting already had started, and the network and producer asked us to hold off and take a look at the finished product. But that didn't change our minds.

"Pulling out of sponsorship of this one program doesn't affect our over-all attitude toward the series, which we think is terrific.

"But," concluded the senior vice-president, "I think this belongs solely in your hands. You make the decision in the way that you think best."

Saga of Ships*†

HOW UNION OIL DIRECTOR HELPED
FAMILY, AIDES TO PROFIT ON TANKERS

The building of a fortune of nearly $1 million from
a $20,000 investment would make a dramatic story under any cir-
cumstances, but this is especially true when the tale includes such
ingredients as these:

An oil company director who arranges for his wife and son to
profit from personal transactions with the company. Ocean-going
tankers equipped with swimming pools. A Liberian company. The
Secretary of the Treasury. A rebuke from the Securities and Exchange Commission. And top executives of the Wall Street investment banking house of Dillon, Read & Co., Inc.

The profitable $20,000 investment was arranged by Dillon Read

* This case was prepared by Professor George Albert Smith of Harvard University Graduate School of Business Administration, as the basis for class discussion rather than to illustrate either effective or ineffective handling of an administrative situation.
† This story was based on reporting by Ed Cony and Lee Siberman in New
York, by Louis Kohlmeier in Washington, and by Charles Stabler and Mitchell
Gordon in Los Angeles. *The Wall Street Journal,* June 13, 1961. Used by permission.

executives—not for their corporation but for a group of 27 present and past Dillon Read officials, stockholders, and their relatives. They formed a company, Barracuda Tanker Corp., to build tankers with borrowed money and charter them exclusively to Union Oil Company of California under an arrangement that would yield almost $50,000 a year profit. The owners are letting the profits accumulate; if the arrangement goes according to plan, they will take out nearly $1 million after 20 years.

Frederic Brandi, President of Dillon Read and husband and father of two of Barracuda's owners, was a director of Union Oil at the time the tanker arrangement was set up. (He left the board a month ago.) Peter Flanigan, a Dillon Read vice president and another owner of Barracuda, is also the son of a present Union Oil director, Horace Flanigan, chairman of Manufacturers Trust Company of New York.

Barracuda is one of seven companies that Dillon Read executives, their families, and charitable organizations own and operate to supply Union Oil with leasing services, which also cover buildings, pipelines, and plants. Total pre-tax profits from these companies are about $250,000 a year, or $3,750,000 after 15 years, the shortest term of any of the leases. Mr. Brandi declines to say precisely how much total capital was put up by the owners of these seven companies, but he says it was less than $300,000.

Treasury Secretary Dillon, before assuming his present Government post, was a trustee for two minors who were among the owners of Barracuda which is incorporated in Liberia—one of the nations that Treasury officials describe as "tax havens." Mr. Dillon, who was head of Dillon, Read & Co., Inc., before entering Government service in 1953, severed all connections with Barracuda when he joined the Cabinet this year. He is now trying to get Congress to restrict use of tax havens by U.S. investors.

Mr. Brandi and Reese Taylor, Union Oil chairman, assert there is nothing unusual about the Dillon Read group's arrangements and that they are in the best interests of Union Oil and were approved by the oil company's directors. Certainly there is nothing illegal about the transactions.

Still, some Union Oil stockholders, who say they are unconvinced that the arrangements are in Union Oil's best interests, have complained to the S.E.C., which has been looking into the matter.

The S.E.C. already has required that Union Oil disclose information about the transactions in an amendment to a new securities registration statement that had omitted details of these arrangements.

The registration statement was filed in connection with Union Oil's plan to sell $120 million worth of debentures, with Dillon Read as the underwriter. Mr. Brandi's resignation from the oil company's board last month was occasioned by this offering. Directors of companies subject to Federal Power Commission regulation are forbidden to participate in or profit from underwriting of the companies' securities.

A LOAN FROM METROPOLITAN

The amendment Union Oil filed with the S.E.C. says the seven companies organized by the Dillon Read group borrowed the approximately $125 million needed to build and acquire the facilities leased or chartered to Union Oil. Mr. Brandi says the funds were borrowed from three insurance companies and two banks: Metropolitan Life Insurance Co., Mutual Life Insurance Co. of New York, New York Life Insurance Co., Security-First National Bank of Los Angeles, and the Manufacturers Trust Co. of New York. In the case of Barracuda, the three tankers built for Union Oil were financed with a $51 million loan granted by Metropolitan Life to an intermediary company.

When the tankers were completed at Newport News, Va., in 1958 and 1959, Union Oil chartered them as agreed. The oil company's payments to Barracuda are designed to cover the costs of paying off the loan, including interest; to cover other expenses incurred by Barracuda, and to yield an annual pre-tax profit to Barracuda equal to about 0.1 per cent of the cost of the tankers—or nearly $50,000 a year.

The three Barracuda tankers, the San Sinera, the Torrey Canyon and the Palourde (named for oil fields of Union Oil), are up to date in every way. Each is 810 feet long, completely air-conditioned and equipped with a swimming pool. Union Oil officials say they are delighted with the chartering arrangement worked out with the Dillon Read group on these fast, efficient tankers.

And yet mutterings of dissent arise from some stockholders. A week or so ago, after receiving a visit from an antimanagement attorney, the S.E.C. sent a "deficiency letter" to Union Oil questioning whether the company in its registration statement on the debenture offering had made all the disclosures called for by S.E.C. rules concerning transactions of officers, directors, and their associates with Union Oil.

AN AMENDMENT

As a consequence, Union Oil amended its statement, disclosing a series of transactions between the Dillon Read group and Union Oil. All of them were similar to the Barracuda arrangement, and all but one were consummated during Mr. Brandi's eight years on Union Oil's board. Annual reports and proxy statements mailed to Union Oil stockholders while Mr. Brandi was on the board did not tell the details of these transactions.

The Union Oil registration statement, as amended, tells of 11 lease or charter transactions between Union and seven companies set up by the Dillon Read group. Each of the seven companies, according to the amendment, is owned by Dillon Read officers, stockholders, employees, or members of their families, "or charitable organizations founded by certain of such persons." Mr. Brandi says the charitable groups hold "about 30 per cent" of the stock of the seven companies.

These seven companies provided Union Oil with "a method of financing the construction or acquisition" of tankers, its office building in Los Angeles, two pipelines, two chemical plants and a number of service stations, all of which Union Oil has under lease or charter, instead of owning them outright, according to the new material Union filed with the S.E.C. It is not unusual these days for a company to lease or charter equipment.

The annual rentals and charter payments which the seven companies receive from Union Oil "are designed to amortize the cost of said properties, to cover interest, and to cover the expenses of and profits to" these concerns, Union Oil told the S.E.C. The total profits, before corporate income taxes, amount annually to about 0.2 per cent of the $125 million borrowed by the seven companies according to the amendment. This would total about $250,000 yearly. The leases and charters run from 15 years up to 40 years, with 20 years being the most common term.

MR. BRANDI'S DEFENSE

In his tastefully-appointed Wall Street office, Mr. Brandi defends the propriety of the transactions between the seven companies and Union Oil.

Mr. Brandi maintains there can be no question of conflict of interest, because the arrangement is such a reasonable one for Union Oil. He says, for instance, that the Barracuda charter arrangement is a better one for Union Oil than the company could obtain from others in the open market. He says Barracuda profits "are less than the going rates."

The Dillon Read executive says there is an element of risk for stockholders in Barracuda and the other companies set up by the group. He says the 0.2 percent figure in the amended registration statement is only a profit goal, and that there is no guarantee that over a long period profits will remain at that level. He says inflation could add to certain unspecified costs incurred by the seven companies.

There's nothing at all unusual about such transactions, Mr. Brandi says. Dillon Read performs such services for other oil companies, he adds. "We have a regular department doing this," he says.

Mr. Brandi says one feature of the tanker transaction is especially attractive from Union Oil's standpoint: At the end of the 20-year lease, Union will be able to buy the tankers from Barracuda for a nominal sum—something like $10,000. He says that Union would not obtain ownership of ships it chartered from other tanker owners.

The Dillon Read executive also stresses that officers and directors of the seven companies serve without pay.

PROFITS ACCUMULATE

Mr. Brandi's wife, Juliette, and son, E. Bruce, own about 12 percent of Barracuda's stock. The company pays no dividends. Since it is a foreign corporation, its profits are not subject to U.S. tax as they accumulate. At the end of 20 years, according to

Mr. Brandi, the corporation will be dissolved and the profits distributed. Under present tax laws, the profits then would be taxed at the capital gains rate, rather than at the higher ordinary income rate.

Mr. Brandi says his wife and children have an interest in all seven companies set up by the Dillon Read group, and he adds: "The arrangement works out better for my children than for me." He says that in all seven corporations each stockholder's interest in the company reflects exactly the interest he or his relatives has in Dillon Read itself.

The Dillon Read president argues that it is unfair to compare the small equity contributed by each of the Barracuda stockholders with the profits their company is accumulating. "You have to consider the services we are rendering to Union Oil," he says.

In Los Angeles, Mr. Taylor of Union Oil makes the same observation. He maintains the profits of the seven companies are merely "a commission for arranging the financing." He says the total profit is less than Union Oil would have had to pay in interest and other costs if it had adopted another method of financing.

"AS GOOD OR BETTER"

"The deals are as good or better than similar deals we've made with other (non-Dillon-Read-group) companies," he adds. "Every one could stand on his own feet."

Mr. Brandi says he does not see any grounds for criticism that the transactions were not arranged at arm's length. Is it proper for Union Oil to make an arrangement that allows relatives of a Union Oil director to profit, instead of dealing with outsiders? Mr. Brandi says he thinks it more appropriate to ask this question: Should Union Oil be prevented from setting up such an arrangement merely because the family of a director might profit from it?

On the subject of conflict of interest in general, Mr. Brandi comments, "There is no law against it, of course." He maintains further that "the best judge as to whether there is a conflict of interest is the board of directors of a company." He says the Union Oil board approved all the arrangements with the Dillon Read group and that he personally refrained from voting on them.

Mr. Taylor's views on any possible conflict of interest are similar. He says that one reason for placing influential men on the board of directors is that they may come up with transactions beneficial to Union Oil, even if the transactions may also benefit the directors.

In March, Union Oil distributed to its employees a pamphlet, printed in the company colors of blue and orange and entitled: Conflict of Interest Policy. In broad terms, Union Oil described a "conflict of company interest" as "an involvement in which an employee (or member of his immediate family) benefits personally from transactions between the company and others." The pamphlet warned employees against accepting "any compensation or other benefits" in any transaction with "any person, corporation, partnership, or other business firm which renders any services to the company."

The pamphlet adds: "A personal or family interest in organizations doing business with the company does not necessarily in itself involve a conflict of interest, depending on the facts."

As for arm's length bargaining, Mr. Taylor says Union Oil, if anything, has been tougher in transactions with directors than with outsiders. Asked if the Dillon Read group's proposals had been compared with what outside financing firms might have been willing to offer, Mr. Taylor replies that all such considerations were made. But he does go on to say that no "formal" attempts were made to get competitive proposals. He says this was largely because of the long-standing relationship Union Oil has had with Dillon Read, which dates back to 1908.

Some stockholders are contending that the full board of directors did not pass on all the transactions with the companies set up by the Dillon Read group. Mr. Taylor says: "The executive committee (of the board) studies all these proposals."

A NURSE'S CURIOSITY

One Union Oil stockholder who is curious about the extent of the full board's knowledge of these transactions is Mrs. Willis Gortner, a trained nurse who lives in Honolulu and who owns 132 shares of Union Oil stock. Mrs. Gortner's attorneys, the San Francisco firm of Slack and Zook, have received copies of lease agreements between Union Oil and the Dillon Read groups' companies.

They also have received minutes of board meetings, including those at which the agreements could have been discussed.

A nurse's interest in the intricacies of high finance has aroused the curiosity of Union Oil's officials. They speculate privately that a proxy fight may be launched to try to gain control of the company.

Government agencies have been approached by a Canadian lawyer who has raised questions about the propriety of alleged actions of Union Oil officers and directors. This lawyer in the past has specialized in representing buyers and sellers of companies.

The possibility of a proxy fight is a matter of concern to the S.E.C. If it were determined that a proxy fight were brewing, this would have to be disclosed in another amendment to the company's registration statement.

At stake in any such proxy fight would be control of a company that Mr. Taylor recently described as "the 15th largest among oil companies and 56th among all U.S. industrial corporations."

In 1960, Union Oil had revenues of $535.6 million and earnings of $34.5 million. The company does all of its refining and most of its marketing in 12 Western states.

Business and Ideology*

At 43, Patrick Joseph Frawley, Jr., has already attained all the material success most men would ever dream of. While still in his twenties, he gambled hugely in business and won. Today, he has a multi-million-dollar personal fortune and the satisfaction of having contributed to the growth of a corporate complex that posted sales of $176 million last year.

But Patrick Frawley, a restless man of diverse enthusiasms, has not been content with merely amassing money and building up his companies. Since 1960, when he became deeply concerned over Castro's takeover in Cuba, he has been a passionate advocate of anticommunism and political conservatism—causes also supported by units of the companies he leads. Over the past few years, this involvement has embroiled both the men and the companies in controversy.

Most large, publicly-held concerns shy away from deep commitment to political causes. To the ruddy-faced executive who guides the affairs of Eversharp, Inc., Technicolor, Inc., and Schick Electric, Inc., this is a harmful policy. He strongly believes that adherence to it, and to the conciliatory lessons in Dale Carnegie's old success manual, How to Win Friends and Influence People, have "neutralized"

* "Battling Blade Man," *Wall Street Journal,* June 24, 1966. Used by permission.

American businessmen into silence on the Communist threat. Mr. Frawley and the companies he guides, particularly Eversharp, spend several hundred thousand dollars a year to fight this "neutralization."

There are, of course, many individual businessmen who hold strong views of one kind or another, and some openly ally themselves with the causes they champion. Multimillionaire Cleveland industrialist Cyrus S. Eaton, for example, has long advocated more communication and trade between the U.S. and the Communist bloc, including Red China. And the John Birch Society lists three business executives connected with fair-sized, publicly-held firms as members of its "Council," a top policy-making group.

(Though a conservative, Mr. Frawley himself is not connected with the Birch Society; he is a strong admirer of former President Eisenhower, who has been attacked by Birch chieftain Robert Welch.)

Some corporations, as well as individual executives, have chosen to take sides on ideological or otherwise controversial matters. Warner & Swasey Co., the big machine-tool maker, regularly runs magazine ads praising the free enterprise system and occasionally taking a slap at political liberalism and government's increasing role in business; the campaign has generated "a lot of letters indeed," both pro and con, according to a spokesman. Xerox Corp. got 61,000 denunciatory letters compared with 14,500 favorable ones when it publicly praised the work of the United Nations and agreed to sponsor a series of TV dramas about the world body.

While only a small minority of the heads of large concerns are willing to stick the corporate neck out—by taking strong positions on controversial subjects—there is some evidence of a growing willingness to do so. Witness the Xerox move. For corporate executives who must decide whether to "play things safe" or become open advocates on political and social issues, a close look at how Mr. Frawley operates, and how his companies have fared, may be instructive.

As chairman of Eversharp, Mr. Frawley has not hesitated to involve the company, one way or another, in his crusade against communism and those elements in our society he considers soft on communism. In some cases, he picks up most of the tab himself.

Just before the 1964 Presidential election, for example, 40,000 Roman Catholic priests got a letter and a book from Mr. Frawley. The book was Phyllis Schlafly's *A Choice not an Echo*, written originally as a plea for the Republican nomination of Barry Goldwater.

Mr. Frawley's letter, written on stationery of Eversharp's Schick Safety Razor Co. division, urged the priests to read the book and went on to criticize the press ("false information . . . brought Communists to power in China and Cuba"), attack the "tragically muddled foreign policy of the liberals," and question the legislative approach to civil rights ("the solution must be of an incentive nature").

Mr. Frawley explains, "I was worried; there seemed to be a lot of Democratic activity among Catholics, and I wanted something to balance it."

He paid for the books and the postage himself out of a personal fortune which he estimates runs to about $10 million, and which other sources place as high as $20 million. He says he lives on his capital and gives away an annual income of "several hundred thousand dollars," 90% of it to charity and the rest to political causes. In 1965, this annual income included a total of $222,567 in Eversharp and Technicolor salaries.

While in the case of the Schlafly book, Mr. Frawley himself took care of the expenses, in a good many other instances Eversharp pays. Sometimes it's an outright grant or contribution, other times a "public service" newspaper ad, sponsorship of a TV show or perhaps the actual production of a show for TV or radio—all directly or indirectly aiding the anti-Communist cause.

Mr. Frawley has no doubts that this is a proper use of stockholders' money. In his machine-gun mode of speech, he says such corporate involvement is "good for the country, good for the company, and good for the stockholders."

He has personally chosen five organizations which he says "fight communism full time" as recipients for Eversharp contributions. Each has been getting $5,000 a year from the company, not a particularly large amount as corporate contributions go; but Eversharp's support of these groups goes well beyond direct donations.

One of the first to get backing from Eversharp was the Christian Anti-Communism Crusade, headquartered in Long Beach, California, and run by Dr. Frederick Schwarz, an Australian physician and fervid battler against communism. Dr. Schwarz does much of his Red-fighting at lectures and rallies; in the past, most recently 1963, says Dr. Schwarz, some of these rallies were televised with the help of Eversharp and Technicolor, which bought the TV time to show them. The rallies generally are built around patriotic speeches by various public figures, and often include testimonials from former agents and informers of the FBI on the threat posed by communism at home and abroad.

A more recent recipient of Eversharp support is the American Security Council, Chicago, an organization which publishes and broadcasts studies on "national security" and maintains voluminous files packed with political and other information on individuals and organizations. The ASC will send such information on request to any of its member business firms which might want a line on various "subjects" or organizations.

Besides outright grants, Eversharp foots the monthly $20,000 bill for production of a five-minute ASC radio show each weekday evening which says it gives "the news behind the news" on some aspect of communism. The show, Washington Report, is distributed free to about 1,000 independent and network stations, says ASC; Schick commercials are included in some locations.

The show features former Congressman Walter Judd and Senator Thomas Dodd (D, Conn.), whose relationship with a lobbyist for West German businesses is now being investigated by the Senate Ethics Committee. The ASC says it has paid Sen. Dodd an "honorarium" of $6,373.69 for his broadcast editing of the news show; this money was drawn from Eversharp's contributions for production expenses.

Recently, Mr. Frawley further urged Eversharp to give ASC $100,000 to finance a contest aimed at bringing the merchandising skills of American businessmen to bear against communism. The grant was approved and the contest has been launched.

Cash prizes totaling $50,000 will be awarded to those five entrants who offer "the best ideas on how Schick and other businesses might better meet their responsibilities in this conflict." Another $50,000 will then be given to "cooperating" colleges and other organizations designated by the five winners.

Eversharp also makes direct contributions to the Freedoms Foundation, a patriotic, awards-giving organization which has former President Eisenhower as its honorary chairman. In the spring of 1965, Eversharp paid a total of $175,000 for sponsorship and promotion of the telecast of the Freedoms Foundation Award Ball. The show—filmed in technicolor and shown on the National Broadcasting Co. network—carried no advertising and was billed as a Schick public service.

Other recipients of Eversharp grants include the Cardinal Mindszenty Foundation, a Catholic organization in St. Louis which encourages the formation of anti-Communist groups, and the Jewish Council Against Communism, a Los Angeles group, now nearly defunct, which played its most active role in the search for Communists in the movie industry in the early 1950s. The latter organization is no longer getting its $5,000 but has assurance of Eversharp support when it needs it.

Some moves are carried out with no publicity. Last fall, for example, Mr. Frawley authorized the shooting of a film, done at Berkeley, California, and Oakland, California, which he says attempts to show the influence of Communists on demonstrations by college students. "If it turns out well, it will be a television show sponsored by Schick and Technicolor," the executive notes. Mr. Frawley says the filming was done secretly because he did not want to alert "Communist sympathizers."

His anti-Communist activities have not been without impact on Mr. Frawley, his companies, and even the Republican Party in California. "I've been called things like 'fascist beast' and 'bloodthirsty monster' in letters," he says—quickly adding, however, that he has received about 100,000 laudatory letters since he began his efforts and only 5,000 derogatory ones.

If some people have called Mr. Frawley nasty names, there's little indication that Eversharp itself has fared badly over the years because some individuals were upset with its crusading chairman. It's true that the company has been struggling a bit lately; though sales rose to $53.4 million in 1965 from $47.7 million the year before, net income declined to $3.6 million from $3.8 million. First-quarter earnings this year were below those of the like 1965 period, and the company omitted its dividend earlier this month, citing high costs of plant expansion, promotion, and research.

Over the long pull, however, Eversharp has done very well indeed. Despite the slight decline in 1965, the company's earnings for the year were still well over double net income back in 1960.

There is one case on record in which Eversharp products were removed from stores. Fed-Mart Corp., a San Diego-based discount chain with 37 outlets in California, Arizona, and Texas, yanked Schick razor blades from its counters late in 1964. Sol Price, Fed-Mart chairman, says they weren't selling. Mr. Frawley contends that ideology, not sales, was the reason, and that Mr. Price told him as much in a tense San Diego confrontation.

Few stockholders have made any complaints about Mr. Frawley involving their companies in ideological causes. But Lewis Gilbert, a New Yorker who is quick to question the management at the annual meetings of many companies, had this to say in his most current published report: "One corporate contribution that should not have been made is the paid 'public service' advertisement on issues that have nothing to do with the company, such as the ad for the Christian Anti-Communism Crusade sponsored by Eversharp in the October 30, 1964, issue of the *New York Times.*"

Mr. Frawley, far from detecting any measurable adverse effects on his companies' financial performance, finds that "anticommunism is very good business." He does say, however, that he has been seriously embarrassed by the so-called Fergus incident. It all began in 1964, when Eversharp's Schick division hired John Fergus in a sales capacity. His principal duty was not to sell razor blades, but to lecture on the evils of communism and the virtues of free enterprise.

Mr. Fergus got into hot water for his part in putting out a widely-circulated affidavit which indicated that Senator Thomas Kuchel, liberal Republican from California, had been one of two men arrested on a drunken driving charge in 1950. The affidavit further said that an arresting officer had noticed signs of "an immoral act" between the two.

As it developed, neither of the men arrested had been Senator Kuchel. Mr. Fergus was eventually indicted for his part in the affair, on the following charge: That he "willfully and wrongfully used the name of United States Senator Thomas Kuchel in a manner that will and did have a tendency to affect his moral reputation generally and in the estimation of the person and persons to whom it was so used." Mr. Fergus pleaded nolo contendere (no contest) and was fined $500, given a suspended sentence of 180 days, and placed on three years' probation. He was also fired by Eversharp.

The Fergus incident has contributed to the friction between the liberal and conservative wings of the California GOP. Senator Kuchel withheld endorsement of fellow Republican George Murphy (at the time a vice president and director of Technicolor) when the former actor ran successfully for the Senate in 1964. The reason, he said recently, was that Technicolor, which had employed Senator Murphy, was linked to Eversharp, which had employed Mr. Fergus.

Mr. Murphy retained his $35,000-a-year vice presidency until he took his Senate seat. Another Technicolor vice president ran the financial end of his campaign, and the Technicolor office lobby was stocked with Murphy literature. Senator Murphy was re-elected a director at the annual meeting May 3, and has increased his holdings of Technicolor stock.

Among other Technicolor executives, there has been considerable turnover. At least five of vice-presidential rank and above have left the company since early 1965.

They are Edward Ettinger, who resigned as executive vice president and a director in March, 1965; Richard J. Goldberg, Wadsworth E. Pohl, and Delbert K. Smith, who resigned as vice-presidents around mid-1965; and Melvin H. Jacobs, who resigned as president and chief executive officer in January, 1966. He did not stand for re-election as a director at the May 3 annual meeting.

Mr. Jacobs says he resigned because he "didn't want all the responsibility" he was carrying. A Democrat, he did not share Mr. Frawley's political enthusiasms; he has said he "can't stand" Dr. Schwarz of the Anti-Communism Crusade, and by his own and Mr. Frawley's accounts he had been a restraining influence on Technicolor's involvement in political activity.

Technicolor is still far less involved in ideology than Eversharp. One of the officers who left the company attributes this moderation to fear that deep involvement could alienate many liberals in the movie industry. Another ex-officer suggests that Mr. Ettinger (who will not comment himself) was removed partly because he expressed dissatisfaction with involvement by Technicolor in political matters, and says some of the others "were taken by surprise" by their own resignations.

Former heavyweight champion Gene Tunney, an Eversharp director and an intimate of Mr. Frawley, adds that one of the three left Technicolor "because he didn't want Frawley to stay involved with Schwarz and the Anti-Communism Crusade." He adds flatly: "Patrick has some execs who don't agree with him politically, but they don't last long."

Despite the lack of longevity among Technicolor executives, this company, too, has enjoyed general prosperity under the Frawley administration. Like Eversharp, Technicolor has had its problems recently; 1965 sales dipped to $96.4 million from $108.7 million in 1964, and earnings fell to $3.8 million from $5.2 million (including a special credit of $518,000) in 1964. First-quarter earnings this year were also off from the 1965 period.

But over the past five years, the company has shown a general pattern of earnings improvement. In 1960, for example, earnings were only $346,000 on sales of $28.5 million.

At the same time he was busy making his companies grow, Mr. Frawley was showing concern for the welfare of his employes. In 1961, he began a "citizenship development program" for Eversharp workers, including the use of films, brochures, and lectures by Congressmen who had made names as fervent anti-Communists.

Lobbies at both Eversharp and Technicolor have been stocked with anti-Communist literature (though this has been de-emphasized at Technicolor now), and bulletin boards have been hung with "stuff that has clearly political overtones, including letters by Mr. Frawley himself," says a middle-management official of one company.

Other businesses have been exposed to Mr. Frawley's ideology, too. In 1962, after the American Broadcasting Co. televised a show in which Richard Nixon was criticized, Eversharp tried to cancel more than $1 million of advertising it had contracted for on other ABC shows. Mr. Frawley said he was "shocked and alarmed at the extreme poor taste and judgment shown" by ABC in permitting Alger Hiss to appear on the program. In 1949, Hiss was convicted of perjury for denying he had played a role in a Communist spy ring; Mr. Nixon played a key role in the prior Congressional investigation.

ABC kept Eversharp to its ad commitments. Vincent Frances, an ABC official, said: "Never in my 26 years of broadcasting have I received a similar request" for ad cancellations "on political grounds." ABC and Eversharp have patched up their differences since; the latter has sponsored some ABC-TV shows recently.

The political activities of Mr. Frawley have sometimes tended to draw attention away from his considerable abilities as a businessman. He started young; born in Nicaragua of an Irish father and an American mother, he went to the U.S. for his education, but left high school before graduating to join his father's successful Nicaraguan export, banking and insurance businesses.

He says he spent two years "as the whirlwind of Nicaragua," selling American goods and gaining his first experience in, as he puts it, "wearing people down, arriving at 7:30 if a shop opened at 8." Then war came, and he went north to serve in the Royal Canadian Air Force.

After military service and marriage, he set up a successful export business in San Francisco. In 1949, he took the gamble that propelled him into big-time business in the U.S.; he invested $100,000 in tiny Paper-Mate Pen Co. Through aggressive marketing and imaginative advertising, he built Paper-Mate into an industry leader and sold it six years later to Gillette Co. for $15.5 million. He owned 80% of Paper-Mate at the time.

In 1958, he moved into the presidency of Eversharp. At about that time, he also became an American citizen by naturalization. In 1960, he gained control of Technicolor from the founders of the film processing concern after threatening a proxy fight, and shortly afterward, in 1961, strengthened his influence at Eversharp with heavy purchases of its stock and a reshuffling of directors that gave him effective control.

Schick Electric, a maker of electric shavers and other electrical products (not to be confused with Eversharp's Schick division), became part of the Frawley complex only last June, when Eversharp and Technicolor combined to purchase 27% of its stock. Mr. Frawley holds only a director's job at Schick, but his Eversharp and Technicolor associates control the board and no one doubts that Mr. Frawley exerts major influence over policy. Schick Electric earned $531,000 on sales of $26 million in 1965 compared with earnings of $606,000 on sales of $23 million the previous year.

To help keep corporate profits fat, Mr. Frawley requires his executives to take the Dale Carnegie success course, the very instruction he calls politically neutralizing—but he does it only to hone their business talents. Absorbing Carnegie, he says, is good for self-development "as long as you're aware he blinds people to everything but pursuit of the dollar."

Mr. Frawley lives with his wife and nine children in a low-slung, 10-bedroom home in the exclusive Bel-Air section of Los Angeles. Down to the youngest child, the Frawleys are chess fiends ("a good self-developer") and make extensive use of their swimming pool.

The master of the house leaves late each morning for Eversharp's sales office in Culver City, riding in a chauffeur-driven limousine he calls "the bus." Even as he rides, he is mapping new enterprises for the diverse complex of companies he guides.

One is the drug business. In 1963, Mr. Frawley stopped what he frankly admits was "problem drinking" after a course of treatment at Shadel Hospital in Seattle. Shadel doctors have been treating alcoholism as an enzyme deficiency, and have been attempting to remedy it by administering an enzyme drug, diphosphopyridine nucleotide (DPN).

In 1964, Eversharp purchased Shale and formed a subsidiary, Enzomedic Laboratories, to produce DPN and other enzyme drugs for the treatment of alcoholism and narcotics addiction. Medical opinion is still skeptical on the merits of treating these disorders with enzyme compounds, though the Eversharp research caused a flurry of trading in its stock when one physician, not connected with hospitals, indicated DPN was of remarkable help in treating schizophrenia.

Much of the decline in Eversharp's 1965 earnings stem from heavy costs in the research and development of these drugs. Mr. Frawley says his own experience had no bearing on the decision to commit Eversharp in this field and that the business opportunity in the "uncharted sea" of anti-addiction pharmaceuticals was what attracted him.

Outside the business field, Mr. Frawley has recently given much support to Moral Rearmament, an international movement aimed primarily at youth and stressing strict morality as a political and economic, as well as an individual, way of life.

MRA boasts many singing groups of young people who have "inspired patriotism" at songfests at dozens of military bases, according to a spokesman for MRA's "Pace" magazine. One of the best of these groups entertained 1,200 guests at a black-tie dinner in the Waldorf-Astoria ballroom recently; the dinner was hosted by the boards of Schick Electric, Eversharp, and Technicolor.

Eversharp has now become a prime supporter of MRA. One of the group's songfests has been produced as a TV show, "Up With People," which will be televised locally in 31 cities; the show will be repeated five times in each city. All production expenses and sponsorship costs as well as much of the promotional expenses will be picked up by Eversharp.

XII

International Business

A Japanese Businessman
Speaks

Hirouki Takeno is a 30-year-old Japanese sales representative of the Fujimura Trading Company, Ltd. of Osaka. Fujimura, capitalized at $20 million and employing 6,000 people, is one of the largest export-import firms in Japan. Takeno studied English language and literature at a private university in Tokyo but was obliged to seek employment in his third year of college, when his father's printing shop joined the list of bankrupt small businesses during the government's 1962 tight money program. He was hired by Fujimura and worked in the Tokyo branch for four years as a translator and interpreter for visiting foreign businessmen. Because of his proficiency in English, a talent in short supply in his company, he was assigned in 1966 to the New York office where he now directs the six-man sales force of the office machines department. He is looking forward eagerly to the time three months from now when his wife and two sons will join him. It is the company policy not to pay the expenses of the family's travel until after the employee has been away from Japan for 15 months.

In an interview with a university professor who was investigating businessmen's attitudes about ethics, Takeno expressed these thoughts:

"I have regularly inquired of American businessmen with whom I had business about their notions of ethics. Last week I talked to the president of an engineering company from Stamford. He was typical. He said that if he had to do unethical deeds to stay in business, he would quit. So I asked him what he would do if a robber came into his house and threatened his family. He said he would fight, even killing the robber if necessary. So I asked, 'If a businessman is willing to fight to the death to save his family, why not the same for his business?' His answer did not satisfy me.

"But he was like most American businessmen in saying that he would quit rather than be forced to deal unethically as a regular thing. This is probably realistic in the United States, and I think they would quit. But if they were living in place of Japanese in Japan, they would not. This is a big difference between the two countries. In Japan there is no allowance, no cushion, no money in the bank, nothing to fall back on. Japanese have no savings; many business decisions are matters of financial life or death. Unlike the U.S., many people in Japan are critically poor, absolutely poor. Business decisions often mean food in the baby's mouth. Always in Japan, and sometimes in U.S., the businessman is walking on the edge of ethics because of too much competition."

The American Way Abroad*

I regret, too, that in all candor I must record the unsavory fact that there is a related area of business endeavor where the state of morality is very low indeed, and where there is a stain on the conscience of industry which needs to be removed, and removed soon. I mean the bribery of officials in the governments of new countries in the underdeveloped parts of the world.

In the course of my government service, I visited many of these areas. I know whereof I speak, and I say that there are many otherwise respectable companies which still buy their way in when it comes to securing a mineral concession or establishing an operation in a remote part of the world.

This must stop, and it can only be accomplished by self-discipline. Surprisingly enough, I happen to have grave doubt whether it is a violation of any present Federal law for an American citizen to corrupt an officer of a foreign government, but that fact merely highlights the challenge to our business leadership. I reject the argument that other nations are doing it, and therefore we must if we

* From an article by Clarence B. Randall, former president and chairman of the board of Inland Steel Company. "For A New Code Of Business Ethics," *The New York Times Magazine,* April 8, 1962, p. 24 ff. © 1962 by The New York Times Company. Reprinted by permisson.

are to compete. Better to lose the business than to deny our heritage. The entire prestige of our country, and its ability to preserve our way of life in the world, is at stake. Those precious values must not be jeopardized by individual dishonor.

In the host countries, someone always knows the facts. What could be more tragic than for us to lose an air base that is vital to our national security because of moral turpitude on the part of American business? What will be our position when some demagogue from the desert calls his people to arms with the cry, "Drive the filthy Americans into the sea. We have been robbed of our ancient heritage"?

Either we have a code of morals, or we do not. If we do, it is for universal application, and must be adhered to in all circumstances, regardless of the impact on earnings. This is the acid test of our integrity.

Whose Customs are Ethical?

Management of international chains of hotels must decide whose ethics they will follow in operating their businesses. An executive in one such chain put it this way.

"We try to interject our own ethical ideas into the nationals who work for us. I don't know that U.S. standards are more objectively right than theirs. But we are an international organization and we want the same standards in our properties all over the world. If the hotel were only for the local population, I think that we might run it by their ethical standards. But we have people from all over the world staying at our hotels, and we want them to know what they can expect. As a result, I think we have upgraded standards in some lands.

"To illustrate, we built a hotel in Localia. The government cooperated fully. At first there were the usual attempts to extort bribes from us, but when we resisted, things went ahead without a hitch. It looked like a profitable venture for the first year since our net profit was about fifteen percent above even our best run hotels elsewhere. Then the government changed hands, and a corrupt, left-of-center group took over. Shortly after this, we found that the general manager of the hotel was providing government officials with free rooms and sending food and liquor to their homes. He was an American who was married to a national, and was trying to get an 'in' with the new government. Profits were still high, but we decided to fire him. Government officials intervened and told us to keep him or they would confiscate the hotel.

"We must operate according to our ethics, not theirs, so we stuck to our decision and let him go. This action caused us to lose the hotel. Later the government changed hands again, and the new administration has promised to provide us with some indemnity. Our losses as of now are about $80,000 cash and $240,000 on our legitimate claims and inventories. We have been able to write off most of the loss, but some of our stockholders have complained. Perhaps one should follow local customs even in these matters, but we don't think so."

A Case of Empty Bottles*

In November, 1966 the Boycott-Israel Office in Kuwait notified the Coca-Cola Export Corporation that its products were banned in the thirteen Arab states and sheikdoms represented by the Office. The action culminated seven difficult months for the management of Coca-Cola.

The Coca-Cola Export Corporation, a subsidiary of the Coca-Cola Company, sells syrup and concentrate to over 800 bottlers in foreign countries, 50 of which are subsidiaries of the company. Foreign operations account for 45 percent of the company's sales, which totalled $864,041,454 in 1965.

The Arab nations provide an unusually large market for soft drinks, including Coca-Cola, since Moslems shun alcohol. Coca-Cola sales account for a substantial percentage of Arab-United States trade in such countries as Egypt and Iraq. The company sells its syrup to 29 franchised bottlers in Arab states.

Since 1949 the Arabs' Boycott-Israel Office has blacklisted about 600 foreign companies for doing business with Israel. Members of the office meet frequently to consider cases of foreign companies doing business with Israel. A vote to boycott a company leaves implementation of the boycott up to member countries. The countries

* With the permission of the author, William H. Brown, S.J., Sophia University, Tokyo.

usually cancel franchises and import privileges, and order the sale of property. Rachad Mourad, an Egyptian stationed at the United Nations as permanent observer with the rank of ambassador for the 13-nation Arab League, sums up the boycott rules this way: "No company can establish a plant in Israel and do business with the Arab world. No country can sell capital goods to Israel and to the Arab countries too." King Faisal of Saudi Arabia in his visit to New York in June, 1966 explained the Arab attitude: "We consider those who provide assistance to our enemies as our own enemies." In its letters to foreign companies, the Boycott-Israel Office is accustomed to warn them that, "We believe it is of mutual interest to both of us to draw attention to the fact that Arab countries are still in a state of war with Israel. Foreign companies should not contribute to the promotion of Israeli economy."

In spite of the boycott threat, many companies are able to do business with Israel and with members of the Arab League. An international sales executive of an American company says, "One of the ways we manage to sell to both the Arabs and Israelis is to avoid calling attention to ourselves." United States Beverage Company, already boycotted by the Arabs because of an investment in Israel, fills Arab orders by using a little-known trade name. The utilization of independent distributors is another means of circumventing the boycott. "If some distributors are able to do business with Arabs, technically we don't know about it," says a spokesman for a large United States industrial equipment concern. Some companies with investments with Israel are said to do business with Arab nations through dummy corporations set up on the island of Malta.

According to Edwin J. Lukas, legal counselor for the American Jewish Committee in New York, "The Arabs rise above principle from time to time when it serves their best interest to do so." There are companies which do business with Israel and Arab nations with permission of the Boycott-Israel Office. Chase-Manhattan Bank has long dealt with the Arab world and maintains a branch in Beirut. In 1964 Chase ignored a warning from the Office to terminate its activities as fiscal agent for the sale of Israeli government bonds in the United States. The Arabs finally decided that the bank was not helping the Israeli economy since it hadn't invested its own funds, but was acting merely as an agent, and therefore was not violating the boycott. In 1961 Conrad Hilton was warned that the Nile Hilton in Cairo would come under the boycott if he went ahead with plans for the Tel-A-Viv Hilton. The hotel opened in 1965 but there were no reprisals; the Arabs seemed to feel that since Hilton merely operated the hotel and had not invested funds in it, the boycott did not apply.

In April, 1966 the Tempo Beverage Company of Israel, which dominates the domestic soft-drink market, requested a bottling franchise from Coca-Cola. This was not the first time Tempo had made this request. As on each previous occasion, the Coca-Cola Company refused. This time, however, the refusal was followed by charges that the Coca-Cola Company was discriminating against Israel.

On April 12, 1966 James A. Farley, Chairman of the Board of the Coca-Cola Export Corporation, replied to the charges of discrimination against Israel in denying a franchise to the Tempo Beverage Company. He stated that over the years Coca-Cola has considered many requests for franchises from new areas, including Israel, and the "basic criterion for accepting or rejecting such requests has been whether in the judgment of the company the investment would be successful." These decisions are not permanent, he said, and the company is "more than willing for purely business reasons to change its decisions."

In connection with the charges that Coca-Cola had rejected a franchise for an Israeli company, Mr. Farley stated that the Tempo Beverage Company was found guilty in 1963 by Israeli courts of infringement of the Coca-Cola trademark and bottle design. "This unhappy experience with the subject company obviously precludes our entering into a business arrangement with it," he said. Mr. Farley concluded his statement with the assurance that his corporation would not conduct its affairs in response to any boycott, including the Arab boycott.

A few months later the Coca-Cola Export Corporation agreed to franchise a bottling plant in Israel.

In June, 1966 Coca-Cola was warned about plans for commencing operations in Israel. In November of the same year, at its 24th regional conference in Kuwait, the Boycott-Israel Office voted unanimously to ban Coca-Cola for refusing to conform to boycott regulations. The conference had earlier asked the company for detailed clarification of its plans in Israel but had received "unconvincing replies."

Dilemmas Abroad

Nordsud is an American company of diversified interests, with a history of involvement in South America. Its investments have contributed to the growth of the host countries in which it operates as well as to its own profit figures. Indeed, the rate of return on the South American operations is almost double that on the company's investment at home.

Nordsud's contributions are varied. It runs training schools for artisans; employs thousands of workers at wages equal to the highest going rates in the host nation; and has contributed to the development of local health facilities. In one country, the Nordsud hospital is the largest and best in the entire nation. On the whole, the company has always adopted what it considered to be an enlightened policy, which respects local customs and traditions.

At a recent meeting of businessmen interested in aiding underdeveloped countries, Nordsud came under severe attack by both American and South American businessmen. The charges centered on the fact that Nordsud policy adapted itself to both the good and the bad in South America. The attackers felt that Nordsud as a leader in many areas should lead in all. In particular, Nordsud was urged to use its most advanced American methods in South American operations rather than settle for a sort of compromise.

Item: Although Nordsud pays wages which compare with the best in the host country, the general level is still exploitative since wages in the host country are very low. One businessman operating in the same country pointed out that his company had upped both its production and local reputation by "busting rates upward." Why could not Nordsud do the same thing?

The Nordsud representative answered that smaller firms could raise wages and bust rates upward, but that bigger companies did not dare to do so. The reason was simply that influential local businesses would get the government to harass a large company if it were too progressive. In short, Nordsud was so big that its wage scale had real political implications and Nordsud wanted to stay out of politics as much as possible.

Item: A law in one country makes it practically impossible to fire a man after he has been on the company payroll for a period of ten years. Nordsud fires many employees just before they have completed ten years with the company in order to avoid trouble. This is a relatively common practice in that particular country, so Nordsud is really only following local custom.

It was objected that such practices negate the law and deprive workers of job security even when they have done nothing to warrant dismissal. The Nordsud representative replied that the dismissals were selective and made in the interests of work discipline. The workers were dismissed only when there was a grounded suspicion that they might cause problems once they were secure in their jobs. There was no policy of wholesale layoffs to circumvent the law, and the company felt it was justified on the basis of both local customs and the need to maintain control of the work force.

Item: Nordsud pays American executives much higher wages than their native counterparts. This is somewhat concealed by the fact that the Americans are paid a local currency salary which is approximately equal, while the difference is banked in the United States. It was objected that this was discriminatory.

The company representative replied that Nordsud had not been able to obtain all the local management it needed. American managers could be tempted to work abroad only if their income were secure. Certainly there was discrimination. This was a fact of life and there was nothing that could be done about it so long as local managers were in short supply.

Those who objected claimed that Nordsud was creating its own problems. If they paid equal wages to both Americans and local executives, they would soon have plenty of local management. Nordsud countered that it did not want to be accused of raiding local companies for talent. "After all, we have to live with those people."

When the meeting was over, the South American representatives agreed that there was a certain wisdom to the answers of the Nordsud executive. "The trouble is," said one South American, "this sort of policy making just encourages those local businessmen who want to continue the old system, and the old system—let's face it—is just an invitation to revolution."

American Business in
South Africa

The following notice appeared in *Social Action Notes* for March, 1966.

Msgr. Thomas J. Carey, administrator of Queen of Angels Church in Newark, N. J., declined to pass through a civil rights picket line to accept a special brotherhood award given by the New Jersey Region, National Conference of Christians and Jews. The pickets were protesting the granting of one of the region's three awards to C. W. Engelhard, Jr., president of Engelhard Industries.

Before the demonstration, the organizing groups met at the North Reformed Church in Newark and adopted a resolution drawn by the American Committee on Africa protesting selection of Engelhard because his firms have branches in South Africa.

In a statement Engelhard said: 'I do business with many countries without commenting on internal affairs of these countries. I believe in the American way of life. I accept the right of those outside the hotel to picket and draw their own conclusions. I have the right to receive this brotherhood award which I am happy to accept.'

Msgr. Carey is a member of the board of directors of the Newark chapter, National Association for the Advancement of Colored People. The New Jersey State Conference of NAACP Branches was one of the groups organizing the protest. Others were CORE and the American Committee on Africa.

'It would be very strange for me to cross picket lines of people protesting the deprivation of basic human rights,' Msgr. Carey said.

Two other clergymen accepted special awards. They were Rabbi Max D. Davidson of Perth Amboy, N. J., and Episcopal Bishop Leland Stark of Newark, whose award was accepted by his wife because the ceremony conflicted with a speaking engagement.

The split in clergy reaction to the picketing points to the existence of a difficult situation in which many American companies are involved. In 1960 the New York Stock Exchange listed 85 U.S. companies which had operating plants or subsidiaries in South Africa.

In 1961 when the South African economy was close to panic, the following loans by U.S.-owned or U.S.-influenced institutions stopped the trouble.

International Monetary Fund:	$38 million
World Bank and its affiliates:	$28 million
Chase Manhattan Bank:	$10 million
First National City Bank:	$ 5 million
U. S. lenders not publicly identified:	$70 million

In 1963 new South African investments by the automotive industry included:

General Motors:	$30 million to make engines and accessories
Ford:	$11 million to make engines
Chrysler:	80 percent production increase (cost not revealed)
Firestone:	$7 million to make tires
Goodyear:	$30 million expansion program

Charles W. Engelhard seems to have been singled out for picketing because of his deep involvement in a large number of South African industries.

South African Directorships of Charles W. Engelhard, 1962[1]

Business address: 113 Astor Street, Newark, 2, New Jersey, U.S.A.

Acme Timber Industries	Anglo American of S. A.
American-South African Investment & Co. (Chairman)	Board & Metal Products (S.A.)
	By Products

[1] *Africa Today,* Published by the American Committee on Africa, March, 1964, p. 17. Used by permission.

Central Mining Finance

The Central Mining & Investment Corp.

The Chamber of Mines Building Co.

The Corner House Investment Co. (Chairman)

Investment Advisors and Managers (Pty.)

Native Recruiting Corp.

Plastic Protection (Pty.)

Precious Metals Development

Rand American Investments (Pty.)

Rand Mines (Chairman)

Rand Refinery

Rand Selection Corp.

S. A. Forest Investments

S. A. Investment Adviser (Pty.) (Chairman)

Transvaal G. M. Estates

Virginia-Merriespruit Investments (Pty.)

Witwatersrand Native Labour Association

Source: Beerman's *South African Financial Year Book: Investors' Manual and Cyclopaedia of South Africa Public Companies,* Volume I, 1962, p. xxx.

Rand Mines, Ltd. (Charles W. Engelhard, U.S.A., Chairman)
Principal Companies of the Group, 1962

Financial

The Corner House Investment Co. Ltd.

Transvaal Consolidated Land & Exploration Co., Ltd.

Virginia-Merriespruit Investments (Pty.) ltd.

Mining

Gold and Uranium

Blyvooruitzicht Gold Mining Co., Ltd.

Harmony Gold Mining Co., Ltd.

Merriespruit (O.F.S.) Gold Mining Co., Ltd.

Gold

City Deep, Ltd.

Consolidated Main Reef Mines & Estate, Ltd.

Crown Mines, Ltd.

East Rand Proprietary Mines, Ltd.

Modderfontein East, Ltd.

Durban Roodeport Deep Ltd.

Rose Deep, Ltd.

Transvaal Gold Mining Estates, Ltd.

Coal

Utrecht Colliery (owned by Welgedacht Exploration Co., Ltd.)

Van Dyks Drift Colliery (Owned by Transvaal Consolidated Land & Exploration Co.), Ltd.

Witbank Colliery, Ltd.

Chrome

Rooderand Chrome Mine (Pty.) Ltd.

Winterveld (T.C.L.) Chrome Mines (Pty.) Ltd. Sales Agent: Johannesburg Ore Co. (Pty.) Ltd.

Industrial

Cement	Steel and Concrete Pipes
Pretoria Portland Cement Co., Ltd.	The Hume Pipe Co. (S. Af.) Ltd.
Cape Portland Cement Co., Ltd.	
Premier Portland Cement Co.	Lime
(Rhodesia) Ltd.	The Northern Lime Co., Ltd.
Eastern Province Cement Co., Ltd.	

Source: *State of South Africa, Yearbook,* 1962, opp. p. 32.

The January 1966 issue of *Africa Today* reports:

Charles W. Engelhard directly controls nearly 15 percent of South African gold production and almost 20 percent of uranium production. Through his other directorships, particularly of Anglo-American Corporation, Charter Consolidated and the Rand Selection Corporation, he influences mineral policy decisions of producers of two-thirds of South African gold and uranium.

As a Director of the Chamber of Mines Building Company, Engelhard also has something to say about setting wage rates and controlling working conditions. The average wage of a colored person in the gold mines is 70 cents a day, but the lowest paid underground white worker gets a minimum of $7.82 a day. Even after a ten percent increase in 1964, the minimum for underground African workers was only 46 cents a day. It should be noted that the minimum wage in Zambia is three times as high. The wages in Northern Rhodesia are also considerably higher. Where the miners live in company compounds, food, training, hospital, and other costs add about 27 cents a day to benefits. The housing itself may cost the company as much as 17 cents a day per worker, if the investment is written off rapidly.

The control of discrimination is not really in the hands of private companies. While South African law requires equal pay for equal work, it also excludes equal opportunity. The Mines and Work Act, No. 12 of 1911 reserves skilled positions for white workers. One recent attempt at giving Africans supervisory positions over other colored persons was vetoed by the Ministry of Mines because of pressure applied by white workers. This happened despite the fact that the attempt had been approved by the government, the mine owners, and a majority of the Mine Workers Union.

These problems afflict industries which are short of trained workers. In some industries, such as automobile assembly, there are job restrictions which exclude non-whites from supervisory and control work, welding and brazing. Such laws help neither business nor the African worker, but they are a fact of South African life. Despite these obstacles, the mine owners are trying to negotiate with the white miners' union in an effort to place some 2,000 Africans in skilled jobs. Economic pressures have also led to the government-run railroads hiring 10,000 Africans for what were once jobs reserved for whites.

The facts of South African life must enter into any business decision. Laws have forced professional associations to expel doctors and lawyers for violations of apartheid. Even charitable organizations practice apartheid. Other African states may detest South Africa, but during 1966 they were increasing their purchases from South Africa since its prices were lower than those of competitors. Business in South Africa is good, and American companies have found that they can often get a better return on their investment there than elsewhere. In January, 1966 *Africa Today* stated:

> In 1962 the average net profit to net worth ratio for U.S. firms was 25 percent, rising two years later to 27 percent. The return on 'raw' investment is 13 percent, compared with a world average of 7.7 percent. . . .
> . . . special treatment is offered to new investors in industrial buildings and machinery. An initial allowance of 15 percent and an investment allowance of 20 percent are deductible from the cost of new machinery; and an investment allowance of 10 percent may be deducted from the cost of erecting or improving factory buildings. In the border areas, these allowances are increased up to 30 percent for machinery and 20 percent for buildings. . . .

South Africa has one more advantage that must not be overlooked. As one U.S. investor put it, "It is the only country in Africa with a stable government. Every businessman wants a strong government to back him up, and South Africa has it."

South Africa might have a stable government, but it is hardly a democratic one. The once active Liberal Party has practically been destroyed, since the police have arrested or confined its leaders. Visitors have described South Africa as a police state in which even the Churches which oppose apartheid are hamstrung. A clergyman who speaks too loudly may find himself without a church, or without the passes necessary to work in the native areas. The English-language press speaks out against the situation, but does not appear to have much impact.

Charles W. Engelhard certainly knew all of these things as he was escorted by police through the picket line to accept his award at the Hotel Robert Treat. In an impromptu speech at the dinner, he said:

> As a businessman, you have certain obligations as a guest in the country in which you do business. One of the obligations consists of not criticizing what they do at home, since you do not want them to criticize what we do at home.

On the other hand, Msgr. Carey said that, after reading Engelhard's remarks, he was more than glad that he had not attended the dinner. And Henry P. Van Dusen, President Emeritus of Union Theological Seminary, wrote to the *New York Times* in September, 1963:

> . . . Every American who is a stockholder or depositor in commercial firms doing business in South Africa is indirectly a participant in the cruel repression of the majority of the South African populace, in the aggravation of violence, bloodshed and brutality which daily increase and, it may well be, in the ultimate loss of American investment abroad.

Epilogue

The Challenge to Businessmen and Educators*

Today's enlightened business executive recognizes that making a profit does not necessarily conflict with moral responsibility. He knows that it is part of his job to consider, when making a management decision, whether an action is right, as well as whether it may be profitable.

What's more, I believe that the responsible manager today realizes that it takes somewhat more than lip service to ensure the ethical conduct of a business. It is not enough, he knows, to hang a motto on his wall extolling the rewards of virtue and say, "That's our creed."

He is aware that in any company principles, like policies, work only if top management sets an example. No amount of preaching will convince his employees of his sincerity if his actions do not reflect his words.

Because I feel so strongly about the role of top management in this matter, I have been baffled—and somewhat disappointed—to

* From a pamphlet by Charles A. Perlitz, Jr., Chairman of the Board of Continental Oil Company, entitled "A Look At Business Ethics." Used by permission.

learn the results of a survey of some 100 business schools, which increasingly are the source of tomorrow's corporate managers. In most cases these schools find no place in their curricula for the study of ethics. As a matter of fact, a good many business schools consider ethics a subject that should be studied only in the department of philosophy or religion.

I make no pretense of being an educator, and thus I do not feel competent to suggest how ethical studies' should be presented to business students. There are those in the education field who believe that courses of study specifically oriented toward business ethics are the answer. Others consider that broader training in ethics apart from business courses is a better way.

I do not believe I have to be an educator, however, to stick with my conviction that the students who will run our businesses must be made aware of the necessity of relating morality to business judgment.

As a business manager, I have little contact with business students. However, I do have occasion to deal with a number of young men who recently were students. In many of them I find an unawareness that problems of ethics and morals exist in business situations.

This, to me, is one area in which our business educators can help. I do not know if they can teach students what to do about problems in business ethics; I am not even sure that morality can be taught as an intellectual exercise. I do believe they can make students aware that ethical and social problems arise in the business world.